VIKTOR E. FRANKL
ANTHOLOGY

Viktor E. Frankl Anthology

Edited and Annotated by

Timothy Lent

To order additional copies of this book, contact:
Xlibris Corporation
1-888-795-4274
www.Xlibris.com
Orders@Xlibris.com
24733

CONTENTS

DEDICATION

Dedication

This book is dedicated with love to my wife,
Louise B. Lent.
She has been my friend for twenty years
and continues to be a great source of spiritual support.
I would not be the man that I am without her.

Foreword

In my first book on Viktor E. Frankl's teachings, *Christian Themes in Logotherapy*, I sought to show how certain psychological teachings in logotherapy correspond to themes in Christian theology. It was not my point to make logotherapy "Christian," because it is not. Rather, it is non-sectarian. It is secular in perspective while at the same time not rejecting the religious dimension of the human person.

My second book on Viktor Frankl, which I have entitled *A Viktor E. Frankl Anthology*, is an outcome of two phases of my work. I minister to the elderly, the sick, and the dying in an assisted living community, and I teach part-time at both Cabrini College and Immaculata University. In both capacities, I use relevant principles from logotherapy. In short, I love to quote to others from the various writings of Frankl.

A Viktor E. Frankl Anthology is an anthology of quotations from the various English editions of the writings of the late medical doctor, psychiatrist, philosopher, psychologist, and Holocaust survivor, Viktor E. Frankl. I have selected quotations which are particularly relevant to men and women living in the twenty-first century. It may be used by priests, ministers, rabbis, psychiatrists, psychologists, social workers, educators, journalists, public speakers, and even politicians.

A Viktor E. Frankl Anthology is a book meant for all human beings, because logotherapy is for everyone. It is not only a philosophy for a select few, but it is also for "the man in the street," to borrow a phrase from Frankl. In short, the purpose of the anthology is to make Frankl's ideas readily available to virtually anyone.

How to Understand and Use This Book

Understanding the Symbols
and Abbreviations

There are several abbreviations in the book which need to be explained. A three-period ellipsis before a quotation (. . .) means that the quotation is not at the beginning of a sentence. For example, a quotation under the section Anthropology reads: " . . . responsibility and freedom comprise the spiritual domain of man."

A three-period ellipsis, followed by a bracketed word or phrase, followed by another three-period ellipsis (. . . [ ] . . .) means that a word or phrase has been deleted from the quotation and that a word or phrase has been added to the quotation in order to clarify its meaning. For example, a quotation under the section Anthropology reads: "It is time that . . . [the] . . . decision quality of human existence be included in our definition of man."

A four-period ellipsis at the end of a quotation (. . . .) means that there is more to the sentence but it has been deleted. For example, a quotation under the section Sex reads: "Sex is human if it is experienced as a vehicle of love . . . ."

A period followed by two spaces, followed by three periods, followed by two more spaces (e.g., ...) means that after ending the sentence, Frankl's thought is continued later in the paragraph. For example, a quotation under the section Death reads: "The dullard newspaper reader sitting at his breakfast table is avid for stories of misfortune and death . . . . at such a person really gets out of these vicarious deaths is the contrast effect: it seems as though other people are always the ones who must die."

A bracketed letter, word or phrase (e.g., [ ]) means that it has been supplied by the editor. For example, a quotation under the section Anthropology reads as follows: "It is time that . . . [the] . . . decision quality of human existence be included in our definition of man." The bracketed [the] is not Frankl's but has been supplied by the editor for the sake of clarity.

A bracketed capital letter at the beginning of a sentence (e.g., [I]) means that the editor began the sentence with a capital letter rather than a lowercase letter "i," as in "it," which is in the original English edition. For example, a quotation under the section Anthropology reads: "Wholeness . . . means the integration of somatic, psychic, and spiritual aspects . . . . [I]t is this threefold wholeness that makes man complete."

A bracketed word, phrase or sentence at the beginning of a quotation is not Frankl's; it introduces the theme of the quotation. For example, under the section Anthropology, a quotation reads: [Logotherapy] " . . . regards man as free and responsible . . . . " The bracketed word [Logotherapy] is the editor's, introducing the subject or theme to follow. Under the section Conscience, a quotation reads: [A human being] " . . . can be his own judge, the judge of his own deeds. The bracketed phrase [A human being] is the editor's.

A parenthesis subdivides a general theme, making it more specific. For example, under the section Human Beings, it is subdivided as follows: (On Being Human), (Human Dignity), (Human Potential), and (Human Uniqueness). A parenthesis may also serve to explain a general theme or topic. For example, under the section Anthropology, there is a parenthesis immediately under it, as in Anthropology (Logotherapy's View of the Human Person).

Understanding the Abbreviations of Frankl's Books

I have quoted from all of the English editions of Frankl's books published to date. After each quotation, I give the source of the quotation so that readers may research a topic in Frankl's writings for themselves. I quote from the following books by Dr. Frankl:

Viktor E. Frankl, *Man's Search for Meaning*, 3rd ed. (New York, N.Y.: Simon and Schuster, 1984).

It shall be abbreviated as *MSM*.

————, *Man's Search for Ultimate Meaning* (New York, N.Y.: Insight Books/ Plenum Press, 1997).

It shall be abbreviated as *MSUM*.

————, *Psychotherapy and Existentialism*: *Selected Papers on Logotherapy* (New York, N.Y.: Simon and Schuster, Inc., 1967).

It shall be abbreviated as *PE*.

————, *The Unconscious God* (New York, N.Y.: Washington Square Press/ Pocket Books/ Simon and Schuster, Inc., English ed.1975, 1st Washington Square Press printing 1985).

It shall be abbreviated as *UG*.

_____, *The Doctor and the Soul: From Psychotherapy to Logotherapy*, trans. Richard and Clara Winston, 3rd ed. (New York, N.Y.: Vintage Books/ Random House, 1986).

It shall be abbreviated as *DS*.

_____, *The Unheard Cry for Meaning: Psychotherapy and Humanism*, rev. ed. (New York, N.Y.: Washington Square Press, 1978, Washington Square Press ed. 1985).

It shall be abbreviated as *UCM*.

_____, *The Will of Meaning: Foundations and Applications of Logotherapy* (New York, N.Y.: New American Library, 1969, 1st printing 1970).

It shall be abbreviated as *WM*.

_____, *Viktor Frankl Recollections: An Autobiography*, trans. Joseph Fabry and Judith Fabry (New York, N.Y.: Plenum Press, 1997).

It shall be abbreviated as *VFR*.

The Man and His Message

Philosopher of Meaning

Viktor Emil Frankl was a philosopher of meaning. Even from his childhood days and into his adolescent years, Frankl was concerned with meaning. At the early age of four, he vividly remembered the thought of his own mortality. In his autobiography, he recalled:

> One evening just before falling asleep, I was startled by the unexpected thought that one day I too would have to die. What troubled me then—as it has done throughout my life—was not the fear of dying, but the question of whether the transitory nature of life might destroy its meaning.[1]

Even as a teenager, Frankl was on a quest for meaning, searching for the answer to the question: "What is the meaning of life?" He wrote:

> I well remember how I felt when I was exposed to reductionism in education as a junior high school student at the age of thirteen. Once our natural science teacher told us that life in the final analysis

was nothing but a combustion process, an oxidation process, I sprang to my feet and said, "Professor Fritz, if this is the case, what meaning does life have?"[2]

In 1921, as a high school student at the age of sixteen, he gave his first public lecture to an adult education school. It was entitled: "The Meaning of Life."[3]

For Frankl, all of life was imbued with meaning, no matter what situation in which one may find oneself, no matter how well or ill (chronically or terminally) one was, no matter where one was along life's journey, no matter how badly a person may have wrecked his or her life. In all of its various conditions, life still has meaning, as Frankl often said, "[E]very life, in every situation and to the last breath, has a meaning, retains a meaning."[4] He was emphatic: *The so-called life not worth living does not exist.*[5]

Frankl was an amazing man who had an amazing message to tell men and women in the twentieth century. He was an extremely gifted human being, a physician, psychiatrist, and philosopher.

Holocaust Survivor

Virtually everyone Frankl loved and everything he enjoyed was taken from him by Hitler's Nazi regime. Shortly after he married his firs wife, Tilly Grosser, in 1941, she conceived a child. However, because the Frankls were Jews, they were forbidden to have children, so the Nazis forced Tilly to have an abortion.[6] Frankl dedicated his book *The Unheard Cry for Meaning* to their unborn child with the words "To Harry or Marion, an unborn child."[7]

Nine months after their wedding, Viktor and Tilly were deported to Theresienstadt. After that, they were transported to Auschwitz. They became separated, because the women's camp was separated from the men's. Upon his release from the concentration camps and his return to Vienna in August 1945, Viktor learned that his wife Tilly also died.[8] He wrote:

> Tilly had died with many others after the liberation of Bergen—Belsen by English soldiers. They had discovered 17,000 corpses and, during the following six weeks, another 17,000 prisoners died from sickness, starvation, and exhaustion. Tilly must have been among them.[9]

Frankl took the first draft of the manuscript of his book, *The Doctor and the Soul,* into the concentration camp at Auschwitz. However, it was either lost or destroyed there.[10] When he became sick with typhus in the concentration camp at Turkheim, he decided to reconstruct the manuscript.[11] When *The Doctor and the Soul* was published, he dedicated it "To the Memory of Tilly."[12]

Frankl's mother, Elsa, died in the gas chamber at the concentration camp in Auschwitz.[13] He dedicated his book *Man's Search for Meaning* "to the memory of my mother."[14] His father, Gabriel, died from starvation and pneumonia at the concentration camp in Theresienstadt.[15] His brother Walter perished in Auschwitz.[16] His sister Stella, however, was not deported to a concentration camp, because she had already gone to live in Australia.[17]

As for Viktor Frankl, he had survived imprisonment in four concentration camps for a total of three years: Theresienstadt, Auschwitz, Kaufering III, and Turkheim.[18] Although Frankl's life story demonstrates the "defiant power of the human spirit" to survive such miserable conditions, it was also a candid story about a real human being. He struggled with depression, pessimism, and the temptation to succumb to despair, which led to the deaths of so many prisoners. He recalled:

> [I]n the camp, Kaufering III, Benscher, the Munich
> television actor-to-be, . . . saved my life . . . . [H]e
> talked to me with great urgency, imploring me to
> get over my pessimism. The mood that had
> overcome me was the mood I had observed in other
> inmates, which almost inevitably led to giving up
> and sooner or later, to death.[19]

Frankl was transported to the Turkheim concentration
camp where he came down with typhus and nearly died.
Frankl's logotherapeutic principle of self-transcendence
was confirmed by his own experience in the concentration
camps.[20] He realized that he had to focus outwardly on
someone or something instead of focusing inwardly on
the hell he was undergoing. His manuscript of *The Doctor
and the Soul* was destroyed in Auschwitz.[21] So he
determined to reconstruct the manuscript in the Turkheim
camp, even though he was near death. He recalled: "I am
convinced that I owe my survival, among other things, to
my resolve to reconstruct that lost manuscript. I started to
work on it when I was sick with typhus and tried to stay
awake, even in the night, to prevent vascular collapse."[22]
As a result of his determination, he eventually became
well.

Another reason he had to stay alive was the love he
had for his beloved wife, Tilly, and the hope that he would
see her again after his release from the concentration
camp. He would often think about her, imagine her
beautiful face and her talking to him. It was his love for her
that kept him going, kept him alive. He wrote:

> In position of utter desolation, when man cannot
> express himself in positive action, when his only
> achievement may consist in enduring his sufferings
> in the right way—an honorable way—in such a
> position man can, through loving contemplation of

the image he carries of his beloved, achieve fulfillment . . . .

My mind still clung to the image of my wife . . . I didn't even know if she were alive. I knew only one thing—which I have learned well by now: Love goes very far beyond the physical person of the beloved. It finds its deepest meaning in his spiritual being, his inner self.[23]

Viktor Frankl learned various psychological methods of survival. There is a proverb in the Hebrew Scriptures which says, "Where there is no vision, the people perish" (Proverbs 29:18a, KJV). A vision of the future gives a person who is undergoing some kind of difficulty, hardship or suffering (either emotional or physical or both) in the present hope. That is what Frankl had. He practiced mental "imaging" or what he called "self-distancing" in the concentration camps. Frankl explained:

I repeatedly tried to distance myself from the misery that surrounded me by externalizing it. I remember marching one morning from the camp to the work site, hardly able to bear the hunger, the cold, and the pain of my frozen and festering feet, so swollen from hunger edema and squeezed into my shoes. My situation seemed bleak, even hopeless. Then I imagined that I stood at the lectern in a large, beautiful, warm, and bright hall. I was about to give a lecture to an interested audience on "Psychotherapeutic Experiences in a Concentration Camp" (the actual title I later used at that congress). In the imaginary lecture I reported the things that I am now living through.[24]

Upon Frankl's release from the concentration camp and upon learning of the horrible news of the deaths of his wife, father, mother, and brother, he was filled with an overwhelming sense of sadness and mourning. He recalled his conversation with his friend, Paul Polak:

> Paul, I must tell you, that when all this happens to someone, to be tested in such a way, that it must have, that it must have some meaning. I have a feeling—and I don't' how else to say it—that something waits for me. That something is expected of me, that I am destined for something.[25]

Now Frankl was challenged by life, questioned by life. Now he had to find a reason to go on living. Why was his life spared? What was the meaning of his survival? He had to discover a new meaning to his life and, indeed, he did! This was amply demonstrated over the next forty years of his life by all of his lectures on logotherapy throughout the world, his inspirational story of his survival of the concentrations camps, his counseling of patients, and all his books on logotherapy.

Contrary to popular misconception, Frankl did not develop logotherapy, the Third Viennese School of Psychotherapy, as a result of his experiences in the concentration camps. Before he went into the camps, he had already developed, in his words, "the essentials of logotherapy" in the first draft of his manuscript *The Doctor and the Soul*.[26] He wrote: "I *entered* the camp with a full-length book manuscript (hidden under the lining of my overcoat) which was indeed an outline of the basic concepts of logotherapy."[27] However, his experiences in the concentration camps confirmed, in his own words,

> One of the main tenets of logotherapy, the theory that the basic meaning orientation of an individual—or, as I am used to calling it, the "will to meaning"—has actual survival value. Under comparable circumstances, those inmates who

were oriented toward the future, whether it was a task to complete in the future, or a beloved person to be reunited with, were most likely to survive the horrors of the camps (I say "camps" because the same lessons can be learned from the psychiatric literature on American soldiers kept in Japanese, North Korean, and North Vietnamese Prisoner of War camps).[28]

Frankl would not say that evil events in which human beings suffer and die are good; nor would he say that evil acts, which are committed by human beings against other human beings, are in themselves (intrinsically) good. But Frankl would say that a new meaning may emerge or result for a person from even the bad things which happen in life, depending on one's attitude. One may choose to turn a tragedy into a triumph. One may choose to become bitter or better.

Frankl's was a triumphant story, but his painful experiences in the concentration camps were deeply etched in his psyche. Much later in his life, he wrote in his autobiography: "I still have nightmares about life in the concentration camps . . . ."[29] But those experiences, as evil as they were in themselves, as painful as they were, actually resulted in much good, both for himself and for millions of others who have been fortunate to have read his books and heard his lectures. Even more fortunate were those who actually knew the man, such as his family, friends, and colleagues.

Frankl practiced many of the principles of logotherapy, which he himself had "preached" to others. Life is not always good, but it can result in good, depending on the attitude (hence, attitudinal values) of the person who suffers from its "slings and arrows of outrageous fortune." Frankl's life experiences in the concentration in concentration camps verified some of his logotherapeutic principles, which he had already developed before having gone into the camps. He said, "The two basic human capacities, self-transcendence and self-distancing, were verified and validated in the concentration camps."[30] They were the "scientific laboratories" of human experience. They were "tried and proven" in the lives and deaths of many inmates in the camps.

Counseling the Suicidal

In 1928-1930, Frankl organized youth counseling centers, first, in Vienna and in six other European cities. He wanted to help "young people in personal and psychological distress . . . ," especially high school students.[31] He helped many confused young people make sense of their lives. As a result of the youth counseling, for "the first time in many years . . . no student suicides were reported in Vienna."[32]

Two years after graduating from medical school, from 1933 to 1937, Frankl was "in charge of the 'pavilion for suicidal women . . .'" at Steinhof Mental Hospital.[33] For four years, then, Frankl "was responsible for no less than 3000 patients each year."[34] He was qualified to work with the suicidal not only because he was a medical doctor but also because of the experience he had gained from counseling patients. In fact, he developed a diagnostic method to determine whether or not a suicidal patient was ready to be released from the hospital. Frankl writes:

> The patient is asked two questions, the first of which is: "Are you planning to commit suicide?" The answer is invariably in the negative, for if the patient truly has no such intention, he will say so, and if he is merely dissimulating his real intention, he will also deny that he plans to commit suicide.
>
> The second question is designed to catch the dissimulating patient off guard and so identify him: "Why not?" The patient who has answered the first

question truthfully will have a ready answer for the second. He may assert his responsibility to himself, to his family, to his vocation, or, perhaps, to his religious convictions.

On the other hand, the patient who is trying to deceive, in order to avoid having his plans thwarted, or perhaps to obtain a discharge from the hospital, will have no such ready answer. Moreover, he will display a typical behavior pattern in which he stirs restlessly in his chair and is unable to give any plausible answer to this unexpected question, any substantial argument in favor of continued living . . . . [35]

Shortly after Hitler's troops entered Vienna on March 15, 1938, Frankl held the position of chief of neurology at Rothschild Hospital. Again, he found himself working with suicidal patients. He recalled: "Up to ten suicide attempts came in every day—so catastrophic was the mood of the Jewish population in Vienna!"[36]

In the concentration camp, Frankl found himself again involved with suicide prevention, counseling the suicidal. He recalled a particular incident in which the general mood of the inmates was gloomy, pessimistic, almost at an all-time low. Many of them had succumbed either to sickness or suicide, because they had given up all hope of being liberated from the camp. Frankl's responsibility was to encourage the prisoners, to give them reasons to go on living. One night he gave a talk to encourage them, to attempt to strengthen their resolve to live, using some of the principles of logotherapy.[37] Frankl said, "The purpose of my words was to find a full meaning in our life, then and there, in that hut and in that practically hopeless situation."[38] They had to find a meaning in the moment—in their present situation in the concentration camp—no matter how miserable it was. Frankl's talk worked! He wrote: "I saw that my efforts had been successful."[39] It did not completely stop all suicides from occurring in the concentration camp, but it did help to prevent many from occurring.

Frankl's Opposition to Suicide

As a physician and a philosopher, Frankl was opposed to suicide. He opposed suicide as a physician, because he was bound in conscience by the ethical code of the Hippocratic Oath. "I do respect the decision of people to end their lives," he wrote.[40] However, he added, "But I also wish others respect the principle that I have to save lives as long as I am able."[41]

As a philosopher, Frankl opposed suicide, because it was contrary to logotherapy's principle of the unconditional meaningfulness of human life. For him, life has meaning in any condition (e.g., whether sick or well, whether chronically ill or terminally ill) and in any circumstance (e.g., whether with a disability or without one, whether in prison or out of it, whether in a nursing home or in one's own home).

But it was not only Frankl, the physician and philosopher, who was opposed to suicide but also Frankl, the man himself, a human being who was concerned about the plight of others. For example, he once received a phone call from a woman at three o'clock in the morning. She said to him that she was going to commit suicide. He tried to talk her out of it for half an hour, giving her different arguments against suicide. Finally, she agreed to put off her decision and see Frankl at nine o'clock in the morning on the same day. When she arrived at his office, she said to him:

> You would be mistaken, doctor, if you thought that any of your arguments last night has the least impact on me. If anything helped me, it was this.

Here I disturbed a man's sleep in the middle of the night, and instead of getting angry, he listens patiently to me for half an hour and encourages me. I thought to myself: If this can happen, then it may be worthwhile to give my life another chance.[42]

Frankl the Communicator

Frankl was well educated, having received his Doctor of Medicine (MD) and his Doctor of Philosophy (PhD) degrees from the University of Vienna. But he wrote and spoke so as to be understood by scholars and layman alike. Gerald F. Kreyche, professor emeritus at De Paul University, was right when he wrote: "Frankl . . . possesses the rare ability to write in a layman's language."[43] It is, indeed, "a rare ability" for scholars to write in a lay person's language. It may be difficult for them to communicate in that way, because each academic discipline has its own vocabulary. It is a challenge for a scholar to take his or her own highly specialized education and translate it into words that can be understood by women and women in general, the general public. One is not diminished as a scholar by doing so. In fact, it is a sign that one knows his or her highly specialized subject really well. Frankl's philosophy of logotherapy, then, is not only for the academically or intellectually elite but also for "the man in the street," to borrow a phrase from Frankl. In a sense, logotherapy is for all human beings, because every man and woman needs to find a meaning in life.

Frankl in America

Frankl understood something about the unfolding of history and its potential meaning later in a person's life. He was convinced that there would have been no logotherapy were it not for the fact that he, along with millions of others, was liberated by the allied soldiers during World War II. Frankl was grateful for the many thousands of American soldiers who gave their lives during that war. Upon becoming an honorary citizen of Austin, Texas, in 1975, Frankl said,

> It really is not appropriate that you make me an honorary citizen. It would be more fitting if I make you an honorary logotherapist. Had not so many young soldiers from Texas, among them several from your city, risked and even sacrificed their lives, there would be no Frankl and no logotherapy today. You see, it was your Texas soldiers who liberated me and many others from the camp at Turkheim.[44]

He was a guest lecturer on more than two hundred colleges and/or university campuses throughout the world.[45] He was a visiting professor at Harvard University in 1961, Southern Methodist University in 1966, and Duquesne University in 1972.[46] Honorary doctorate degrees were conferred on him by Loyola University, in Chicago, Illinois (1970); Edgecliffe College, in Cincinnati, Ohio (1970); Rockford College, in Rockford, Illinois (1972); Mount Mary College, in Milwaukee, Wisconsin (1984); Santa Clara University, in Santa Clara, California (1991) and Ohio State University, in Columbus, Ohio (1997). In 1970, a chair for logotherapy was installed by the United States International University in San Diego, California, which has combined with Alliant University to become Alliant International University.[47] In 1971, the Viktor Frankl Institute of Logotherapy was founded in Berkeley, California. Since then, it has relocated to Abilene, Texas.[48]

The Oskar Pfister Award was given to Frankl by the American Psychiatric Association.[49] Frankl's logotherapy has been described as "perhaps the most significant thinking since Freud and Adler," according to the *American Journal of Psychiatry*.[50] *Man's Search for Meaning*, Frankl's most popular book, "has sold over nine million copies in the English editions alone. The United States Library of Congress has listed it as 'one of the ten most influential books in America.'"[51] Logotherapy has been officially recognized as a scientifically based school of psychotherapy by the American Medical Society, the American Psychiatric Association, and the American Psychological Association.

Although Frankl enjoyed being in America and there was much that he admired about it, he had a few criticisms of some cherished American values (at least the popular understanding of them). First, he took exception to the popular or commonly accepted notion of freedom today, which equates it with a license to do virtually anything that one wants. To this, he often would say, "The Statue of Liberty on the East Coast should be supplemented by a Statue of Responsibility on the West Coast."[52]

Second, Frankl was critical of a popular understanding of the phrase "the pursuit of happiness" in the Declaration of Independence. If the pursuit of happiness means living deliberately or intentionally just to seek one's own happiness, being concerned only with pleasing oneself to the exclusion of others, then it is wrong. For Frankl, the pursuit of happiness is self-defeating. He writes: "The very 'pursuit of happiness' is what thwarts it."[53]

Frankl taught that happiness should not be deliberately pursued. Rather, it must ensue, that is, it should happen as a result of forgetting about it, not intentionally or deliberately making it one's aim.[54] Happiness usually happens by giving oneself to a good cause or by helping others, by taking the focus off of oneself and placing it on something or someone else. Then a person experiences fulfillment, inner satisfaction, a sense that his or her life is worthwhile.

Frankl's Legacy

Frankl would often say that logotherapy "is not a panacea."[55] It is not a cure-all to the problems of human beings. It needs to be supplemented by other approaches to psychotherapy, each of which has its own particular value. Frankl's logotherapy is not a religion. It does not address the issue of eternal life. It is not a message of salvation for the human race. It is not concerned with saving souls.

Although logotherapy was founded by Frankl in the early part of the twentieth century and addressed the psychological problems of that century, Frankl's legacy will continue into the twenty-first century, because most of the issues and problems which he addressed in the twentieth century are present today, especially the "existential vacuum" or lack of meaning in life; the often frustrated search for meaning by young people in drugs, sex, and violence; the financially secure man or woman who has means without meaning, who has everything for living and nothing for which to live.

Frankl would not want to be regarded as some kind of guru, nor would he want to be idolized by anyone. He was not a savior. Rather, he was just a man, but a good man. The world is a better place, because he lived in it. Hopefully, his legacy will continue for centuries to come.

A Chronology
of
Viktor Emil Frankl[56]

1907-1997

1905	On March 26, Viktor Emil Frankl is born in Vienna, Austria. He is the second of three children. His mother, Elsa Frankl, nee Lion, comes from Prague; his father, Gabriel Frankl, director in the Ministry of Social Service, comes from Southern Moravia.
1914-1918	During the First World War, the Frankl family experiences bitter deprivation; sometimes the children beg for food from farmers.[57]
1915-1923	In his high school years, Frankl eagerly reads the "Nature Philosophers" and attends public lectures on applied psychology. He comes into contact with psychoanalysis.
1921	Frankl delivers his first public lecture, entitled "On the Meaning of Life."[58] He becomes a functionary of the Young Socialist Workers.
1923	He writes his high school graduation essay entitled, "On the Psychology of Philosophical Thought" (a psycho

analytically oriented study on Arthur Schopenhauer).[59] His writings become published in the youth section of a daily newspaper. He often corresponds with Sigmund Freud.[60]

1924   Frankl's essay "On the Mimic Movements of Affirmation and Negation" is published in the *International Journal of Psycho analysis*.[61] He studies medicine and acts as spokesman of the Austrian Socialist High School Students' Association. A year later, he meets Freud in person, but becomes more and more involved with Alfred Adler.[62]

1925   Frankl's article "Psychotherapy and World View" is published in the *International Journal of Individual Psychology*.[63] He strives to explore the frontier between psychotherapy and philosophy, focusing on the fundamental question of meaning and values—a topic that will become a major theme in his life work.[64]

1926   Frankl presents public lectures on congresses in Duesseldorf, Frankfurt, Berlin.[65] For the first time, he uses the word "logotherapy."[66]

1927   Frankl's relationship to Alfred Adler is declining. Frankl becomes involved with Rudolf Allers and Oswald Schwarz (the founder of psychosomatic medicine). He is enthusiastic about Max Scheler's book, *Formalism in Ethics and Non-formal Ethics of Values*.[67] Against his intention, he is excluded from the Adler circle.[68] However, Adler's daughter Alexandra, Rudolf Dreikurs, and other important Adlerians keep up friendly relations with him.

1928-1929   In Vienna and in six other European cities, Frankl organizes youth counseling centers where adolescents in need may obtain advice and help free of cost. Individual psychologists such as Charlotte Buehler and Erwin Wexberg join Frankl's project, and the anatomy professor and Vienna councilman Julius Tandler provides financial support.[69]

1930   Frankl organizes a special counseling program at the end of the school term; as a result, for the first time in years, no student suicide occurs in Vienna. Frankl gains international attention: Wilhelm Reich invites him to Berlin, the universities of Prague and Budapest want him for lecturing.[70] At the Adult Education Center, he presents a course on psychological hygiene.[71] Shortly before earning his MD, he starts to work at the Psychotherapeutic Department of the Psychiatric University Clinic.[72] He graduates from the University of Vienna Medical School. After his doctorate, he is promoted to "assistant" at the Psychotherapeutic Department of the Psychiatric University Clinic.

1931-1932   Frankl obtains training in neurology. He Works at the Maria TheresienSchloessl in Vienna.

1933-1937   Frankl becomes chief of the Female Suicidals Pavilion at the Psychiatric Hospital in Vienna, with some three thousand patients annually passing through it.[73]

1937   Frankl opens a practice as doctor of neurology and psychiatry.[74]

1938   Hitler's troops invade Austria.[75]

1939   Frankl coins the expression "existential analysis" in his paper "Philosophy and Psychotherapy: On the Foundation of an Existential Analysis."[76] He obtains an immigration visa to America but lets it pass unused, not wanting to desert his elderly parents.[77]

1940-1942   He becomes director of the Neurological Department of the Rothschild Hospital, a clinic for Jewish patients.[78] In spite of the danger to his own life, he sabotages Nazi procedures by making false diagnoses to prevent the euthanasia of mentally ill patients.[79] He publishes several articles in Swiss medical journals and starts writing the first version of his book, *The Doctor and the Soul*.

1942   Frankl marries Tilly Grosser. She conceives their child, but the Nazis force them to have the child aborted.[80] In September, they are arrested—together with Frankl's family—and deported to the Theresienstadt camp in Bohemia.[81] Frankl's sister Stella immigrates to Australia. Frankl's brother Walter and his wife attempt to escape through Italy. After a half a year in Theresienstadt, Frankl's father, Gabriel, dies of starvation and pneumonia.[82]

1944   Frankl and Tilly (and shortly thereafter his mother, Elsa) are transported to Auschwitz; upon entry, his book manuscript is destroyed. In Auschwitz, his mother dies in the gas chamber and his brother Walter dies. Tilly is deported to Bergen-Belsen, where she later perishes.[83] Frankl is later brought to Kaufering und Tuerkheim (extension camps of Dachau).[84] Under the extreme conditions of the camps, Frankl finds his theses on fate and freedom corroborated.[85]

1945 In the last camp, Tuerkheim, he comes down with typhoid fever. To avoid fatal collapse during the nights, he keeps himself awake by reconstructing his book manuscript, *The Doctor and the Soul*, on slips of paper stolen from the camp office.[86] On April 27, the camp is liberated. Frankl returns to Vienna in August. There he learns about the death of his wife, Tilly; his mother, Elsa; and his brother Walter.[87]

1946 Frankl becomes director of the Vienna Neurological Policlinic. He holds this position for twenty-five years, until his retirement.[88] With his reconstructed book, *The Doctor and the Soul*, he attains his teaching appointment at the University of Vienna Medical School. Within nine days, he dictates a book in German, which would later be translated into English and published as *Man's Search for Meaning*. By 1997, more than nine million copies of this book had been sold.[89]

1947 Frankl marries Eleonore B. Schwindt. In December, their daughter Gabriele is born.[90] He publishes his most practice-oriented book *Psychotherapy in Practice: A Casuistic Introduction for Physicians*.[91] In addition, the books *Time and Responsibility* and *Existential Analysis and the Problems of Our Age* are published.[92]

1948 Frankl obtains his Doctor of Philosophy degree (PhD) from the University of Vienna with a dissertation on **"The Unconscious God."**

1948-1949   Frankl becomes associate professor of neurology and psychiatry at the University of Vienna. He presents his "Metaclinical Lectures," which are published under the title, **"Unconditional Man."**

1950   Frankl creates the "Austrian Medical Society for Psychotherapy" and becomes its first president. On the basis of a lecture series, he writes the book *Suffering Man: An Essay on the Problem of Suffering*; its central theme is how to give support and comfort to suffering people. At the Salzburger University Weeks, Frankl expounds his **"10 Theses on the Human Person."**

1951   In his book *Logos and Existence*, Frankl completes the anthropological foundation of logotherapy.[93]

1952   Together with Otto Pöötzl, Frankl publishes a psychophysiological study about the experiences of a falling mountain climber.

1954   Universities in London, Holland, and Argentina invite Frankl to give lectures. In the USA, Gordon Allport promotes Frankl and the publication of his books.[94]

1955   Frankl becomes professor at the University of Vienna. He begins guest professorships at overseas universities.

1956   The theoretical and practical aspects of neuroses from the viewpoint of logotherapy are treated in the book, *Theory and Therapy of Neuroses*.

1959   A very systematic treatment of logotherapy and existential analysis appears as the book chapter **"Outline of Existential Analysis and Logotherapy,"** in *Handbook of Psychotherapy and the Theory of*

Neuroses, edited by Frankl, Gebsattel and Schultz.

1961   Frankl is guest professor at Harvard University in Cambridge, Massachusetts.

1966   He becomes professor at the Southern Methodist University in Dallas, Texas. Based on his lecture manuscripts, Frankl publishes *The Will to Meaning,* which he regards as his most systematic book in English.

1970   In San Diego, California, the United States International University installs a chair for logotherapy.

1972   Frankl becomes guest professor at Duquesne University in Pittsburgh, Pennsylvania.

1988   At the Memorial Day, commemorating the fiftieth year after the invasion by Hitler's troops, Frankl presents a widely noted public address at the Vienna Town Hall Square.

1992   The Viktor Frankl Institute is founded in Vienna by a number of academic friends and members of the Frankl family.

1995   The German edition of Frankl's autobiography, *What is Not in My Books,* is published. In 1997, the English translation is published in the United States under the title *Viktor Frankl—Recollections.*

1997   Frankl's last book, *Man's Search for Ultimate Meaning,* is published. On September 2, Viktor Frankl dies of heart failure in Vienna, Austria.

++++++++++

The meaning of Viktor Frankl's life was to help others find meaning in their lives.[95]

A1
Achievements
(Judging One's Achievements in Life)

a.   "The runner who has started behind his competitor with such-and-such a handicap may emerge from the race as the better runner, even though he does not cross the finish line first . . . . [T]he English . . . have made the phrase "to do one's best" one of their commonest maxims. To do one's best implies that one also includes the relativity of an accomplishment in the judgment of its value. The accomplishment must be judged in reference to the starting-point, to the concrete situation with all its difficulties, all its outward obstacles and inner inhibitions."[96]

b.   "[E]ach human being is not comparable with any other in his innermost being. To compare yourself with anyone else is to do an injustice either to yourself or to the other person . . . . For everyone has a different kind of start. But the person whose start was more difficult, whose fate was less kind, can be credited with the greater personal achievement . . . . Since, however, all aspects of the situation imposed by fate can never be assessed, there is simply no basis and no standard for a comparison of achievements."[97]

See Defiant Power of the Human Spirit, Human Uniqueness.

A 2
Abstinence
(Sexual)

a.   "The shibboleth of sexual frustration is occasionally called for purposes of sexual propaganda . . . . The harmfulness of sexual abstinence has been preached to youth. Such doctrines have done a good deal of injury by nourishing neurotic sexual anxiety. The slogan has been sexual intercourse at any cost, even among young people . . . ."[98]

b.   "[S]exuality should be permitted to mature tranquilly and to advance toward a healthy and meaningful eroticism consonant with human dignity, eroticism in which the sexual element is the expression and crown of a love relationship. This kind of eroticism must necessarily precede the commencement of sexual relations."[99]

See Love, Sex.

A 3
Addiction

To support his theory that addiction in certain instances may be traced back to the existential vacuum, Frankl refers to the studies of alcoholics by Annemarie von Forstmeyer and of drug addicts by Stanley Krippner: "[T]he findings presented by Annemarie von Forstmeyer . . . noted that, as evidenced by tests and statistics, 90 percent of the alcoholics she studied had suffered from an abysmal feeling of meaninglessness. Of the drug addicts studied by Stanley Krippner, 100 percent believed that "things seemed meaningless."[100]

See Existential Vacuum, Mass Neurotic Triad.

A 4
Adler, Alfred
(1870-1937)
(Medical Doctor, Psychiatrist and Psychologist)

"Adlerian psychology . . . considers man a being who is out to overcome . . . the feeling of inferiority which he tries to get rid of by developing the striving for superiority . . . ."[101]

See Freud, Potzl, Psychoanalysis, Viennese Schools of Psychotherapy.

A 5
Affluence

"Affluent society has given vast segments of population *the means*, but people cannot see an *end*, a meaning to live for."[102]

See Materialism, Purpose.

A 6
Aggression[103]

Frankl refers to an experimental study by Carolyn Wood Sherif to show that a sense of purpose gives meaning to life and helps to overcome aggressive tendencies in youth:

"She had succeeded in artificially building up mutual aggressions between groups of boy scouts, and observed that the aggressions only subsided when the youngsters dedicated themselves to a collective purpose—that is, the joint task of dragging out of the mud a carriage in which food had to be brought to their camp. Immediately, they were only challenged but also united by a meaning they had to fulfill."[104]

See Mass Neurotic Triad.

A 7
Alienation

"[A]lienation concerns not only others but also oneself. There is a social alienation, and there is an emotional alienation—alienation from one's own emotions."[105]

A 8
Allport, Gordon W.
(American Psychologist, Formerly Professor of Psychology at Harvard University)
(1897-1967)

[Allport calls logotherapy] "the most significant psychological movement of our day."[106]

See Logotherapy, *Man's Search for Meaning*.

A 9
Anthropology
(Logotherapy's View of the Human Person)[107]

a.   Dimensional Ontology

   "[T]he . . . way to cope with the age-old psychophysical problem in man without disrupting his wholeness and unity seems to be the approach which I have termed "dimensional ontology." This means that we no longer speak of the physical, psychical, and spiritual layers, because as long as we do so it would appear that the layers could be separated from one another. On the other hand, if we try to understand body, psyche, and mind as different dimensions of one and the same being, its wholeness is not in the least destroyed."[108]

b.   Embodied Human Person[109]

"A person's body expresses his character, and his character expresses the person as spiritual being. The spirit attains to expression—and demands expression—in the body and the psyche."[110]

c.   Freedom and Responsibility

1. "[R]esponsibility and freedom comprise the spiritual domain of man."

2. "It is time that . . . [the] . . . decision quality of human existence be included in our definition of man."[111]

3. "[L]ogotherapy sees in responsibleness the very essence of human existence."[112]

4. Frankl quotes from Vatican II: "Note . . . a statement in the documents of Vatican II: 'We are witnesses of the birth of a new humanism, one in which man is defined first of all by his responsibility.'"[113]

5. [Logotherapy] "regards man as free and responsible . . . ."[114]

6. "[F]reedom and responsibility together make man a spiritual being."[115]

d.   More Than an Animal

In a sense, he [the human person] remains an animal, and yet he infinitely surpasses his animal properties."[116]

e.   Noetic or Noological Dimension of the Human Person[117]

1. [The noological dimension is] "in contradistinction to the biological and psychological ones [dimensions]. It is that dimension in which the uniquely human phenomena are located."[118]

2. "This specifically human dimension, which I have entitled noological, is not accessible to a beast. A dog, for example, after wetting the carpet may well sink under the couch but this would not yet be a sign of bad conscience; it is some sort of anticipatory anxiety—namely, fearful anticipation of punishment."[119]

3. "[L]ogotherapy might . . . make a contribution toward the completion of psychotherapy's picture of man, toward a picture of man that . . . includes the genuinely human, that is, the noological dimension."[120]

f.   Psychosomatic Unity of the Human Person

1. "[B]oth mind and matter are part of man, . . .

both are contingent upon one another in his existence. For man is a citizen of more than one realm . . . ."[121]

2. "Those who know how close the connection is between the state of mind of man—his courage and hope, or lack of them—and the state of immunity of his body will understand that the sudden loss of hope and courage can have a deadly effect."[122]

3. "I don not 'have' a self, but I 'am' a self."[123]

4. "Speaking of man in terms of his spiritual, mental, and bodily levels, or layers, may well prompt one to assume that each of these aspects can be separated from others. Nobody, however, can claim that viewing a human being in his manifold dimensions would destroy the wholeness and oneness inherent in man."[124]

5. "Wholeness . . . means the integration of somatic, psychic, and spiritual aspects . . . . [I]t is this threefold wholeness that makes man complete . . . . Body and psyche may form a unity—psychophysical unity—but this does not yet represent the wholeness of man. Without the spiritual as its essential ground, this wholeness cannot exist."[125]

6. "The challenge [today] is how to attain, how to maintain, and how to restore a unified concept of man in the face of the scattered data, facts, and findings supplied by a compartmentalized science of man."[126]

g.   Three Dimensions of the Human Person

    1.   "[W]e see man as a physical-psychic-spiritual totality. We have called on psychotherapy to recognize this totality as such, so that not only the psyche, but the spiritual aspects of man will be taken into account."[127]

    2.   "Man lives in three dimensions: the somatic, the mental, and the spiritual. The spiritual dimension cannot be ignored, for it is what makes us human."[128]

    3.   [S]piritual' does not have a religious connotation but refers to the specifically human dimension."[129]

See Free-Will, Logotherapy, Psychotherapy, Purpose in Life, Responsibility, Spirit/ Spirituality, World View.

A 10
Anticipatory Anxiety

a.   The 'mechanism' of what is termed anticipatory anxiety is all too familiar to the psychotherapist. Something goes wrong when the consciousness attempts to regulate acts which normally take place . . . without thought."[130]

b.   Example of Insomnia

"If a person mistakenly fixes his mind upon the process of falling asleep, if he desperately wills sleep, he creates an inner tension which makes sleep impossible. Fear of sleeplessness is an anticipatory anxiety which in such cases hinders falling asleep, thus confirming the fact of insomnia, which in turn reinforces anticipatory anxiety—a vicious circle."[131]

c.   Example of Stuttering

"The stutterer is acutely conscious of the way he speaks—he concentrates on saying, not on what he wants to say; he observes the how instead of the what. And so he inhibits himself—as though his speech were a motor into which he attempts to poke his fingers when he should simply start it up and let it run of its own accord . . . . If only he will think aloud, the mouth will talk of its own accord— the more fluently when the least observed."[132]

See Hyperreflection, Self-Transcendence, Unconscious.

A 11
Arnold, Magda B.

Frankl quotes Magda B. Arnold: "All choices are caused but they are caused by the chooser."[133]

See Conditioning, Free-Will, Self-Transcendence.

A 12
Arousal
(Sexual Arousal)

"The bodily appearance of the other person . . . [may happen] . . . to be sexually arousing, and this arousal sets off the sex drive in the sexually disposed person, directly affecting that person's physical being."[134]

See Love, Sex.

A 13
Art

"[A]nother definitely human capacity . . . [is] . . . creating and using symbols . . . . [I]t is a characteristic of humanness . . . ."[135]

See Distinctively Human Phenomena.

A 14
Atheism[136]

a.   Frankl quotes from the atheistic philosopher Friedrich Nietzsche: "He who has a *why* to live for can bear almost any *how*."[137]

b.   [It is not surprising to find] "religious motifs in dreams of people who are manifestly irreligious, because . . . there is . . . repressed and unconscious *religio*."[138]

c.   "[A] religious sense is existent and present in each and every person, albeit buried, not to say repressed, in the unconscious . . . ."[139]

d.   "In North Korean prisoner of war camps the prisoners were told that if they did not yield to brainwashing, they would die without anybody knowing about them and their heroism. To someone who is not religious, it must seem senseless to be heroic if no one gets anything out if it, and not even a single person ever knows anything about it."[140]

See Empiricism, God, Nietzsche, Religion, Unconscious.

A 15
Attitudinal Values[141]

a.   "It is through attitudinal values that even the negative, tragic aspects of human existence, or what I call the 'tragic triad'—pain, guilt, and death—may be turned into something positive and creative. Caught in a hopeless situation as its helpless victim, facing a fate that cannot be changed, man still may turn his predicament into an achievement and accomplishment at the human level. He thus may bear witness to the human potential at its best, which is to turn tragedy into triumph."[142]

b.   "[W]hat matters is to make the best of any given situation."[143]

c.   "Through the right attitude, unavoidable suffering is transmitted into a heroic and victorious achievement."[144]

d.   "Facing a fate we cannot change, we are called upon to make the best of it by rising above ourselves and growing beyond ourselves, in a word, by changing ourselves."[145]

e.   [A patient whose leg was amputated because of gangrene learned that] "human life is not so poor a thing that the loss of a limb would make it meaningless."[146]

f.   "A human being, by the very attitude he chooses, is capable of finding and fulfilling meaning in even a hopeless situation."[147]

g.   "[M]eaning rests on the attitude the patient chooses toward suffering."[148]

h.   "[P]atients . . . can learn that difficulties only make life more meaningful, never meaningless."[149]

i.   "Destiny appears to man in three principal forms: (1) as his natural *disposition* or endowment . . . 'somatic fate'; (2) as his *situation*, the total of his external environments; (3) disposition and situation together make up man's *position*. This 'position taken' or attitude is . . . a matter of free choice . . . . [M]an can 'change his position,' take another attitude (as soon as we include the time dimension in our scheme, since a change of position means an alteration of attitude in the course of time)."[150]

j.   "What is significant is the person's attitude toward an unalterable fate. The opportunity to realize such attitudinal values is therefore always present whenever a person finds himself confronted by a destiny toward which he can act only by acceptance. The way in which he accepts, the way in which he bears his cross, what courage he manifests in suffering, what dignity he displays in doom and disaster, is the measure of his human fulfillment."[151]

k.   "I would like to quote Rabbi Earl A. Grollman who once received a call from a woman dying of an incurable disease. 'How can I meet the thought and reality of death?' she asked. The rabbi reports: 'I . . . mentioned the attitudinal values concept of Dr.

Frankl . . . . [S]he learned that the founder of this concept was a psychiatrist who was incarcerated in a concentration camp. This man and his teaching captured her imagination for he knew more than just theoretical application of suffering. She resolved then and there [that] if she could not avoid the inescapable suffering, she would determine the manner and the mode in which she would meet the illness. She became a tower of strength to those around her, whose hearts were lacerated with pain . . . . She died in dignity and is remembered in our community for her indomitable courage.'"[152]

l.   Frankl quotes Czechoslovakian psychologists S. Kratochvil and I. Planova: "Unfavorable circumstances in life may but do not have to frustrate one existentially; it depends on one's value system."[153]

m.   "[I]n the final analysis . . . the sort of person the prisoner became was the result of an inner decision, and not the result of camp influences alone."[154]

n.   "How crucial is an affirmative attitude toward life . . . is . . . illustrated by the following example: A large-scale statistical survey of longevity showed that all the long-lived subjects had a 'serene'—that is, an affirmative view of life."[155]

See Concentration Camps, Conditioning, Defiant Power of the Human Spirit, Free-Will, Happiness, Medical

Ministry, Negative Attitude, Optimism, Questioning the Meaning of Life, Suffering.

A 16
Augustine, Saint
(Bishop of Hippo, theologian, and philosopher)
(354-430)

[Frankl paraphrases Saint Augustine] "[M]an's heart is restless unless he has found, and fulfilled, meaning and purpose in life."[156]

A 17
Auschwitz

a.   "Auschwitz—the very name stood for all that was horrible: gas chambers, crematoriums, massacres."[157]

b.   "[A]mong those who actually went through the experience of Auschwitz, the number of those whose religious life was deepened—in spite of, not because of, this experience—by far exceeds the number of those who gave up their belief."[158]

c.   "God is not dead . . . , not even 'after Auschwitz' . . . ."[159]

d.   "Since Auschwitz we know what man is capable of."[160]

See Concentration Camps, Faith, God, Kolbe, Father Maximilian, Nobility and Misery of Human Beings, Religion.

B 1
Bacon, Yehuda
(Jewish Artist/ Holocaust survivor)
(1929-)

Frankl quotes Yehuda Bacon: "[S]uffering . . . can have a meaning if it changes *you* for the better."[161]

See Suffering.

B 2
Being

a.   "[M]eaning must not coincide with being: meaning must be ahead of being. Meaning sets the pace for being. Existence falters unless it is lived in terms of transcendence toward something beyond itself."[162]

b.   "Meaning is more than being."[163]

See Moses, Self-Transcendence, Tension.

B 3
Boredom

a.   "The existential vacuum manifests itself mainly in a state of boredom."[164]

b.   "What threatens contemporary man is the alleged meaninglessness of his life, or as I call it, the existential vacuum within him. And when does this vacuum open up, when does this so often latent vacuum become manifest? In the state of boredom."[165]

See Existential Vacuum, Meaninglessness.

B 4
Buber, Martin
(Austrian/Jewish Philosopher and Theologian)
(1878-1965)

Using the language of Martin Buber, Frankl talks about a concentration-camp prisoner's loved one: "[I]n the consciousness of every single . . . [prisoner] . . . somebody was present, was invisibly there, perhaps not even living any longer but yet present and at hand, somehow 'there' as the Thou of the most intimate dialogue. For many it was the first, last, and ultimate Thou: God." [166]

See Encounter, God, Personalism.

B 5
Buhler, Charlotte
(1893-1974)
(German Psychologist)[167]

Frankl quotes Charlotte Buhler: "[M]an . . . [lives] . . . with

intentionality, which means living with purpose. The purpose is to give meaning to life . . . ."[168]

See Purpose.

C 1
Certainty[169]

"The normal person is satisfied with the given results of his acts of thinking and does not question them any further; but the obsessional neurotic lacks that simple feeling of satisfaction which follows the thought, and which in the case of the arithmetic example 'two times two equals four' would be followed by: 'Of course that's right.' The normal person experiences the sense of certainty that comes from obviousness . . . ."[170]

See Obsessive-Compulsive Neurotic, Security.

C 2
Change
(The Possibility of Changing Oneself)

a.   "[T]o be human means not only to be different, but also to be able to become different, that is, to change."[171]

b.   "Man . . . may well change himself, otherwise he would not be man. It is a prerogative of being human, and a constituent of human existence, to be capable of shaping and reshaping oneself."[172]

See Fatalism, Free-Will, Human.

C 3
Christianity

"Christianity has placed in the foreground of man's moral consciousness the kind of values we have called 'attitudinal'—the third of the three main categories of possible values. For the Christian existence, taken in the perspective of the cross, of the Crucified One, becomes ultimately and essentially a freely chosen imitation of Christ, a 'passion.'"[173]

See Attitudinal Values, Values (Three General Groups of).

C 4
Clergy

a.   "Western humanity has turned from the priest to the doctor . . . . [N]owadays too many patients come to the medical man with problems which should really be put to a priest."[174]

b.   "[S]ome of the people who nowadays call on the psychiatrist in former days would have seen a pastor, priest, or rabbi. But now they refuse to go to a priest, so that the doctor is forced into what I call medical ministry. It is a ministry occupied not only by the neurologist or by the psychiatrist, but by every doctor."[175]

See Medical Ministry.

C 5
College (or University) Graduates

"As a former teaching assistant of mine at Harvard University could show, among graduates of that university who went on to lead quite successful, ostensibly happy lives, a huge percentage complained of a deep sense of futility, asking themselves what all their success had been for."[176]

See College (or University) Students Existential Vacuum, Success.

C 6
College (or University) Students

a.   "Consider the staggering suicide rates among American college students, second only to traffic accidents as the most frequent cause of death."[177]

b.   "At an American university 60 students who had attempted suicide were screened afterward, and 85 percent said the reason had been that 'life seemed meaningless.' Most important, however, 93 percent of these students suffering from the apparent meaninglessness of life 'were actively engaged socially, were performing well academically, and were on good terms with their family groups.' What we have here . . . is an unheard cry for meaning."[178]

See College (or University) Graduates, Education, Existential Vacuum, Success, Suicide.

C 7
Concentration Camps
(During the Holocaust)

a.   "Most of the camp inmates suffered from certain complexes. The majority were tormented by inferiority feelings. These people had once been 'somebodies' and were now being treated worse than 'nobodies.'"[179]

b.   "But what about human liberty? Is there no spiritual freedom in regard to behavior and reaction to any given surroundings? Is that theory true which would have us believe that man is no more than a product of many conditional and environmental factors— be they of a biological, psychological or sociological nature? Is man but an accidental product of these? Most important, do the prisoners' reactions to the singular world of the concentration camp prove that man cannot escape the influences of his surroundings? Does man have no choice of action in the face of such circumstances?"[180]

c. "The experiences of camp life show that man does have a choice of action. There were enough examples, often of a heroic nature, which proved that apathy could be overcome, irritability suppressed. Man *can* preserve a vestige of spiritual freedom, of independence of mind, even in such terrible conditions of psychic and physical stress."[181]

d. "Sigmund Freud once asserted: 'Let one attempt to expose a number of the most diverse people uniformly to hunger. With the increase of the imperative urge of hunger all individual differences will blur, and in their stead will appear the uniform expression of the one unstilled urge.' Thank heaven, Sigmund Freud was spared knowing the concentration camps from the inside. His subjects lay on a couch designed in the plush style of Victorian culture, not in the filth of Auschwitz. *There*, the 'individual differences' did *not* 'blur' but, on the contrary, people became more different; people unmasked themselves, both the swine and the saints. And today you need no longer hesitate to use the word 'saints': think of Father Maximilian Kolbe who was starved and finally murdered by an injection of carbolic acid at Auschwitz and who in 1983 was canonized."[182]

e. "We who lived in the concentration camps can remember the men who walked through the huts comforting others, giving away their last piece of bread. There may have been few in number, but they offer sufficient proof that everything can be taken from a man but one thing: the last of the human freedoms— to choose one's attitude in any given set of circumstances, to choose one's own way."[183]

f.   [The different reactions to suffering by the inmates in the concentration camps prove that a person] "may remain brave, dignified and unselfish. Or in the bitter fight for self-preservation he may forget his human dignity and become no more than an animal."[184]

g.   "In the living laboratories of the concentration camps we watched comrades behaving like swine while others behaved like saints. Man has both these potentialities within himself. Which one he actualizes depends on decisions, not on conditions. It is time that this decision quality of human existence be included in our definition of man."[185]

h.   "[A] good many men learned in concentration camp, and as the result of concentration camp, to believe in God again."[186]

i.   "[T]here broke out in many a prisoner in confinement, and because of confinement, . . . a subconscious or a repressed relationship to God. "Let no one . . . dispose of it as 'foxhole religion,' as Anglo-Saxon countries term that religiosity which does not show until one is in danger. [T]he religion which one does not have until things go badly is . . . still preferable to that which one has only as long as things go well—I call that a 'bargainer's religion.'"[187]

j.   "In a sense, living through the concentration camps was one big experiment—a crucial experiment. Our dead colleagues [referring the Viennese physicians who expressed the highest professional or ethical standards and conducted themselves with dignity in the concentration camp] passed the test with honors. They proved to us that even under the most depraved, the most humiliating conditions, man can still remain man . . . . [188]

k.   "[T]he concentration camp was nothing more than a microcosmic mirroring of the human world as a whole. And so we may be justified in applying what is to be learned from the experiences of the concentration camp to conditions in the world today."[189]

l.   Referring to the experiences of the prisoners in the concentration camp, Frankl says: "Whatever we had gone through could still be an asset to us in the future."[190]

See Attitude, Auschwitz, Conditioning, Forgiveness, Free-Will, Freud, Gas Chambers, God, (Human Survival), Kolbe, Nobility and Misery of Human Beings, Religion, Spirit.

C 8
Conditioning

a.   "Man is not free from conditions. But he is free to take a stand in regard to them. The conditions do not completely condition him. Within limits it is up to him whether or not he succumbs and surrenders to the conditions. He may as well rise above them and by so doing open up and enter the human dimension."[191]

b.   "Man, as the finite being he basically is, will never be able to free himself completely from the ties which bind him to the various realms wherein he is confronted by unalterable conditions. Nevertheless, there is always a certain residue of freedom left to his decisions. For within the limits—however restricted they may be—he can move freely; and only by this very stand which he takes toward whatever conditions he may face does he prove to be a truly human being. This holds true with regard to biological and psychological as well as sociological facts and factors. Social environment, hereditary endowment, and instinctual drives can limit the scope of man's freedom, but in themselves they can never totally blur the human capacity to take a stand toward all those conditions."[192]

See Anthropology, Attitudinal Values, Concentration Camps, Determinism, Free-Will, Noological Dimension of the Human Person, Self-Transcendence, Soul, Spirit, Survival.

C 9
Conscience

a. "Man passes [to] the noological dimension whenever he is reflecting upon himself—whenever he displays his being conscious of himself—or whenever he exhibits his being conscientious. In fact, being conscientious presupposes the uniquely human capacity to rise above oneself, to judge and evaluate one's own deeds in moral and ethical terms."[193]

b. "I may ask whether . . . conscience has not to be something other than I myself; might it not be something higher than he who merely perceives its 'voice?' In other words, . . . I understand conscience as a phenomenon transcendent of man."[194]

c. [There is a] "transcendent quality of conscience."[195]

d. "Conscience not only refers to transcendence; it also originates in transcendence."[196]

e. [There is a transhuman or] "transpersonal agent

of . . . [conscience] . . . of which the human person is but the 'image.'"[197]

f.   "Hitler would never have become what he did unless he had *suppressed* within himself the voice of conscience"[198]

g.   "[C]onscience is . . . an irreducible thing-in-itself."[199]

h.   [True conscience cannot] "be dismissed as a conditioning process. Conscience is a definitely human phenomenon."[200]

i.   [A human being] "can be his own judge, the judge of his own deeds."[201]

j.   "Time and again, an individual's conscience commands him to do something which contradicts what is preached by the society to which the individual belongs . . . ."[202]

k.   "[O]nly a[n] erroneous conscience will ever command a person to commit suicide . . . . [O]nly an erroneous conscience will ever command a person to commit homicide, or— . . . to refer to Hitler—genocide"[203]

See also Anthropology, Humor, *Imago Dei*, Noological Dimension, Psychotherapist, Suicide, Transcendence.

D 1
Death

a.   [In death], "the person . . . has no mind, no body; he has lost his psychophysical ego. What is left, and what remains, is the self, the spiritual self."[204]

b.   [A human being] "is 'creating' himself at the moment of his death. His self is not something that 'is' but something that is becoming, and therefore becomes itself fully only when life has been completed by death."[205]

c.   [We are sleeping and suddenly the alarm clock goes off,] "and, still caught in our dreams, we often do not (at least not immediately) realize that the alarm wakes us up to our real existence, our existence in the real world. But do we mortals no[t] act similarly when we approach death? Do we not equally forget that death awakens us to the true reality of our selves?"[206]

d.   "Death . . . is not wiped off the slate by being pushed out of consciousness . . . ."[207]

e.   "[M]an is a being which sooner or later must die and before doing so, must suffer—despite the advances of science . . . ."[208]

f.   "[W]hat about death—does it not completely cancel the meaning of our life? By no means. As the end belongs to the story, so death belongs to life."[209]

g.   "The dullard newspaper-reader sitting at his breakfast table is avid for stories of misfortune and death . . . . What such a person really gets out of these vicarious deaths is the contrast effect: it seems as though other people are always the ones who must die. For this type of person is fleeing what most horrifies him: the certainty of his own death—which his existential vacuum makes unbearable to him . . . . This type of person takes refuge in the delusion that nothing can happen to him personally; death and disaster are trials that only affect others."[210]

See Diversions, Dying Young, Self-Creation, Tragic Triad.

D 2
Decisions

"Man cannot avoid decisions. Reality inescapably forces man to decide . . . . Through . . . decisions man decides upon himself. Continually and incessantly he shapes and reshapes himself."[211]

See Anthropology, Free-Will, Responsibility, Self-Creation.

D 3
Defiant Power of the Human Spirit

At the age of seventeen, Jerry Long became a quadriplegic by a diving accident. He remained that way for the rest of his life. His body became paralyzed, but his spirit did not. He eventually went on to college and graduated. Then he went to graduate school and earned a PhD. Jerry is a witness to the defiant power of the human spirit. For example, he wrote a letter to Dr. Frankl, which, in part, reads:

> "I view my life as being abundant with meaning and purpose. The attitude that I adopted on that fateful day has become my personal credo: I broke my neck, it didn't break me . . . . I believe that my handicap will only enhance my ability to help others. I know that without the suffering, the growth that I have achieved would have been impossible."[212]

See Accomplishments, Attitudinal Values, Meaning, Purpose, Spirit.

D 4
Democracy

"Responsibleness has two intentional referents. It refers to a meaning for whose fulfillment we are responsible, and also to a being before whom we are responsible. Therefore the sound spirit of democracy is but one-sidedly conceived of if understood as freedom without responsibleness."[213]

See Freedom, Responsibility Self-Creation.

D 5
Depression

a. "A Carmelite sister was suffering from a depression which proved to be somatogenic [related to bodily causes]. She was admitted to the Department of Neurology at the Poliklinik Hospital. Before a specific drug treatment decreased her depression this depression was increased by a psychic trauma. A Catholic priest told her that if she were a true Carmelite sister she would have overcome the depression long before. Of course this was nonsense . . . I was able to free the patient of the effects of the traumatic experience and thus relieve her depression over being depressed. The priest had told her that a Carmelite sister cannot be depressed."[214]

b. "[D]epression often results in suicide, and there is ample evidence that, particularly among the young generation, the number of suicides is increasing."[215]

c. "[N]ot each and every case of depression is to be traced back to a feeling of meaninglessness, nor does suicide—in which depression sometimes eventuates—always result from an existential vacuum."[216]

d.   "[T]here are cases of depression who commit suicide, and there are cases who manage to overcome the suicidal impulse for the sake of a cause or a person. They are too committed to commit suicide . . . ."[217]

See Existential Vacuum, Despair, Self-Transcendence, Suicide, Youth.

D 6
Despair

a.   The following words illustrate one of the reasons that Frankl wrote his book *Man's Search for Meaning:* "I had wanted simply to convey to the reader by way of a concrete example that life holds a potential meaning under any conditions, even the most miserable ones. And I thought that if the point were demonstrated in a situation as extreme as that in a concentration camp, my book might gain a hearing. I therefore felt responsible for writing down what I had gone through, for I thought it might be helpful to people who are prone to despair."[218]

b.   "One must go through his own existential despair if he is to immunize his patients against it."[219]

c.   "There is no need to feel ashamed of existential despair [over life's meaning] because of the assumption that it is an emotional disease, for it is . . . a human achievement and accomplishment. Above all, it is a manifestation of intellectual sincerity and honesty.

"However, if a young man . . . challenges life's meaning, he must have patience—enough patience to wait until meaning dawns upon him."[220]

d. Viktor Frankl recalls a conversation he had with a man who was in despair, because, although he was searching for a meaning to his life, he could not find it. "[Y]ou need not despair because of your despair. You should rather take this despair as evidence of the existence of . . . 'the will to meaning.' And in a sense, the very fact of your will to meaning justifies your faith in meaning. Or, as the famous Austrian novelist Franz Werfel once said, 'Thirst is the surest proof for the existence of water.' He meant, how could a man experience thirst unless water were in the world."[221]

e. "[D]espair is suffering without meaning."[222]

f. "A doctor [that is, a psychiatrist or psychotherapist] should not prescribe a tranquilizer cure for the despair of a man who is grappling with spiritual problems."[223]

See Depression, Existential Vacuum, Man's Search for Meaning, Meaning, Questioning the Meaning of Life, Suffering, Suicide, Will to Meaning.

D 7
Determinism

a. "Man has been presented as constrained by biological, by psychological, by sociological factors. Inherent human freedom, which obtains in spite of all these constraints, the freedom of the spirit in spite of nature, has been overlooked."[224]

b.   "Pan-determinism serves the criminal as an alibi:
it is the mechanisms within him that are blamed.
Such an argument, however, proves to be self-
defeating. If the defendant alleges that he really
was not free and responsible when he committed
his crime, the judge may claim the same when
passing sentence."[225]

See Anthropology, Conditioning, Fatalism, Free-Will,
Responsibility, Spirit/ Spirituality.

D 8
Distinctively Human Phenomena[226]

a.   "[T]he search for meaning is a distinctive
characteristic of being human. No other animal has
ever cared whether or not there is a meaning to
life . . . But man does."[227]

b.   "[T]he sense of humor is exclusively human—after
all, no animal but man is capable of laughing."[228]

c.   "[T]here are no computers that laugh at themselves,
nor are there animals that care about meaning and
purpose in their existence."[229]

d.   [No] "rat . . . [is] . . . capable of asking itself whether
its existence has a meaning."[230]

e.   "Challenging the meaning of life can therefore
never be taken as a manifestation of morbidity
or abnormality; it is rather the truest expression
of the state of being human, the mark of the most
human nature in man. For we can easily imagine

highly developed animals or insects—say bees or ants—which in many aspects of their social organization are actually superior to man. But we can never imagine any such creature raising the question of the meaning of its own existence, and thus challenging this existence. It is reserved for man alone to find his very existence questionable, to experience the whole dubiousness of being. More than such faculties as power of speech, conceptual thinking, or walking erect, this factor of doubting the significance of his own existence is what sets man apart from animals."[231]

f.   "[T]his most radical challenging of oneself, to the extent not only of doubting the meaning of life, but of taking action against that life—this fundamental possibility of choosing suicide, this liberty of man to decide whether he shall be at all, distinguishes his being from all other kinds of being and marks its contrast with the mode of being of animals."[232]

g.   "Conscience is a human phenomenon, and we must see to it that it is preserved in its humanness rather than being dealt with reductionistically. Reductionism is a pseudoscientific procedure that either reduces human phenomena to, or deduces them from, subhuman phenomena. For example, conscience is reductionistically interpreted as nothing but the result of conditioning processes."[233]

See Anthropology, Art, Conscience, Free-Will, Human, Humor, *Imago Dei*, Meaning, Paradoxical Intention, Purpose, Reductionism, Self-Detachment, Spirit, Suicide.

D 9
Diversions[234]

a.   "[M]an is afraid of his inner void, of the existential vacuum, and runs away from it into work or pleasure."[235]

b.   "Flight from the self allows for avoiding a confrontation with the void in the self."[236]

c.   "I consider the pace, the haste of our times, to be . . . an attempt—albeit an unsuccessful one—to cure ourselves of existential frustration. The less a man is able to discover a goal for his life, the more he speeds the pace of his living."[237]

d.   "People vacillating between professional overactivity and centrifugal leisure have no time to finish their thoughts. When they begin to think, a secretary comes in and asks for a signature, or a telephone call must be answered."[238]

See Existential Vacuum, Lonely, Money, Sunday Neurosis, Purpose in Life, Workaholic.

D 10
Doctor
(or Physician's Role in Saving Human Lives)

a.   "[T]he duty of the doctor to save life wherever he can remains binding even when he confronts a patient who has tried to destroy himself and whose life now hangs by a thread."[239]

b.   "It might be said that the doctor who intervenes in an attempt at suicide is taking on himself the role of arbiter of destiny, instead of letting destiny take its course. To which we reply: If 'destiny'—or Providence—were intent on letting a person weary of life die, it would have found ways to make the doctor's intervention come too late. If destiny places the would-be suicide in the hands of a doctor before it is too late, this doctor must act as a physician, must never assume the role of judge and decide on personal philosophical grounds, or simply arbitrarily, whether his patient is to be or not to be."[240]

See Euthanasia, Hippocratic Oath, Suicide.

D 11
Doctor and the Soul
(or The Doctor and the Soul)[241]

a. "[U]pon my arrival at Auschwitz, the manuscript [*The Doctor and the Soul*] was sewn into the lining of my overcoat, hidden there . . . . [I]t was lost when I had to throw everything on the ground: my clothing, my last few belongings . . . ."[242]

b. "I am convinced that I owe my survival, among other things, to my resolve to reconstruct that lost manuscript. I started to work on it when I was sick with typhus and tried to keep awake, even in the night, to prevent a vascular collapse."[243]

c. "I will never forget the sense of deep reward that I experienced when I went to my publisher in Vienna with the manuscript whose first version I had carried to Auschwitz. I felt like the man in the psalm: 'he that goeth forth weeping, bearing precious seed, shall doubtless come again with rejoicing, bringing his sheaves with him."

The first printing of the book sold out within three days. But it still took nine years before an English translation was published . . . ."[244]

See Frankl, *Man's Search for Meaning.*

D 12
Don Juan[245]

There is a type of aberrant (abnormal) sexual behavior in which the man does not even "try to respect or love the sexual partner."

"The so-called Don Juan type belongs to this class. Simple souls are impressed by him, think of him as an erotic hero. But in reality he is a weakling who has never dared to attempt a truly fulfilling love life. For all the amount of sexual pleasure and the numbers of sexual partners he can total up, he remains inwardly empty. His world is emptier than that of the real lover and his life more unfulfilled than other lives."[246]

See Existential Vacuum, Love, Sex.

D 13
Dostoevski (or Dostoyevski), Fyodor (Russian Novelist) (1821-1881)

Frankl quotes Dostoevski: "There is only one thing that I dread: not to be worthy of my sufferings."[247]

See Nobility and Misery of Human Beings, Suffering.

D 14
Dress
(A Woman's Dress)

"An evening dress . . . does not affect a man 'in itself'; he thinks it beautiful only when the woman he loves is wearing it."[248]

D 15
Drives[249]

"[M]an is pushed by drives but pulled by meaning, and this implies that it is always up to him to decide whether or not he wishes to fulfill the latter. Thus, meaning fulfillment always implies decision-making."[250]

See Free-Will, Instincts, Meaning.

D 16
Drugs

a.   "[T]he drug scene is one aspect of a more general mass phenomenon, namely the feeling of meaninglessness resulting from a frustration of our existential needs . . . ."[251]

b.   "[P]eople who are caught in the existential vacuum are eager, if meanings cannot be acquired, to provide themselves at least with mere feelings of meaningfulness—such as those that are available in the state of intoxication that is induced by LSD."[252]

c.   [Dr. Betty Lou Padelford] "reports that Nowlis addressed the quxestion of why students were interested in and took drugs. Among the reasons often listed was 'the desire to find meaning in life. [253]

See Existential Vacuum, Meaning, Youth.

D 17
Dullness

"Life never ceases to put new questions to us, never permits us to come to rest. Only self-narcotization keeps us insensible to the eternal pricks with which life with its endless succession of demands stings our consciences."[254]

D 18
Dying Young

a.   "[E]ven a life of short duration . . . could be so rich in joy and love that it contained more meaning than some life that lasts eighty years."[255]

b.   "It is not from the length of its span that we can ever draw conclusions as to a life's meaningfulness. We cannot, after all, judge a biography by its length, by the number of pages in it; we must judge by the richness of the contents. The heroic life of one who has died young certainly has more content and meaning than the existence of some long-lived dullard. Sometimes the 'unfinisheds' are among the most beautiful symphonies."[256]

See Death, Meaning.

E 1
Education

a.   Frankl quotes James C. Crumbaugh: "[E]ducation alone by no means assures the attainment of meaning in life.'"[257]

b.   "Education avoids confronting young people with ideals and values. They are shunned. There is a feature of American culture that is striking in the eyes of the European. I refer to the obsession to avoid being authoritarian, to avoid even being directive."[258]

c.   "[E]ducation often adds to the existential vacuum. The students' sense of emptiness and meaninglessness is reinforced by the way in which scientific findings are presented to them, by the reductionist way, that is. The students are exposed to an indoctrination along the lines of a mechanistic theory of man plus a relativistic philosophy of life."[259]

d.   "I well remember how I felt when I was exposed to reductionism in education as a junior high school student at the age of thirteen. Once our natural science teacher told us that life in the final analysis was nothing but a combustion process, an oxidation process, I sprang to my feet and said, 'Professor Fritz, if this is the case, what meaning does life have?'"[260]

See College Students, Existential Vacuum, Meaning, Meaninglessness, Youth.

E 2
Einstein, Albert
(Physicist)
(1879-1955)

Frankl quotes Albert Einstein: "What is the meaning of human life, or for that matter of the life of any creature? To find a satisfying answer to this question means to be religious."[261]

See Existential Vacuum, Meaninglessness, Reductionism.

E 3
Emotions

a.   "Consistent suppression of intrinsically meaningful emotional impulses because of their possible unpleasurable tone ends in the 'killing' of a person's inner life. A sense of the meaning of emotional experiences is deeply rooted in human beings . . . ."[262]

b.   "[M]an is actually always striving, whether his emotions be joyful or sad, to remain psychically alive' and not to sink into apathy."[263]

See Grief.

E 4
Empiricism
(The Radical Form)

a.   "[There are certain] "people who insist that nothing can be real unless it is tangible."[264]

b.   "People who limit reality to what is tangible and visible and for this reason tend *a priori* to deny the existence of an ultimate being, also repress religious feelings."[265]

See Atheism, God, Religion, Repression, Soul.

E 5
Encounter

"[T]he concept of encounter has been derived from existentialist . . . literature . . . . [Existentialists interpret] . . . existence in terms of coexistence. In this context, encounter is understood as a relationship between an I and a Thou—a relationship which, by its very nature, can be established only on the human and personal level."[266]

See Kant, Love, Personalism, Rogers, Sex.

E 6
End Justifies the Means
(Critique of)

"[T]here are means which desecrate even the most sacred ends."[267]

E 7
Euthanasia[268]

a. [Logotherapy affirms] "the unconditional value of each and every person. It is that which warrants the indelible quality of the dignity of man. Just as life remains potentially meaningful under any conditions, even those which are the most miserable, so too does the value of each and every person stay with him or her, and it . . . is not contingent on the usefulness that he or she may or may not retain in the present."[269]

b.   [The quality of life or usefulness notion in today's society] "blurs the decisive difference between being valuable in the sense of dignity and being valuable in the sense of usefulness."[270]

c.   "If one . . . holds that an individual's value stems only from his present usefulness, then, believe me, one owes it only to personal inconsistency not to plead for euthanasia along the lines of Hitler's program, that is to say, 'mercy' killing of all those who have lost their social usefulness, be it because of old age, incurable illness, mental deterioration, or whatever handicap they may suffer."[271]

d.   "[I]t is not the doctor's province to sit in judgment on the value or lack of value of a human life."[272]

e.   "The doctor must act as agent of the sick man's will to live and as supporter of his right to live. It is not for the doctor to deny him that will or retract that right."[273]

f.   Referring to a doctor's mission as a healer of the sick, Frankl says: "The task assigned to him by society is solely that of helping wherever he can, and alleviating pain where he must; of healing to the extent that he can, and nursing illness which is beyond cure. If patients and their near and dear were not convinced that the doctor takes this mandate seriously and literally, they would never trust him again. A patient would never know whether the doctor was still coming to him as a helper—or as an executioner."[274]

g.   [Frankl was critical of the attempt, which] "has repeatedly been made in various quarters to legalize the ending of *lives supposedly no longer worth living.*"[275]

h.   "[E]very life, in every situation and to the last breath, has a meaning, retains a meaning. This is equally true of the life of a sick person, even the mentally sick. *The so-called life not worth living does not exist.*"[276]

i.   "[A] person surrounded by loving relatives, a person who is the irreplaceable object of their love, is a person whose life has meaning, though that meaning may be only passive."[277]

See Doctor, Existential Personalism, Hippocratic Oath, Human Uniqueness, Meaning, Suicide.

E 8
Example

"Example is more powerful than talk, as modern psychological research on 'modeling' has shown us."[278]

E 9
Executive's Disease

a.   "In 'Executive's Disease' the frustrated will to meaning is vicariously compensated by the will to power. The professional work into which the executive plunges with such maniacal zest . . . is a means to self-stupefaction."[279]

b.   "I know of a patient, a big industrialist, who presented the classical picture of Executive's Disease. His entire life was dominated by one single desire to the point where he overlooked himself and thereby ruined his health; although he possessed a sports plane, he was not satisfied, but wished for a jet plane. Apparently his existential vacuum was so great that it could only be overcome by supersonic speed."[280]

See Diversions, Sunday Neurosis.

E 10
Existential Analysis[281]

a. "At the time we introduced the term 'existential analysis' in 1938, contemporary philosophy offered the word 'existence' to denote that specific mode of being that is basically characterized by being responsible."[282]

b. "What comes to consciousness in existential analysis . . . is not drive or instinct, . . . but self . . . . [T]he self . . . becomes conscious of itself."[283]

See Responsibility.

E 11
Existentialism

a. "To contemporary existentialist philosophy goes the honor of having shown that the existence of man is essentially concrete and subjective. It took the existentialist stress on these qualities to restore moral responsibility to the modern scene."[284]

b. In the Preface to the book *Man's Search for Meaning*, psychologist Gordon Allport comments on Frankl's account of the sufferings of the prisoners in the concentration camps: "It is here that we encounter the central theme of existentialism: to live is to suffer, to survive is to find meaning in the suffering. If there is a purpose in life at all, there must be a purpose in suffering and in dying."[285]

c.   "[T]his objectivity [of each person's meaning of life] is frequently neglected by some of those writers who call themselves existentialists. Though they never weary of repeating ad nauseam that man is 'being in the world,' they seem to forget that meaning is also 'in the world' and thus not merely a subjective factor. It is more than a mere self-expression, or a projection of the self *into* the world."[286]

d.   [To some existentialists,] "man is a being who, in all his cognitive acts and efforts, can never reach a real world. His world is but a design projected by himself and mirroring the structure of his being."[287]

e.   "Existentialism places the emphasis on the present—however transitory the present might be."[288]

f.   "[A] human being is no thing. This *no-thingness, rather than nothingness, is the lesson to learn from existentialism*."[289]

g.   "[T]here are as many existentialisms as there are existentialists."[290]

See Death, Free-Will, Meaning, Responsibility, Suffering, Truth.

E 12
Existential Frustration[291]

a. [Existential frustration may be caused by] "a lack of knowledge about a meaning to [one's] existence which alone can make life worth living . . . ."[292]

b. "Inasmuch as we may define as existential whatever is connected not only with man's existence but also with the meaning of man's existence, we can speak of existential frustration . . . ."[293]

c. "[M]an's existential vacuum . . . [is] . . . the result of the frustration of the . . . 'will to meaning.'"[294]

See Existential Vacuum.

E 13
Existential Psychiatry

"Logotherapy represents one of the schools in the field of psychotherapy, and, more specifically, . . . fall[s] under the category of . . . 'existential psychiatry.'"[295]

See Psychotherapy.

E 14
Existential Vacuum

a. "The director of the Behavior Therapy Center in New York, Leonard Bachelis, . . . has been quoted to the effect that many undergoing therapy at the center have good jobs and are successful but want to kill themselves because they find life meaningless"[296]

b. "At an American university, 60 students who had attempted suicide were screened afterward, and 85 percent said the reason had been that 'life seemed meaningless.' Most important, however, 93 percent of these students suffering from the apparent meaninglessness of life 'were actively engaged socially, were performing well academically, and were on good terms with their family groups.' What we have here . . . is an unheard cry for meaning . . . ."[297]

c.   "Rolf H. Von Eckartsberg conducted a study at Harvard University to investigate the life adjustment of Harvard's graduates. The result offers statistical evidence among 100 subjects, who had graduated twenty years before, there was a huge percentage of people who complained of a crisis. They felt that their lives were pointless and meaningless—and this they did although they had been very successful in their professional lives—as lawyers, doctors, surgeons, and, last but not least, analysts, we may suppose—as well as in their marital lives. They were caught in an existential vacuum."[298]

d.   "[S]o many patients complain today . . . [about] . . . the feeling of the total and ultimate meaninglessness of their lives. They lack the awareness of a meaning worth living for. They are haunted by the experience of their inner emptiness, a void within themselves; they are caught in that situation which I have called the 'existential vacuum.'"[299]

e.   [The existential vacuum means] "the experience of a total lack, or loss, of an ultimate meaning to one's existence that would make life worthwhile."[300]

f.   [The existential vacuum may be called] "'existential frustration' or the frustration of the 'will to meaning.'"[301]

g.   [The existential vacuum may also be called an] "abyss experience . . ."[302]

h.   "[T]here are various masks and guises under which the existential vacuum appears. Sometimes the frustrated will to meaning is vicariously compensated for by a will to power, including the most primitive form of the will to power, the will to money. In other cases, the place of frustrated will to meaning is taken by the will to pleasure. That is why existential frustration often eventuates in sexual compensation. We can observe in such cases that the sexual libido becomes rampant in the existential vacuum."[303]

i.   "One might enjoy a life full of pleasure and power and yet be caught in the feeling of its ultimate meaninglessness."[304]

j.   "In our present culture we are witnessing . . . an inflation of sex . . . .

k.   [S]exual inflation is associated with a devaluation: sex is devalued inasmuch as it is dehumanized. Thus, we observe a trend to living a sexual life that . . . is lived out for the sake of pleasure. Such a depersonalization of sex is a symptom of existential frustration: the frustration of man's search for meaning."[305]

l.   " Not *eros* [that is, sex] but *logos* [that is, meaning] is the victim of repression. Once the will to meaning is repressed, however, the existence of meaning is no longer perceived."[306]

m.   "In contrast to the findings of Sigmund Freud, man

is no longer sexually frustrated, in the first place, but rather 'existentially frustrated.' And in contrast to the findings of Alfred Adler, his main complaint is no longer a feeling of inferiority but rather a feeling of futility, a feeling of meaninglessness and emptiness, which I have termed the 'existential vacuum.'"[307]

n.   "[T]he feeling of meaninglessness . . . is an existential despair and a spiritual distress rather than an emotional disease or a mental illness."[308]

o.   "[M]an is a being in search of meaning . . . . [T]oday his search is unsatisfied . . . and that . . . constitutes the pathology of our age."[309]

p.   Effects of the Existential Vacuum

1.   "[L]et us turn . . . to the effects of the existential vacuum . . . . Among the worldwide effects is what one might call the *mass neurotic triad*, which consists of *depression, addiction*, and *aggression*. I once took a taxi to a university whose student body had invited me to give a lecture on the question of whether 'the new generation is mad.' I asked the cab driver to answer that question. He . . . [said]: 'Of course they are mad; they kill themselves, they kill each other, and they take dope.'"[310]

2.   "[A]longside depression and aggression, addiction too is at least partially to be traced back to the feeling of meaninglessness."[311]

See Drugs, Meaning, Meaninglessness, Mass Neurotic Triad, Money, Neurosis, Sex, Suicide, Youth.

F 1
Faith

a. "[W]e may . . . define belief and faith as *trust* in ultimate meaning."[312]

b. "Man . . . can reach out for the ultimate meaning through faith which is mediated by trust in the ultimate being."[313]

c. "[O]ut of an unconditional trust in ultimate meaning and an unconditional faith in ultimate being, Habakkuk chanted his triumphant hymn: 'Although the fig tree shall not blossom, neither shall fruit be in the vines; the labor of the olive shall fail, and the fields shall yield no meat; the flock shall be cut off from the fold, and there shall be no herd in the stalls: Yet I will rejoice in the Lord, I will joy in the God of my salvation.'"[314]

d. "For either belief in God is unconditional or it is not belief at all. If it is unconditional it will stand and face the fact that six million died in the Nazi holocaust; if it is not unconditional it will fall away if only a single innocent child has to die . . . ."[315]

See also God, Religion, Ultimate Meaning.

F 2
Fatalism

a. "The man who believes his fate is sealed is incapable of repealing it."[316]

b. "Neurotic fatalists . . . are prone to blame childhood educational and environmental influences for 'making' them what they are and having determined their destinies. These persons are attempting to excuse their weaknesses of character. They accept these weaknesses as given facts, instead of seeing that having had such unfortunate early influences only makes it more incumbent upon them to practice self-restraint and seek to school themselves differently."[317]

c.   "Neurotic Fatalism is only another disguised form of escape from responsibility . . . ."[318]

See Attitudinal Values, Change, Determinism, Free-Will, Responsibility.

F 3
Finitude

a.   [Conscience] "is subject to the human condition in that it is stamped by the finiteness of man. For he is not only guided by conscience in his search for meaning, he is sometimes misled by it as well."[319]

b.   "Man has to accept his finiteness in its three aspects: He has to face the fact (1) that he has failed; (2) that he is suffering; and (3) that he will die."[320]

See Conscience, Death, Guilt, Suffering, Tragic Triad, Transitoriness of Life.

F 4
Forgiveness
(of the Perpetrators of the Holocaust)

a.   Frankl recalls his conversation with Dr. Paul Furst and Dr. Ernst Rosenberg—two medical doctors—before they died in the concentration camp: "[I]n their last words there was not a single word of hate, only words of longing came from their lips and words of forgiveness, because what they hated was not human beings—a person must be able to forgive humans—but what they hated and what we all hate was the system, . . . which brought others to death."[321]

b.   "[W]e do not only want to remember the dead, but also to forgive the living. As we extend our hand to the dead, across the graves, so we also extend our hand to the living, across all hatred. And if we say, 'Honor to the dead,' we want to add, 'and peace to all the living, who are of good will.'"[322]

c.   "[T]he jury of Vienna is absolutely against me, because I'm too much for reconciling-very mean to me. They are fearing that I'm one who has forgotten the Holocaust. In my whole book *Man's Search for Meaning*, you will not find the word Jew.' I don't capitalize from being a Jew and having suffered as a Jew . . . ."[323]

See Concentration Camps, Nobility, and Misery of Human Beings.

F 5
Frankl, Viktor E.

a.   Accomplishments in His Life since Auschwitz

"While others may look at what I may have accomplished, or rather at what turned out well by good fortune, I realize at such moments how much . . . I owe to God's grace, granted to me for all these years beyond the time I was forced to walk through the gates of Auschwitz."[324]

b.   Childhood, Puberty, and Youth

1. "When I was three, I decided to become a physician, and this probably pleased my father much."[325]

2. "As a child I was religious, but then, during puberty, I passed through an atheistic period."[326]

3. "As a youth I remained enthusiastic about psychiatry, and about psychoanalysis particularly. I was also fascinated by philosophy."[327]

c.   Existentialist Philosopher

Gordon Allport, referring to Frankl, said: "Unlike many European existentialists, Frankl is neither pessimistic nor anti-religious. On the contrary, for a writer who faces fully the ubiquity of suffering and the forces of evil, he takes a surprisingly hopeful view of man's capacity to transcend his predicament and discover an adequate guiding truth."[328]

d.   Hobbies

1. "[A]t age 67, I took my first flying lessons during my professorship in San Diego, California . . . . After a few months I took my first solo flights."[329]

2. "Until my 80th year, mountain climbing was my most passionate hobby."[330]

e.   Holocaust Survivor

1. "I am a survivor of four . . . concentration

camps . . . and as such I also bear witness to the unexpected extent to which man is capable of defying and braving even the worst conditions conceivable."[331]

2. "[T]he will to meaning has 'survival value.' This was the lesson I had learned in three years spent in Auschwitz and Dachau: . . . those most apt to survive the camps were those oriented toward the future—toward a task, or a person, waiting for them in the future, toward a meaning to be fulfilled by them in the future."[332]

f.   Humility

Frankl was granted a private audience with Pope Paul VI. Frankl said to the pope: "While others may look at what I may have accomplished, or rather at what turned out well by good fortune, I realize at such moments how much more I should have done, but failed to do. In other words, how much do I owe to God's grace, granted to me for all these years beyond the time I was forced to walk through the gates of Auschwitz."[333]

g.   Junior High School Student

"I well remember how I felt when I was exposed to reductionism in education as a junior high school student at the age of thirteen. Once our natural science teacher told us that life in the final analysis was nothing but a combustion process, an oxidation process, I sprang to my feet and said, 'Professor Fritz, if this is the case, what meaning does life have?'"[334]

h.   Liberation from the Concentration Camps

"One day, a few days after the liberation, I walked through the country past the flowering meadows, for miles and miles, toward the market town near the camp. Larks rose to the sky and I could hear their joyous songs. There was no one to be seen for miles around; there was nothing but the wide earth and sky and the larks' jubilation and the freedom of space. I stopped, looked around, and up to the sky—and then I went down on my knees. At that moment . . . I had but one sentence in mind—always the same: 'I called to the Lord from my narrow prison and He answered me in the freedom of space.'"[335]

i.   Medical Doctor

"[L]et me remind myself of being an M.D. in the first place. Day by day I am confronted with people who are incurable, men who become senile, and women who remain sterile. I am besieged by their cry for an answer to the question of an ultimate meaning to suffering."[336]

j.   Meaning of His Life

[One morning, I was] "greeted by a small group of American professors, psychiatrists, and students who has come to Vienna to do research. I had just responded to *Who's Who in America* by returning the questionnaire they had sent. It had asked that I express, in one sentence, the meaning of my life. So I asked the group to guess what response I had made. Some quiet reflection. Then a student from

Berkeley said . . . : 'The meaning of your life is to help others find the meaning of theirs.' "That was it, exactly. Those are the very words I had written."[337]

k.   Meaning of His Suffering and Possible Death in the Concentration Camp

"As far as I was concerned, I felt duty-bound to my mother to stay alive. We two loved one another beyond all else. Therefore my life had a meaning—in spite of everything. But I had to count upon death any minute of every day. And therefore my death also should somehow have meaning—as well as all the suffering that I would have to go through before it came. And so I made a pact with Heaven: if I should have to die, then let my death preserve my mother's life; and whatever I should have to suffer up until the time of my death was to purchase for her a sweet and easy death when her time came. Only by imagining it in terms of such a sacrifice was my tormented existence endurable. I could live my life only if it had a meaning; but I also wanted to suffer my suffering and die my death only if suffering and death also had a meaning."[338]

l.   Neurologist

"[A]s a neurologist, I stand for the justification of using the computer as a model, say, for the activity of the central nervous system. It is perfectly legitimate to use such an analogy. Thus, in a certain sense the statement is valid: man is a computer. However, at the same time he also is infinitely more than a computer. The statement is erroneous only insofar as man is defined as 'nothing but' a computer."[339]

m.   Overcoming His Own Sense of Meaninglessness

"I have had to overcome nihilism within myself. And that is perhaps why I am so capable of smelling it out, wherever it may hide.
"And . . . out of the school of my own existential self-analysis, perhaps I can see the mote in the other's eyes so well because I have had to tear the beam out of my own."[340]

n.   Philosopher and Physician

"I was qualified to speak both as a medical man and as a philosopher . . . I had a doctorate in each field."[341]

o.   Philosopher of Meaning

"There is nothing in the world, I venture to say, that would so effectively help one to survive even the worst conditions as the knowledge that there is a meaning in one's life."[342]

p.   Professor

"As a professor in two fields, neurology and psychiatry, I am fully aware of the extent to which man is subject to biological, psychological and sociological conditions."[343]

q.   Psychiatrist and Psychologist

"[M]y investigation moves within the frame of reference of psychology, or rather anthropology: that is to say, on the human level. Grace, however, dwells in the supra-human dimension . . . . In other words, what on the natural plane takes on the appearance of being man's decision might well be interpreted on the supra-natural plane as the sustaining assistance of God."[344]

r.   Psychological Test

"I was once given the Rorschach inkblot test by a psychologist at an Innsbruck psychiatric clinic. He claimed that he had never seen such a range between rationality and deep emotions. The former I probably inherited from father, and the latter from mother."[345]

s.   Psychotherapist[346]

[As a psychotherapist,] "I tried to forget what I had learned from psychoanalysis and individual psychology so that I could learn from listening to my patients. I wanted to find out how they managed to improve their conditions."[347]

t.   Rationality and Emotions

"I am for the most part a rational person, a man of the mind. At the same time, . . . I am a person of deep feelings as well."[348]

See Adler, Conditioning, *Doctor and the Soul*, Frankl, Freud, Psychoanalysis, Reductionism.

F 6
Free-Will[349]
(Freedom of Choice)

a.   "If I really am the victim of outer and inner circumstances and influences—the product of environment and heredity—and my behavior, decision, and action are 'nothing but' the result of operant conditioning, conditioned reflexes, and learning processes, who is justified to demand that I improve or to expect that I change? There is no need for apologies; there are plenty of excuses . . . . And as for myself, I am neither free nor responsible."[350]

b. "[A] human being is . . . finite . . . and his freedom is restricted."[351]

c. "[T]he freedom of a finite being such as man is a freedom within limits. Man is not free from conditions, be they biological or psychological or sociological in nature. But he is, and always remains, free to take a stand toward these conditions; he always retains the freedom to choose his attitude toward them. Man is free to rise above the plane of the somatic (bodily) and psychic (mind) determinants of his existence."[352]

d. "Freedom is not something we 'have' and therefore can lose; freedom is what we 'are.'"[353]

e. Frankl quotes Magda B. Arnold: "All choices are caused but they are caused by the chooser."[354]

f. "[B]eing human is . . . 'deciding what one is going to be,' to quote Jaspers . . . ."[355]

g. "A human being is not one thing among others: Things are determining each other, but man is self-determining."[356]

h. "During no moment of his life does man escape the mandate to choose among possibilities. Yet he can pretend to act 'as if' he had no choice and no freedom of decision."[357]

i.   "Whether any circumstances, be they inner or outer
       ones, have an influence on a given individual or
       not, and in which direction this influence takes its
       way—all that depends on the individual's free
       choice. The conditions do not determine me, but I
       determine whether I yield to them or brave them."[358]

j.   "[A] person is free to shape his own character, and
       man is responsible for what he may have made out
       of himself. What matters is not the features of our
       character or the drives and instincts per se, but rather
       the stand we take toward them. And the capacity to
       take such a stand is what makes us human beings."[359]

k.   "[I]n the final analysis it becomes clear that the sort of
       person the prisoner became was the result of an inner
       decision, and not the result of camp influences alone.
       Fundamentally, therefore, any man can, even under
       such circumstances, decide what shall become of
       him—mentally and spiritually. He may retain his
       human dignity even in a concentration camp."[360]

See Attitude, Concentration Camps, Change, Conditioning,
Determinism, Fatalism, Grace, Reductionism,
Responsibility, Self-Creation.

F 7
Freud, Sigmund
(Medical Doctor, Psychologist and "Father of Psychoanalysis")[361]
(1856-1939)

a.   Frankl praises the man Sigmund Freud and his work
       by paraphrasing William Stekel's remark about
       Freud: "[A] dwarf standing upon the shoulders of a
       giant can see farther than the giant himself."[362]

b. Frankl compares Freud's greatness to Rabbi Loew's: "The place still reserved to Freud . . . reminds me of a story they tell at the oldest synagogue in the world, Prague's medieval Alt Neu Synagogue. When the guide there shows you the interior, he tells you that the seat once occupied by the famous Rabbi Loew has never been taken over by any of his followers; another seat has been set up for them, because Rabbi Loew could never be replaced, no one could match him. For centuries no one was allowed to sit down on his seat. The chair of Freud should also be kept empty."[363]

c. Frankl quotes Freud: "'Men are strong as long as they stand for a strong idea.'"[364]

d. "Those who know me also know that my opposition to Freud's ideas never kept me from showing him the respect he deserves."[365]

e. "[T]he concept for everything pertaining to the spirit and religion in particular is made very easy . . . by the help of a misconceived psychoanalysis. With all due respect for the genius of Sigmund Freud and his pioneering achievement, we must not close our eyes to the fact that Freud himself was a child of his time and not independent of the spirit of his age. Surely, Freud's consideration of religion as an illusion or an obsessional neurosis and God as a father-image was an expression of that spirit."[366]

f. "Freud believed that man could be explained by a mechanistic theory and that his psyche could be cured by means of techniques."[367]

g.   "Freed from the mechanistic ideology of the
      nineteenth century, seen in the light of the
      existentialist philosophy of the twentieth century,
      one could say that psychoanalysis promotes self-
      understanding in man."[368]

h.   "Sigmund Freud once said, 'Let us attempt to expose
      a number of the most diverse people uniformly to
      hunger. With the increase of the imperative urge of
      hunger all individual differences will blur, and in their
      stead will appear the uniform expression of the one
      unstilled urge.' In the concentration camps, however,
      the reverse was true. People became more diverse.
      The beast was unmasked—and so was the saint. The
      hunger was the same but people were different."[369]

i.   Frankl quotes Sigmund Freud: "'The moment a man
      questions the meaning and value of life he is sick.'"[370]

j.   Frankl disagrees with Freud's opinion that
      questioning the meaning of life is a sign of mental
      illness. Frank's reply to Freud was: "I rather think that
      such a man only proves that he is truly a human
      being."[371]

k.   [Freud] "became a victim of reductionism . . . by
      declaring that he had 'already found a place for
      religion, by putting it under the category of the
      neurosis of mankind.'"[372]

l.   "Freud's age was a period of tension, brought
      about by the repression of sex on a mass scale."[373]

m.   Frankl quotes Gordon Allport who, in turn, quotes
      Sigmund Freud: "Gordon W. Allport once rightly said:
      'Freud was a specialist in precisely those motives
      that cannot be taken at their face value.'"[374]

n.   "Freud and . . . [his followers] . . . have taught us always to see something behind, or beneath, human volitions: unconscious motivations, underlying dynamics. Freud never took a human phenomenon at its face valued . . . ."[375]

o.   How wise and cautious was Freud when he once remarked that sometimes a cigar may be a cigar and nothing but a cigar."[376]

See Adler, Concentration Camps, Conditioning, Determinism, Meaning, Motives, Potzl, Psychoanalysis, Techniques, World View, *Zeitgeist*.

G 1
Gas Chambers
(Used by the Nazis to Exterminate the Jews During the Holocaust)

"Man is that being, who . . . invented the gas chambers; but at the same time he is that being who entered into those gas chambers with his head held high and with the 'Our Father' or the Jewish prayer of the dying on his lips."[377]

See Concentration Camps, Nobility and Misery of Human Beings.

G 2
God

a.   "God . . . is not one thing among others but being itself or Being . . . ."[378]

b.   [Using the language of the Jewish philosopher and theologian Martin Buber, Frankl calls God] "the first, last, and ultimate Thou . . . ."[379]

c.   Frankl quotes the Austrian philosopher Ludwig Wittgenstein: "To believe in God is to see that life has a meaning."[380]

d.   "[F]aith in the ultimate meaning is preceded by trust in an ultimate being, by trust in God."[381]

e.   "It was the therapy that led me to God. There is no longer an abyss, this being-in-God carries me and I cannot fall. Life again is wonderful, rich, and full of possibilities. When related to God, everything is bearable and filled with meaning. I think I know what I have to do: bring my daily life in order for the love of God."[382]

f.   "God is not dead . . . , not even 'after Auschwitz' . . . ."[383]

g.   Frankl quotes the Kaddish, a Hebrew prayer for the dead: "God is 'high above all the blessings and hymns, praises and consolations, which are uttered in the world.'"[384]

h.   Frankl quotes Ludwig Wittgenstein: "The famous sentence by which Ludwig Wittgenstein concludes his most famous book reads: 'Whereof one cannot speak, thereof one must be silent.'"[385]

i.   "God may be unconscious to man and . . . man's relation to God may be unconscious."[386]

j.   "[O]ur concept of an unconscious God refers to man's hidden relation to a God who himself is hidden."[387]

k.   "[T]he religious psychiatrist believes not only in God, but also in an unconscious belief on the part of the patient. In other words, he [the psychiatrist] believes . . . [in] . . . 'the unconscious God' of the patient. And . . . this unconscious God is one who has simply *not yet* become conscious to the patient."[388]

See Atheism, Buber, Imago Dei, Meaning, Psychotherapy, Religion, Unconscious, Werfel.

G 3
Goethe, Johann Wolfgang Von
(German Poet and Philosopher)
(1749-1832)

a.   Frankl quotes Goethe: "When we take man as he is, we make him worse; but when we take man as if he were already what he should be, we promote him to what he can be."[389]

b.   Frankl quotes Goethe: "How can we learn to know ourselves? Never by reflection, but by action. Try to do your duty and you will soon find out what you are. But what is your duty? The demands of each day."[390]

c.   Frankl quotes Goethe: "There is no condition which cannot be ennobled either by a deed or by suffering."[391]

See Attitudinal Values, Human Potential, Nobility and Misery of Human Beings, Suffering.

G 4
Grace

a.   "If a man is to believe in God, he has to be helped by grace. But one should not forget that my investigation moves within the frame of reference of psychology, or rather anthropology: that is to say, on the human level. Grace, however, dwells in the supra-human dimension . . . . In other words, what on the natural plane takes on the appearance of being man's decision might well be interpreted on the supra-natural plane as the sustaining assistance of God."[392]

b.   "Time and again I am asked the question, 'Where is a place for grace in logotherapy?' And I answer that a doctor writing up a prescription or performing an operation should do as attentively as possible . . . . The more he pays attention to what he is doing, and the less he cares for grace, the better a vehicle he will be for grace. The more human one is, the more he can be a tool for divine purposes."[393]

See Anthropology, Free-Will, Religion.

G 5
Greatness

Frankl quotes the Jewish philosopher Benedict de Spinoza: "[E]verything great is just as difficult to realize as it is rare to find."[394]

G 6
Grief
(Suppression of the Grief Emotion)

"The person who tries to 'take his mind off' a misfortunate or narcotize his feelings solves no problem, comes to no terms with misfortune; all he does is get rid of a mere aftereffect of the misfortune: the sensation of unpleasure. By diversion or narcotization he makes himself 'ignore' what has happened—he no longer knows it. He tries to escape reality . . . . But this is to commit . . . the error of acting as if what has been banished to non-consciousness were thereby banished to unreality . . . . And so the suppression of an impulse of grief does not annul the thing that is grieved over."[395]

See Diversions, Drugs.

G 7
Guilt[396]

a.   Frankl comments about speaking to the prisoners at San Quentin: "I had simply taken them as human beings and not mistaken them for mechanisms to repair. I had interpreted them . . . as free and responsible. I had not offered them a cheap escape from guilt feelings by conceiving of them as victims of biological, psychological, or sociological conditioning processes . . . . I had not provided them with an alibi. Guilt had not been taken away from them. I had not explained it away . . . . They learned that it was a prerogative of man to become guilty—and his responsibility to overcome guilt."[397]

b.   "[M]an has a *right* to be considered guilty and to be punished. Once we deal with man as the victim of circumstances and their influences, we not only cease to treat him as a human being but also *lame* his will to change."[398]

c.   "Something for which a person cannot be made responsible cannot be accounted to his praise or blame . . . . [A] man can be ethically judged only where he is free to decide and to act responsibly; he is not to be judged where he is no longer free."[399]

See Conditioning, Determinism, Distinctively Human Phenomena, Free-Will, Responsibility, Tragic Triad.

H 1
Happiness

a.   "'Pursuit of happiness' amounts to a self-contradiction: The more we strive for happiness, the less we attain it."[400]

b.   "Happiness must ensue. It cannot be pursued. It is the very pursuit of happiness that thwarts it. The more one makes happiness an aim, the more he misses the aim.
       "And this is most conspicuous in cases of sexual neurosis such as frigidity or impotence. Sexual performance or experience is strangled to the extent to which it is made either an object of attention or an object of intention . . . . [T]he first . . . [is] . . . 'hyperreflection' and the second 'hyperintention.'"[401]

c.   "[H]appiness . . . is the side effect of living out the self-transcendence of existence. Once one has served a cause or is involved in loving another human being, happiness occurs by itself."[402]

d.   Frankl notes that people can be "happy under adverse, even dire, conditions."[403]

e.   Frankl quotes from a letter from Cleve W., Number 049246, who was a prisoner in an American state prison: "Here in prison . . . there are more and more blissful opportunities to serve and grow. I'm really happier now than I've ever been."[404]

See Attitudinal Values, Free-Will, Hyperintention, Hyperreflection, Materialism, Pleasure, Self-Transcendence.

H 2
Health

"[S]omeone who is ill wishes, in the first place, to become healthy. So health will seem to constitute his supreme goal in life. But in actual fact, it is no more than a means to an end, because health is a precondition for attaining whatever might be considered the real meaning in a given instance."[405]

See Meaning, Purpose.

H 3
Heaven

"[I]f there is such a thing as Heaven, and if Heaven ever accepts a prayer, it will hide this behind a sequence of natural facts."[406]

H 4
Height Psychology

a.   "'[H]eight psychology' . . . takes into account the so-called 'higher aspirations' of the human psyche: not only man's seeking pleasure and power but also his search for meaning."[407]

b.   "[R]ather than being a substitute for depth psychology, height psychology is only a supplement (to be sure, a necessary one); but it does focus on the specifically human phenomena—among them man's desire to find and fulfill a meaning in his life, or for that matter in the individual life situations confronting him."[408]

See Distinctively Human Phenomena, Logotherapy.

H 5
Rabbi Hillel[409]
(ca. 75 BCE-15 CE)

a. Frankl quotes Rabbi Hillel: "If I do not do this job—
    who will do it? And if I do not do this job right now—
    when shall I do it? But if I carry it out only for my
    own sake—what am I?"[410]

b. Frankl's Commentary on Hillel.

   1. On Hillel's first question: "If I do not do this job—
       who will do it?" [suggests that] "each man is
       unique and each man's life is singular: . . . no
       man can be replaced and no man's life can be
       repeated."[411]

   2. On Hillel's second question: "And if I do not do
       this job right now—when shall I do it?" suggests
       that in every moment of a person's life, he or
       she has "a specific and particular meaning to
       fulfill . . . ."[412]

   3. On Hillel's third question: "But if I carry it out
       only for my own sake—what am I?" [suggests
       the self-transcendence of human existence;
       in other words, a] "man's life always points
       to something beyond himself; it is always
       directed toward a meaning to fulfill (rather
       than a self to actualize, or one's potentialities
       to develop)."[413]

See Personalism, Human Uniqueness, Self-
Transcendence.

H 6
Hippocratic Oath

"[T]he . . . Hippocratic oath would compel the doctor to prevent the patient from committing suicide. I am personally glad to take the blame for having been directive along the lines of a life-affirming *Weltanschauung* whenever I have had to treat a suicidal patient."[414]

See Doctor, Euthanasia, Psychotherapist, Suicide, *Weltanschauung.*

H 7
Hope[415]

a. Frankl illustrates the need for hope by his own experience in a concentration camp: "When we spoke about attempts to give a man in camp mental courage, we said that he had to be shown something to look forward to in the future. He had to be reminded that life still waited for him, that a human being waited for his return."[416]

b. Frankl recalls how his friend had lost hope of ever leaving the concentration camp, which eventually led to his death: "Those who know how close the connection is between the state of mind of a man—his courage and hope, or lack of them—and the state of immunity of his body will understand that the sudden loss of hope and courage can have a deadly effect. The ultimate cause of my friend's death was that the expected liberation did not come and he was severely disappointed. This suddenly lowered his body's resistance against the latent typhus infection. His faith in the future and his will to live had become paralyzed and his body fell victim to illness . . . ."[417]

c.   "The prisoner who had lost faith in the future—his future—was doomed. With his loss of belief in the future, he also lost his spiritual hold; he let himself decline and became subject to mental and physical decay."[418]

See Meaning, Purpose in Life, Survival.

H 8
Human Beings

a.   Being Human.

1.   "Being human is being always directed, and pointing, to something or someone other than oneself: to a meaning to fulfill or another human being to encounter, a cause to serve or a person to love. Only to the extent that someone is living out this self-transcendence of human existence, is he truly human or does he become his true self. He becomes so, not by concerning himself with his self's actualization, but by forgetting himself and giving himself, overlooking himself and focusing outward."[419]

2.   *"[B]eing human means being conscious and being responsible."*[420]

3.   "[T]he search for meaning is a distinctive characteristic of being human. No other animal has ever cared whether or not there is a meaning to life . . . . But man does."[421]

4. "[B]eing human means being confronted continually with situations, each of which is at once a chance and a challenge, giving us a 'chance' to fulfill ourselves by meeting the 'challenge' to fulfill its meaning."[422]

5. "[A] person is free to shape his own character, and man is responsible for what he may have made out of himself. What matters is not the features of our character or the drives and instincts per se, but rather the stand we take toward them. And the capacity to take such a stand is what makes us human beings."[423]

b.   Human Dignity

1. "The dignity of man does not suffer in the least from the fact that he inhabits the earth, a planet of the sun, and is not born at the center of the universe . . . . [T]he dignity of man depends on grounds other than his location in the material world."[424]

2. "'What is man that you are mindful of him?' 'He is a reed,' said Pascal, 'but a reed which thinks!' And it is in this thinking, this consciousness, this responsibility that constitute the dignity of man, the dignity of each individual human being. And it is always to be ascribed to the individual person whether he preserves this dignity or tarnishes it. Whereas the first behavior is personal merit, the second constitutes personal guilt."[425]

c.   Human Potential[426]

1. "If we are to bring out the human potential at its

best, we must first believe in its existence and presence. Otherwise man . . . will deteriorate. For there is a human potential at its worst as well! And in spite of our belief in the potential humanness of man we must not close our eyes to the fact that *humane* humans are, and probably will always remain, a minority. But it is precisely for this reason that each of us is challenged to *join* the minority."[427]

2. "Socrates confessed that he had within himself the potentiality to become a criminal, but decided to turn away from materializing this potentiality, and this decision . . . made all the difference."[428]

3. "In the living laboratories of the concentration camps we watched comrades behaving like swine while others behaved like saints. Man has both these potentialities within himself. Which one he actualizes depends on decisions, not on conditions."[429]

4. "I prefer to live in a world in which man has the right to make choices, even if they are the wrong choices, rather than a world in which no choice at all is left to him. In other words, I prefer a world in which, on the one hand, a[n] . . . Adolf Hitler can occur, and on the other hand, . . . many saints . . . can occur also."[430]

d.   Human Survival.

Frankl refers to the attempts of prisoners to survive the concentration camps during the Holocaust: "[W]hile the concern of most people was summed up by the question, 'Will we survive the camp?'— for if not, then this suffering has no sense—the question which . . . beset me was, 'Has this whole suffering, this dying, a meaning?'—for if not, then ultimately there is no sense to surviving?"[431]

e.   Human Uniqueness.

1. [Logotherapy affirms] "the unconditional value of each and every person. It is that which warrants the indelible quality of the dignity of man. Just as life remains potentially meaningful under any conditions, even those which are the most miserable, so too does the value of each and every person stay with him or her . . . ."[432]

2. "'[T]o be equals to be different.' . . . For the uniqueness of every individual human being means that he is different from all other human beings."[433]

3. "Each human being is unique . . . and thus neither expendable nor replaceable. In other words, he is a particular individual with his unique personal characteristics who experiences a unique historical context in a world which has special opportunities and obligations reserved for him alone."[434]

4. "Everyone has his own specific vocation or mission in life to carry out a concrete assignment which demands fulfillment. Therein he cannot be replaced, nor can his life be repeated. Thus, everyone's task is as unique as is his specific opportunity to implement it."[435]

5. "In the final analysis, no one can be replaced— by virtue of the uniqueness of each man's existence. And each man's life is unique in that no one can repeat it—by virtue of the

uniqueness of his existence. Sooner or later his life will be over forever, together with all the unique opportunities to fulfill the meanings."[436]

6. "[A] unique person . . . can never be replaced by any double, no matter how perfect a duplicate."[437]

7. "Ultimately every person is irreplaceable, and if for no other person he is so for him by whom he is loved."[438]

See Concentration Camps, Distinctively Human Phenomena, Goethe, Existential Personalism, *Imago Dei*, Nobility and Misery of Human Beings.

H 9
Humor

a.   [Logotherapy] "utilizes a unique and specific aspect of self-detachment, namely, the human sense of humor."[439]

b.   "[H]umor . . . can afford an aloofness and an ability to rise above any situation, even if only for a few seconds."[440]

c.   "[H]umor would . . . be located in the noetic dimension."[441]

d.   "Humor . . . is a uniquely human capacity . . . . Humor is said even to be a divine attribute. In three psalms God is referred to as a 'laughing' one."[442]

e.   "[T]he sense of humor is exclusively human—after all, no animal but man is capable of laughing.

> Specifically, humor is to be regarded as a manifestation of that peculiarly human ability which in logotherapy is called self-detachment . . . ."[443]

f.   "[N]o computer is capable of laughing at itself . . . ."[444]

g.   "[H]umor allows man to create perspective, to put distance between himself and whatever may confront him. By the same token, human allows man to detach himself from himself and thereby to attain the fullest possible control over himself."[445]

h.   "[I]n principle each and every human being, by virtue of his humanness, is capable of detaching himself from himself and laughing about himself."[446]

See Anthropology, Distinctively Human Phenomena, Paradoxical Intention, Self-Detachment.

H 10
Hyperintention[447]

a.   "Nowhere is this [that is, hyperintention] more conspicuous than with regard to happiness: happiness must ensue and cannot be pursued. Happiness must happen, and we must let it happen. Conversely, the more we aim at it, the more we miss our aim."[448]

b.   "[T]he pleasure principle is self-defeating. The more one aims at pleasure, the more his aim is missed . . . . This self-defeating quality of pleasure-seeking accounts for many sexual neuroses. Time and again the psychiatrist is in a position to witness how both orgasm and potency are impaired by being the target of intention."[449]

See Happiness, Intention, Pleasure, Solomon.

H 11
Hyperinterpretation

a. "[H]yperinterpretation . . . proves to be most dangerous when it comes to self-interpretation. We psychiatrists have met many patients who are suffering from, and crippled by, the obsessive compulsion to analyze themselves, to observe and watch themselves, to reflect upon themselves."[450]

b. "As the boomerang returns to the hunter only when it has missed its target, so man returns to himself, reflects upon himself, and becomes overly concerned with self-interpretation only when he has, as it were, missed his target, having been frustrated in his search for meaning."[451]

See Hyperreflection, Self-Transcendence.

H 12
Hyperreflection[452]

a. "Paying too much attention to something is what I am used to calling 'hyper-reflection.'"[453]

b. "A pedestrian will stumble as soon as he focuses too much on the act of walking instead of keeping his eye on the goal. A person may at best initiate some act with excessive awareness, but he cannot carry it out in the same spirit without that awareness being itself a disturbing factor."[454]

c.   "We know a case in which a violinist always tried to play as consciously as possible. From putting his violin in place on his shoulder to the most trifling technical detail, he wanted to do everything consciously, to perform in full self-reflection. This led to a complete artistic breakdown. Therapy had to start with eliminating this tendency to overbearing self-reflection and self-observation, or, in the terminology of logotherapy, 'hyperreflection.' Therapy had to be aimed at what we call in logotherapy 'dereflection.' Treatment had to give back to the patient his trust in the unconscious, by having him realize how much more musical his unconscious was than his conscious."[455]

d.   "Spontaneity and activity are impeded if made a target of too much attention. Consider the centipede who, as a story has it, was asked by his enemy in what sequence he moved his legs. When the centipede paid attention to the problem, he was unable to move his legs at all."[456]

e.   "[O]nce the self reflects on itself, it is no longer the true self that exhibits itself."[457]

See Anticipatory Anxiety, Self-Transcendence, Unconscious.

H 13
Hyper-specialization[458]

a.   "The pictures by which the individual sciences depict reality have become so disparate, so different from each other, that is has become more and more difficult to obtain a fusion of the different pictures."[459]

b.   "What we have to deplore . . . is not that *scientists are specializing but that the specialists are generalizing* . . . . I mean those who cannot resist the temptation to make overgeneralized statements on the grounds of limited findings."[460]

c.   "Science cannot cope with reality in its multidimensionality but must deal with reality as if reality were unidimensional. However, a scientist should remain aware of what he does, if for no other reason than to avoid the pitfalls of reductionism."[461]

See Reductionism.

H 14
Hypochondriacs

"[I]f we make health our main concern we have fallen ill. We have become hypochondriacs."[462]

See Hyperintention.

I 1
Identity
(Knowledge of Whom One is)

a.   "[M]an should not, indeed cannot, struggle for identity in a direct way; he rather finds identity to the extent to which he commits himself to something beyond himself, to a cause greater than himself."[463]

b.   Frankl is talking to a patient named Anna who suffered from a psychological and emotional crisis and she now must go on with her life: "[Y]ou are in a stage where reconstruction of your life is the task awaiting you! But one cannot reconstruct one's life without a life goal, without anything challenging him . . . . What counts is . . . what waits in the future, waits to be actualized by you . . . . [Y]ou are Anna, for whom something is in store . . . . [G]ive yourself to that unborn work which you have to create. And only after you have created it will you come to know what you are like. Anna will be identified as the artist who has accomplished this work. Identity doesn't result from concentration on one's self, but rather from dedication to some cause, from finding one's self through the fulfillment of one's specific work."[464]

See Hyperreflection, Meaning, Purpose, Self-Creation, Self-Transcendence, Values.

I 2
Imago Dei[465]

a. "[O]ur concern with the origin of conscience is anthropological rather than theological. Nonetheless we may be justified in claiming that this transhuman agent must necessarily be of a personal nature. More correctly, however, we would have to speak of a transpersonal agent of which the human person is but the 'image.'"[466]

b. Conscience not only refers to transcendence; it also originates in transcendence. This fact accounts for its irreducible quality."[467]

c. "[M]an, as long as he regarded himself as a creature, interpreted his existence in the image of God, his creator; but as soon as he started considering himself as a creator, began to interpret his existence merely in the image of his own creation, the machine."[468]

d.   "[B]ehavior in animals . . . is *analogous* to moral
        behavior in man . . . . By contrast, the reductionists
        do not recognize a qualitative difference between
        the two type[s] of behavior. They deny that a uniquely
        human phenomenon exists at all. And they do so . . .
        on the basis of an a priori denial. They insist that
        there is nothing in man that cannot be found in
        animals as well."[469]

See also Anthropology, Conscience, Distinctively
Human Phenomenon, Existential Vacuum, God,
Meaning, Reductionism, Religion, Transcendence,
Werfel.

I 3
Immigration Visa
(Frankl's)[470]

"[S]hortly before Pearl Harbor, I was asked to come to the
American Consulate to pick up my visa. Then I hesitated.
Should I leave my parents behind? I knew what their fate
would be: deportation to a concentration camp. Should I
say goodbye, and leave them to their fate? The visa
applied to me alone.
"Undecided, I left home, took a walk, and had this
thought: 'Isn't this the kind of situation that requires
some hint from heaven?' When I returned home, my eyes
fell on a little piece of marble lying on the table.
"'What's this?' I asked my father.
"'This? Oh, I picked it out of the rubble of the synagogue
they have burned down. It has on it part of the Ten
Commandments. I can even tell you from which
commandment it comes. There is only one commandment
that uses the letter that is chiseled here.'
"'And that is . . . ?' I asked eagerly.
"Then father gave me this answer: 'Honor thy father and

thy mother, that thy days may be long upon the land which the Lord thy God giveth thee.'
"Thus I stayed 'upon the land' with my parents, and let the visa lapse."[471]

See Concentration Camps.

I 4
Infatuation

a.   "[I]n the matter of loving, individuals may deceive themselves. A person may think that love had made him see, when in fact he may be blinded by mere infatuation."[472]

b.   "[I]nfatuation makes us blind; real love enables us to see. Love permits us to see the spiritual core of the other person . . . . Love allows us to experience another's personality as a world in itself, and so extends our own world."[473]

c.   "[M]ere infatuation . . . [is] . . . by its nature a more or less fleeting 'emotional state' . . . ."[474]

d.   "[T]he sexually disposed person or the infatuated person feels attracted by the physical characteristics or psychic traits 'of' the partner—that is, something this other person 'has'—the lover loves the beloved's self—not something the beloved 'has,' but what he 'is.' The lover's gaze looks through the physical and the psychic 'dress' . . . to the core of the other's being. He is . . . concerned with the person, with the partner as unique, irreplaceable, and incomparable."[475]

See Love, Sex.

I 5
Infidelity

"The variety of possible attitudes toward infidelity makes it an occasion for actualizing attitudinal values. One person will avenge the hurt which has been inflicted on him by breaking up the relationship; another will forgive and make up; a third will try to conquer the partner anew, to win him back."[476]

See Attitudinal Values.

I 6
Insomnia

Referring to the words of the psalmist, Frankl says: "'*Vel per noctem me monet cor meum.*' Even at night his heart admonishes him. Today he would say that at night the repressed existential problems remain. Conscience reminds him of them. This is the origin of what I would call 'noogenic sleeplessness.' People suffering from it often take sleeping pills."[477]

I 7
Instincts[478]

"Certainly man has instincts, but these instincts do not have him. We have nothing against instincts, nor against man's accepting them . . . . We [however] are concerned above all with man's freedom to accept or reject his instincts."[479]

See Anthropology, Drives, Free-Will, Logotherapy, Spirit.

I 8
Intention

a.   Frankl quotes, in part, Gordon Allport: "[A]t every moment, . . . man's mind is directed by some intention."[480]

b.   Frankl quotes, in part, Herbert Spiegelberg: "[I]ntention [is] . . . the 'property of an act which points to an object.'"[481]

c.   Frankl quotes Franz Brentano: "[E]very psychical phenomenon is characterized by the reference to a content, the directedness toward an object."[482]

See Allport, Hyperintention, Phenomenology.

I 9
Intoxication

"The essence of intoxication is a turning away from the objective world and a turning to a subjective world."[483]

See Drugs.

J 1
Jaspers, Karl
(German Existentialist Philosopher)
(1883-1969)

Frankl quotes from the existentialist philosopher Karl Jaspers: "What man is, he has become through that cause which he has made his own."[484]

See Meaning.

J 2
Jealousy

"At its root is the attitude toward the object of love as property. The jealous man treats the person he allegedly loves as if this person were his possession; he degrades her to a piece of property. He wants to have her 'only for himself'—thereby proving that he thinks of her in terms of 'having.' There is no room for jealousy within a real love relationship. It is ruled out by very definition, since real love presupposes a mutual feeling of the uniqueness and singularity of the partners. The rivalry so feared by the jealous lover assumes the possibility that he can be replaced by a competitor, assumes that love can be transferred to another. But that is impossible in real love, for the beloved one cannot be compared with any other person."[485]

See Love, Personalism.

J 3
Judging Others

a.   "[W]hoever wishes to condemn . . . a man as a coward must first prove that in the same situation he himself would have been a hero.
       "But it is better and more prudent not to sit in judgment on others."[486]

b.   "No man should judge unless he asks himself in absolute honesty whether in a similar situation he might not have done the same."[487]

K 1
Kant, Immanuel
(German Philosopher)
(1724-1804)

a. Frankl paraphrases Immanuel Kant: "According to the second version of Kant's categorical imperative, no man should ever be taken as a mere means to an end."[488]

b. Frankl applies Kant's imperative to the relationship between the psychotherapist and the patient or client: "Seeing in man a mere means to an end is the same as manipulating him."[489]

c. "[P]sychotherapy can be conducted in such a spirit that the patient is no more 'regarded as a person' but rather his *psyche* considered merely as a set of mechanisms."[490]

See Encounter, Love, Personalism, Reductionism, Rogers, Sex.

K 2
Kolbe, Father Maximilian
(Polish Roman Catholic Priest)
(1894-1941)

a. "[T]oday you need no longer hesitate to use the word 'saints': think of Father Maximilian Kolbe who was starved and finally murdered by an injection of carbolic acid at Auschwitz and who in 1983 was canonized."[491]

b.   "Father Maximilian Kolbe found meaning within the
          fraction of a second when he decided to sacrifice
          his life, asking the SS for permission to let himself
          be sentenced to death instead of a family
          father . . . ."[492]

See Auschwitz, Concentration Camps.

L 1
Life

a.   "[M]an is not he who poses the question, What is
          the meaning of life? but he who is asked this
          question, for it is life itself that poses it to him. And
          man has to answer to life by answering for life; he
          has to respond by being responsible . . . ."[493]

b.   "[D]ay by day life is asking us questions, we are
          interrogated by life, and we have to answer. *Life . . .
          is a life-long question-and-answer period.* As to the
          answers, . . . we can only answer to life by answering
          for our lives. *Responding* to life means *being
          responsible* for our lives."[494]

See Meaning, Responsibility.

L 2
Logos[495]

a.   [In logotherapy,] "logos means 'meaning.'
          However it also means 'spirit.' And logotherapy
          takes the spiritual or noological dimension [of
          the human person] fully into account."[496]

b.   "Logos is deeper than logic. Thus the fact that man
          can no longer be considered as a totally rational
          being has been recognized by logotherapy without

falling prey to the *other* extreme, i.e., idolizing the irrational and the instinctual . . . ."[497]

See Anthropology, Existentialism, Noological Dimension, Truth, Spirit, Supra-Meaning.

L 3
Logotherapy
(The Third Viennese School of Psychotherapy)[498]

a.   Adds a New Dimension to Psychotherapy

"[L]ogotherapy adds a new dimension to psychotherapy: . . . it adds to it the dimension of the distinctively human phenomena. In fact, [it includes] two specifically human phenomena, the capacity of self-transcendence and the capacity of self-detachment . . . ."[499]

b.   Frankl Coined the Term in Public in 1926

"It was in the study group of this society [i.e., the Academic Society for Medical Psychology] that I gave a lecture before an academic audience and first spoke of logotherapy."[500]

c.   Limitations of Logotherapy

"[L]ogotherapy . . . is not a panacea. It therefore is open to cooperation with other approaches to psychotherapy; it is open to its own evolution; and it is open to religion."[501]

d.   Logotheory[502]

[Another theory of logotherapy is:] "What is sick is

not necessarily wrong . . . . As I have said, two times two make four, even if a paranoid patient says it."[503]

e.   Meaning of the Word "Logotherapy"

"Let me explain why I have employed the term 'logotherapy' as the name for my theory. *Logos* is a Greek word that denotes 'meaning'! Logo-therapy or, as it has been called by some authors, 'The Third Viennese School of Psychotherapy,' focuses on the meaning of human existence as well as on man's search for such a meaning. According to logotherapy, the striving to find a meaning in one's life is the primary motivational force in man."[504]

1.   "Logotherapy aims to unlock the will to meaning and to assist the patient in seeing a meaning in his life."[505]

2.   "[L]ogotherapy considers man to be primarily motivated by a search for a meaning to his existence . . . ."[506]

3.   [Logotherapy is] "therapy through meaning" [or] "healing through meaning . . . ."[507]

4.   "Truly, there is a healing force in meaning."[508]

5.   "Logotherapy is concerned not only with being but also with meaning—not only with *ontos* but also with *logos* . . . ."[509]

6.   "Logotherapy insists that man's main concern is not to seek pleasure or to avoid pain, but rather to find a meaning to his life."[510]

f.   Non-Sectarian or Non-Denominational

1. "[L]ogotherapy is not a Protestant, Catholic, or Jewish psychotherapy."[511]

2. "Logotherapy is usually either subsumed under the category of humanistic psychology . . . or identified with phenomenological . . . or existential psychiatry . . ."[512]

g.   Not a Religious Psychotherapy

1. [Logotherapy is] "an essentially secular approach" [to psychotherapy].[513]

2. [Logotherapy is] "available for every patient and useable in the hands of every doctor, whether his *Weltanschauung* (world view) is theistic or agnostic."[514]

h.   Not Opposed to Religion

[Logotherapy may even be] "compatible with religion."[515]

i.   Purpose of Logotherapy

1. "Logotherapy aims to unlock the will to meaning and to assist the patient in seeing a meaning in his life."[516]

2. "[I]n the widest possible sense, logotherapy *is* treatment . . . of the patient's attitude toward his unchangeable fate."[517]

j.   Resistance to Logotherapy by Psychologists and
        Psychotherapists

        "[M]uch of the resistance to . . . logotherapy . . .
        stems from emotional grounds such as loyalty and
        obedience to a [psychological] sect."[518]

k.   Synonym for Logotherapy

        1. "The alternative term [i.e., to logotherapy], . . .
            Existenzanalyse (existential analysis), I used
            from 1930 on."[519]

        2. "[L]ogotherapy . . . falls under the category of
            existential psychiatry."[520]

l.   World View

        "Particularly in an era such as ours, one of
        meaninglessness, depersonalization, and
        dehumanization, it is not possible to cope with the
        ills of the age unless the human dimension, the
        dimension of human phenomena, is included in the
        concept of man, which indispensably underlies
        every sort of psychotherapy, be it on the conscious
        or the unconscious level."[521]

See Distinctively Human Phenomenon, Meaning, Religion,
Self-Transcendence, *Weltanschauung.*

L 4
Loneliness

a.   "We need . . . [to] . . . allow for contemplation and
        meditation. To this end, man needs the courage to
        be lonely."[522]

b.   "There is a . . . creative loneliness which makes it possible to turn something negative—the absence of people—into something positive—an opportunity to meditate."[523]

See Diversions.

L 5
Love[524]

a.   Choosing to Love

1.   "Does love . . . have to do with decision and choice? Certainly it does. To be sure, the choice of a partner is only a true choice when it is not dictated by drives."[525]

2.   "Love is more than an emotional condition; love is an intentional act."[526]

b.   Finding Meaning in Love

1.   Frankl recalls thinking about his wife while being marched by Nazi soldiers to forced labor in a concentration camp: "We stumbled on in the darkness, over big stones and through large puddles, along the one road leading from the camp. The accompanying guards kept shouting at us and driving us with the butts of their rifles. Anyone with very sore feet supported himself on his neighbor's arm. Hardly a word was spoken; the icy wind did not encourage talk. Hiding his hand behind his upturned collar, the man marching next to me whispered suddenly: 'If our wives could see us now! I do hope they are better off in

their camps and don't know what is happening to us.'

"That brought thoughts of my own wife to mind. And as we stumbled on for miles, slipping on icy spots, supporting each other time and again, dragging one another up and onward, nothing was said, but we both knew: each of us was thinking of his wife. Occasionally I looked at the sky, where the stars were fading and the pink light of the morning was beginning to spread behind a dark bank of clouds. But my mind clung to my wife's image, imagining it with an uncanny acuteness. I heard her answering me, saw her smile, her frank and encouraging look. Real or not, her look was then more luminous than the sun which was beginning to rise.

"A thought transfixed me: for the first time in my life I saw the truth as it is set into song by so many poets, proclaimed as the final wisdom by so many thinkers. The truth—that love is the ultimate and highest goal to which man can aspire. Then I grasped the meaning of the greatest secret that human poetry and human thought and belief have to impart: *The salvation of man is through love and in love.*"[527]

2. "[M]an is . . . primarily concerned with . . . something or someone out there in the world, be it a cause to serve or a partner to love—and if he really loves the partner, he certainly does not just use him as a more or less apt means to satisfying his own needs."[528]

3. "[M]an is a being who is reaching out for meanings to fulfill and other human beings to encounter . . . ."[529]

c.   Outlasts Death

"Love is more than an emotional condition; love is an intentional act. What it intends is the essence of the other person. This essence is ultimately independent of existence; *essentia* is not contingent upon *existentia*, and insofar as it has this freedom, it is superior to *existentia*. That is why love can outlast the death of the beloved; in that sense we can understand why love is 'stronger' than death. The existence of the beloved may be annihilated by death, but his essence cannot be touched by death. His unique being is, like all true essences, something timeless and thus imperishable. The 'idea' of a person—which is what the lover sees—belongs to a realm beyond time."[530]

d.   Permanence of Love

"[A] physical state passes, and a psychological state is also impermanent. Sexual excitement is only temporary; the sex drive vanishes promptly after gratification. And infatuation, too, is seldom of long duration. But the spiritual act by which the person comprehends the spiritual core of another outlasts itself; to the degree that the content of that act is valid, it is valid once and for all."[531]

e.   Procreative Love

[Another] "factor enter[s] into love: the miracle of love. For through love the incomprehensible is accomplished—there enters (via a detour through the realm of biology) into life a new person, itself complete with the mystery of the uniqueness and singularity of its existence: a child!"[532]

f.   Spiritual Love.

"Loving represents a coming to relationship with another as a spiritual being . . . . The lover is no longer aroused in his own physical being, nor stirred in his own emotionality, but moved to the depths of his spiritual core, moved by the partner's spiritual core. Love, then, is an entering into direct relationship with the personality of the beloved, with the beloved's uniqueness and singularity."[533]

g.   Uniqueness of Love

1. "[L]ove . . . breaks through to that layer of being in which every individual human being no longer represents a 'type,' but himself alone, not comparable, not replaceable, and possessing all the dignity of his uniqueness. This dignity is the dignity of those angels of whom some scholastics maintained that they do not represent a kind; rather, there is only one of each kind."[534]

2. "[B]odily and temperamental peculiarities . . . are not unique and singular and can be found in other persons . . . ."[535].

3. "In love the beloved person is comprehended in his very essence, as the unique and singular being that he is; he is comprehended as a Thou . . . ."[536]

4. "Love . . . is that capacity which enables . . . [one human being] . . . to grasp the other human being in his very uniqueness . . . . [M]eaning is something unique. So is each and every person. Ultimately every person is irreplaceable, and if

for no other person he is so for him by whom he is loved."[537]

5. "While the sexually disposed person or the infatuated person feels attracted by the physical characteristics or psychic traits 'of' the partner—that is, something this other person 'has'—the lover loves the beloved's self—not something the beloved 'has,' but what he 'is.' The lover's gaze looks through the physical and the psychic 'dress' . . . to the core of the other's being. He is . . . concerned with the person, with the partner as unique, irreplaceable, and incomparable."[538]

h.   Unmerited Love

"Love is not deserved, is unmerited—it is simply grace."[539]

See Human Uniqueness, Marriage, Meaning, Monogamous Marital Love, Personalism, Self-Transcendence, Sex.

M 1
Man's Search for Meaning[540]
(Frankl's Book)

a.   "The publisher of the English edition would never have printed the book at all, had it not been for the effort of Gordon Allport."[541]

b.   Gordon W. Allport, formerly a professor of psychology at Harvard University, introduces *Man's Search for Meaning.* He writes: "I recommend this little book heartily, for it is a gem of dramatic narrative, focused upon the deepest of human problems. It has literary and philosophical merit and provides a compelling introduction to the most significant psychological movement of our day."[542]

c.   Philosopher Karl Jaspers says to Frankl: "I know all your books, but the one about the concentration camp . . . [that is, *Man's Search for Meaning*] . . . belongs among the great books of humankind."[543]

d.   Jerry Long, a quadriplegic—paralyzed in both arms and legs due to a diving accident—typed with a pencil-sized rod, which he held in his mouth. He wrote to Frankl: "I have read with much interest *Man's Search for Meaning* . . . . What a far greater impact your book has because you lived it . . . ."[544]

e.   "In my whole book *Man's Search for Meaning*, you will not find the word 'Jew.' I don't capitalize from being a Jew and having suffered as a Jew . . . ."[545]

f.   "*Man's Search for Meaning* has sold over nine million copies in the English editions alone. The United States Library of Congress has listed it as 'one of the ten most influential books in America.'"[546]

g.   Its Therapeutic Effect on Those Who Read It

        "There may be such a thing as autobibliotherapy— healing through reading—and apparently logotherapy is particularly well suited to it."[547]

See Allport, Concentration Camps, Existentialism, Existential Vacuum, Jaspers, Logotherapy, Meaning, Meaninglessness.

M 2
Marcel, Gabriel
(French Existentialist Philosopher and Playwright)[548]
(1889-1973)

"Marcel . . . wrote the preface to the French edition of *Man's Search for Meaning.*"[549]

M 3
Marriage

"Instinctual gratification and biological reproduction are . . . only two aspects of marriage—and not even the most important ones. The spiritual factor of love is more essential."[550]

See Distinctively Human Phenomena, Love, Sex, Spirit.

M 4
Maslow, Abraham H.
(Psychologist,
Father of Humanistic Psychology)
(1908-1970)

a.   [According to Abraham Maslow, the will to meaning is] "man's primary concern."[551]

b.   Frankl quotes, in part, Abraham Maslow: "[T]he 'business of self-actualization' can best be carried out 'via a commitment to an important job.'"[552]

See Meaning, Self-Actualization, Self-Transcendence.

M 5
Masochism

a.   "The logotherapeutic emphasis on the potential
         meaning of unavoidable suffering has nothing to
         do with masochism. Masochism means accepting
         unnecessary suffering, but I . . . [refer] to 'a fate that
         cannot be changed.' What can be changed should
         be changed."[553]

b.   "[M]eaning is available in spite of—nay, even
         through—suffering, provided . . . that we have to
         deal with unavoidable suffering. If it were
         avoidable, the meaningful things to do would be
         to remove its cause, be it psychological,
         biological, or sociological. Unnecessary
         suffering would be masochistic rather then
         heroic."[554]

See Attitudinal Values, Suffering.

M 6
Mass Neurotic Triad

"Such widespread phenomena as depression,
aggression and addition are not understandable unless
we recognize the existential vacuum underlying them."[555]

See Aggression, Existential Vacuum.

M 7
Masturbation

a.   "We often hear . . . patients speak of 'masturbating
         on a woman,' by which they mean that they
         sometimes 'use' their partners simply for the
         purpose of reducing sexual tension."[556]

b.   "To the individual who really is mature, the partner is in no way a means to an end [that is, a means to reducing sexual tension]. The mature individual's partnership moves on a human level, and the human level precludes the mere use of others."[557]

c.   "Sexuality . . . experienced in an undirected way . . ., the act of masturbation, entirely lacks any object outside of the self, any directedness toward a partner.
"Masturbation is, to be sure, neither a disease nor a cause of disease; rather, it is the sign of a disturbed development of misguided attitude toward the love life. Hypochondriacal ideas about its morbid consequences are unjustified. But the hangover which generally follows the act of masturbation has a reason . . . . The underlying reason is that guilt feeling which comes upon one whenever one flees from active, directional experience to passive, nondirectional experience . . . . [T]his kind of escape . . . [is] . . . the underlying motif of intoxication . . . . [M]asturbation—like drunkenness—is followed by a mood of hangover."[558]

See Love, Sex.

M 8
Materialism

a.   Philosophical Materialism

1.   "People who limit reality to what is tangible and visible and for this reason tend *a priori* to deny the existence of an ultimate being, also repress religious feelings . . . . They insist that God must be visible [in order to believe in him]."[559]

2. "[M]aterialism . . . permeates the psychoanalytic way of thinking . . . ."[560]

b.   Practical Materialism[561]

1. "[T]oday's society . . . gratifies and satisfies virtually every need—except for one, the need for meaning! . . . [T]he need for meaning remains unfulfilled—in the midst of and in spite of all our affluence."[562]

2. In a letter to Frankl, a wealthy young man wrote: "I am a 22-year-old with degree, car, security and the availability of more sex and power than I need. Now I have only to explain to myself what it all means."[563]

3. In a letter to Frankl, another wealthy man wrote: "All of my life I have been in engineering management. I am presently in a salary bracket which puts me in the upper 2 percent of salaries earned in the United States. Yet in spite of my relatively high salary and the responsible positions I have held I felt an emptiness in my life."[564]

4. In still another letter to Frankl, a wealthy man wrote: "As a therapist I was primarily Freudian by training. All that Freudian philosophy had promised, I had received in abundance—sixty-thousand-dollar home with pool, two late-model cars, three healthy, bright children, loving wife and companion and an occupation that brought pride and acceptance from the community—but still something was missing."[565]

5. "For too long we have been dreaming a dream from which we are now waking up: the dream

that if we just improve the socioeconomic situation of people, everything will be okay, people will become happy. The truth is that as the *struggle for survival* has subsided, the question has emerged: *survival for what*? Ever more people today have the means to live, but no meaning to live for."[566]

6. [Even though many people in today's society are grossly materialistic, there are, nevertheless, just as many young people who say,] "What we want is not money but some content to our lives."[567]

See Affluence, Existential Vacuum, Happiness, Meaning, Money.

M 9
Meaning[568]

a.   Common Meanings

"[T]there are . . . meanings which are shared by human beings across society and, even more, throughout history. Rather than being related to unique situations these meanings refer to the human condition. And these meanings are what is understood by values. So that one may define values as those meaning universals which crystallize in the typical situations a society or even humanity has to face."[569]

b.   Meaning in General or Meaning in Life as a Whole

"I will not be elaborating . . . on the meaning of one's life as a whole, although I do not deny that such a long-range meaning does exist."[570]

c.   Objective Meaning[571]

1. "[H]uman existence can never be intrinsically meaningless."[572]

2. "[T]he true meaning of life is to be discovered in the world rather than within man or his own psyche, as though it were a closed system."[573]

3. "Human beings are transcending themselves toward meanings which are something other than themselves, which are more than mere expressions of their selves, more than mere projections of these selves. Meanings are *discovered* but not *invented*."[574]

d.   Personal Meaning[575]

"[I]t is never the task of the therapist to give a meaning to the life of the patient. It is up to the patient himself to find the concrete meaning of his existence. The therapist merely assists him in this endeavor. That he must find the meaning implies that this meaning is to be discovered and not invented. It implies that the meaning of one's life is, in a certain sense, objective."[576]

e.   Search for Meaning

1. "[L]ogotherapy considers man to be primarily motivated by a search for a meaning to his existence . . . ."[577]

2. "Man's search for a meaning is not pathological, but rather the surest sign of being truly human. Even if this search is frustrated, it cannot be

considered a sign of disease. It is spiritual distress, not mental disease."[578]

3. "[M]an's quest for, and even his questioning of, a meaning to his existence, i.e., his spiritual aspirations as well as his spiritual frustrations, should be taken at face value and should not be tranquilized or analyzed away."[579]

4. "[T]here is a meaning of life—a meaning, that is, for which man has been in search all along— and . . . man has the freedom to embark on the fulfillment of this meaning."[580]

5. "[M]eaning must be found and cannot be given."[581]

6. "[M]an is . . . in search of tasks whose completion might add meaning to his existence."[582]

7. "[T]he search for meaning is a distinctive characteristic of being human. No other animal has ever cared whether or not there is a meaning to life . . . . But man does."[583]

8. "[M]an is . . . in search of meaning—a search whose futility seems to account for many of the ills of our age."[584]

9. Even if a person has not yet found the meaning of his or her life after searching for it, and is experiencing the existential vacuum, Frankl's counsel is: "Try to be patient and courageous: patient in leaving the problems unresolved for the time being, and courageous in not giving up the struggle for their final solution."[585]

f.   Taboo to Discuss the Meaning of Life

Frankl quotes Nicholas Mosley: "There is a subject nowadays which is taboo in the way that sexuality was once taboo, which is to talk about life as if it had any meaning."[586]

g.   Unconditional Meaning

1. "[T]here is no situation that does not contain within it the seed of a meaning. To a great extent, this conviction is the basis of logotherapy."[587]

2. [Logotherapy teaches that] "the meaning of life is an unconditional one."[588]

3. [Logotherapy helps a person to see that there is] "a meaning in his (or her) life under any conditions."[589]

4. "[E]very life, in every situation and to the last breath, has a meaning, retains a meaning. This is equally true of the life of a sick person, even the mentally sick. *The so-called life not worth living does not exist.*"[590]

5. "[E]ven a life that has been wasted, may—even in the last moment—still be bestowed with meaning by the very way in which we tackle this situation."[591]

6. Frankl quotes from a letter from Frank E., Number 020640, who was a prisoner in an American prison: "I have found true meaning in my existence even here, in prison. I find purpose

in my life, and this time I have left is just a short wait for the opportunity to do better, and to do more."[592]

7. Frankl quotes from a letter from Greg B., who was a prisoner in a maximum security prison in Florida: "Yes, one of the greatest meanings we can be privileged to experience is suffering. I have just begun to live, and what a glorious feeling it is . . . . [M]y brothers in our group . . . are even now achieving meanings they never thought possible . . . . Lives which heretofore have been hopeless and helpless now have meaning."[593]

h.   Unique Meaning

1. "[T]he meaning of life . . . differ[s] from man to man, and from moment to moment. Thus it is impossible to define the meaning of life in a general way."[594]

2. "[M]eaning is something unique. So is each and every person."[595]

i.   Will to Meaning[596]

1. [The will to meaning] "denotes the fundamental fact that normally . . . man is striving to find, and fulfill, meaning and purpose in life."[597]

2. [A human being is dominated by "the will to meaning,"—that is, a] "deep-seated striving and struggling for a higher and ultimate meaning to his existence."[598]

3. "[M]an's main concern is not to gain pleasure or to avoid pain but rather to see a meaning in his life."[599]

4. "[T]he will to meaning . . . is in greater or smaller degree present in all human beings."[600]

See Anthropology, Attitudinal Values, Euthanasia, Identity, Logotherapy, Questioning the Meaning of Life, Reality, Suffering, Suicide, Truth, Values (Three Chief Groups of Values), Will to Meaning.

M 10
Meaninglessness

a.   "There are people—and this is more manifest today than ever—who consider their life meaningless, who can see no meaning in their existence and therefore think it is valueless."[601]

b.   "The dean of students at a major American university has told me that in his counseling work he is continually being confronted by students who complain about the meaninglessness of life, who are beset by that inner void which I have termed the 'existential vacuum.'"[602]

c.   "George A Sargent . . . promulgated the concept of 'learned meaninglessness.' He . . . remembered a therapist who said, 'George, you must realize that the world is a joke. There is no justice, everything is random . . . . There is no grand purpose in the universe. It just *is*. There is no particular meaning in what decision you make today about how to act."[603]

d.   Frankl explains the problem with a philosophy that teaches life is objectively meaningless—that is, meaningless in and of itself, but that human beings can find meaning subjectively by pro-creating human life: "The only meaning in the life of one generation consists in raising the next. But to perpetuate something in itself meaningless is meaningless. If the thing is meaningless, it does not acquire meaning by being immortalized."[604]

e.   "Either life has meaning and retains this meaning whether it is long or short, whether or not it reproduces itself; or life has no meaning, in which case it takes on none, no matter how long it lasts or can go on reproducing itself."[605]

See Education, Existential Vacuum, Neurosis, Nihilism, Sartre, Values.

M 11
Medical Ministry[606]

a.   [Medical ministry] "is a ministry occupied not only by the neurologist or by the psychiatrist, but by every doctor."[607]

b.   "When the surgeon has completed an amputation, he takes off his rubber gloves and appears to have done his duty as a physician. But if the patient then commits suicide because he cannot bear living as a cripple—of what use has the surgical therapy been? Is it not also part of the physician's work to do something about the patient's attitude toward the pain of surgery or the handicap that results from it? Is it not the physician's right and duty to treat the patient's attitude toward his illness . . . . Where actual surgery comes to an end, the work of medical ministry begins. For something must follow after the surgeon has laid aside his scalpel, or where surgical work is ruled out—as, for example, in an inoperable case."[608]

c.   "Medical ministry is indicated wherever inevitable 'fated' conditions exist in the life of the patient, where he is crippled or faced with an incurable disease or chronic invalidism. It is also useful where persons are in a really inescapable predicament, faced with unalterable difficulties imposed from outside themselves . . . . Medical ministry helps the patient to shape his suffering into inner achievement and so to realize attitudinal values."[609]

d.   "Medical ministry is that aspect within the logotherapeutic system which deals with the treatment of somatogenic cases . . . . [T]he somatic [bodily] cause of trouble cannot be removed. What then matters is the stand a patient takes toward his predicament, the attitude he chooses toward his suffering: in other words, the fulfillment of the potential meaning of suffering . . . . [W]e must give preference to causal treatment of disease, and resort to medical ministry only if causal treatment proves to be of no avail. Then the treatment of the patient's attitude toward his disease is the one thing possible and necessary."[610]

e.   "That aspect of logotherapy which I call medical ministry must not be confused with pastoral ministry."[611]

See Attitudinal Values, Clergy, Pastoral Counseling.

M 12
Midlife Crisis

"As a former teaching assistant of mine at Harvard University could show, among graduates of that university who went on to lead quite successful, ostensibly happy lives, a huge percentage complained of a deep sense of futility, asking themselves what all their success had been for. Does this not suggest that what today is often referred to as 'midlife crisis' is basically a crisis of meaning?"[612]

See Existential Vacuum, Happiness, Materialism.

M 13
Mental Health

a.   "A man's concern, even his despair, over the worthwhileness of life is an *existential distress* but by no means a *mental disease*."[613]

b.   "A sound amount of tension, such as that tension which is aroused by a meaning to fulfill, is inherent in being human and is indispensable for mental well-being."[614]

c.   "[A] strong meaning orientation is a health-promoting and a life-prolonging, if not a life-preserving, agent. It not only makes for physical but also for mental health . . . ."[615]

d.   "[A] mind is healthy when it has achieved a sufficient store of 'meaning.'"[616]

e.   Frankl quotes W. M. Millar, formerly a Professor of Mental Health at Aberdeen University in

Scotland: "There is surely something wrong in the idea that wholeness must be equated with mental health, that an individual in the eyes of God is not complete unless he has a certificate of fitness from a psychiatrist. What about the idiot child, or the withdrawn schizophrenic, or the demented senile patient? What comfort can be brought to them if we commit ourselves to this notion of physical-mental integrity? There must surely be some sense in which these creatures of God can be made whole, although there can be no hope of their medical recovery."[617]

f.   [Frankl mentions] "religion's inestimable contribution to mental health . . . . [R]eligion provides man with a spiritual anchor, with a feeling of security such as he can find nowhere else."[618]

See Meaning, Mental Retardation, Purpose, Religion, Tension.

M 14
Mental Retardation

a.   "[A] retarded child retains the humanness of human beings."[619]

b.   Frankl quotes Carl J. Rote, formerly a resident chaplain in a state institution of about 4,300 mentally retarded patients: "The retardates have taught me more than I can tell. Theirs is a world where hypocrisy is banished; it is a kingdom where a smile is their passport to your affection and the light in their eyes will melt the coldest heart. Perhaps this is God's way of reminding us that the world must rediscover the attributes which the mentally retarded have never lost."[620]

M 15
Mission in Life[621]
(or Life Task)

a. "[W]hen we speak of the meaning of one's existence, we specifically refer to the *concrete* meaning of personal existence. By the same token, we could speak of a mission in life, indicating that every man has a mission in life to carry out."[622]

b. "[M]an is . . . in search of tasks whose completion might add meaning to his existence."[623]

c. "Nothing helps man to survive and keep healthy like the knowledge of a life task."[624]

d. "When the professional task is no longer there, other life tasks must be found . . . ."[625]

e. "Only in the degree to which man accomplishes certain specific tasks in the surrounding world will he fulfill himself."[626]

See Existential Personalism, Human Uniqueness, Meaning, Mental Health, Purpose in Life, Tension.

M 16
Money
(The Inordinate Pursuit of Money)

a. "To those people who are anxious to have money as though it were an end in itself, 'time is money.' They exhibit a need for speed. To them, driving a fast car becomes an end in itself. This is a defense mechanism, an attempt to escape the confrontation with an existential vacuum. The less one is aware of a goal the faster he tries to cover the road."[627]

b.   "Once the will to money takes over, the pursuit of meaning is replaced by the pursuit of means. Money, instead of remaining a means, becomes an end. It ceases to serve a purpose.
"What then is the meaning of money, or for that matter the meaning of possessing money? Most of those people who possess it are really possessed by it, obsessed by the urge to multiply it, and thus they nullify its meaning."[628]

c.   [One may have] "the means—the financial means—but no meaning."[629]

See Affluence, Existential Vacuum, Diversions, Practical Materialism.

M 17
Monogamous Marital Love[630]

"Real love in itself constitutes the decisive factor of a monogamous relationship. But there is another factor, that of exclusiveness . . . . Love means a sense of inward union; the monogamous relationship, in the form of marriage, is the outward tie. Being faithful means maintaining this tie in al its definitiveness. The exclusiveness of this tie, however, makes it the more imperative that a person form the 'right' tie; not only must he be prepared to bind himself, but also he must know whom he is binding himself to. It becomes supremely important that he decide in favor of the right partner. Erotic maturity . . ., being . . . inwardly mature enough for a monogamous relationship, thus involves a dual requirement: the ability to select a partner; and the ability to remain definitively faithful to that partner."[631]

See Love.

M 18
Moses
(Israel's Great Law Giver and Prophet)
(*b. ca.* 1526 B. C. E.)

"[M]eaning must not coincide with being: meaning must be ahead of being. Meaning sets the pace for being. Existence falters unless it is lived in terms of transcendence toward something beyond itself. Viewed from this angle, we might distinguish between people who are pacemakers and those who are peacemakers: the former confront us with meanings and values, thus supporting our meaning orientation; the latter alleviate the burden of meaning confrontation. In this sense Moses was a pacemaker; he did not soothe man's conscience but rather stirred it up. Moses confronted his people with the Ten Commandments and did not spare them confrontation with ideals and values. Peacemakers, on the other hand, appease people . . . ."[633]

See Being, Self-Transcendence, Tension.

M 19
Motivation

a.   "[I]f one is to understand the frustrations of man, one has to understand his motivations, to begin with, and especially the most human of human motivations, which is man's search for meaning."[634]

b.   "According to logotherapy, . . . striving to find a

meaning in one's life is the primary motivational force in man."[635]

See Logotherapy, Meaning.

M 20
Motives

"Gordon W. Allport once rightly said: 'Freud was a specialist in precisely those motives that cannot be taken at their face value.' The fact that such motives exist certainly does not alter the fact that by and large motives can be taken at their face value. And if this is denied, what might be the unconscious and hidden motives behind the denial?"[636]

See Freud, Unmasking.

N 1
Negative Attitude
(Countering It)

"So long as a person makes the mistake of reminding himself constantly, before making an effort, that the effort may fail, he is not likely to succeed—if only because he does not like to disapprove his own expectations. It is therefore all the more important when formulating a resolution to bar from the start all the counter-arguments which spring up with such profusion."[637]

See Attitudinal Values, Optimism.

N 2
Neurology

"In the frame of neurology . . ., man necessarily appears as 'nothing but' a 'closed' system of physiological reflexes without any place left for something like the self-transcendent quality of human existence. We must beware of the self-deception that this dimension of neurology is the only one which exists."[638]

See Anthropology, Reductionism, Self-Transcendence.

N 3
Neurosis

a.   Neurosis of Meaninglessness

"Adler has made us conversant with the important part played by what he called the 'sense of inferiority' in the formation of neuroses. Well, . . . today something else is playing at least as important a part, the sense of meaninglessness: not the feeling of being less valuable than others, but the feeling that life has no longer any meaning."[639]

b.   Religious Neurosis

"Even if it is a neurosis that drives a person to religion, religion may become genuine, in the long run, and finally help the person to overcome the neurosis."[640]

See Existential Vacuum, Meaninglessness, Religion.

N 4
Nietzsche, Friedrich
(German Atheistic Philosopher)
(1844-1900)

a.   Frankl quotes from Friedrich Nietzsche: "He who has a *why* to live for can bear almost any *how*."[641]

b.   Frankl quotes Nietzsche: "That which does not kill me, makes me stronger."[642]

See Purpose in Life.

N 5
Nihilism

a.   "Nihilism does not contend that there is nothing, but it states that everything is meaningless."[643]

b.   "[N]ihilism can be defined as the contention that being has no meaning."[644]

c.   "Today nihilism no longer unmasks itself by speaking of 'nothingness.' Today nihilism is masked by speaking of the 'nothing-but-ness' of man. Reductionism has become the mask of nihilism."[645]

d.   "[I]ndoctrination in a reductionist philosophy of life . . . results in nihilism, to which the reaction is cynicism."[646]

e.   Frankl quotes a letter to him from a graduate student in psychology at the University of California at Berkeley: "It is strange . . . . The nihilists first laugh at your concept of meaning through suffering—and ultimately their tears dissolve them."[647]

See Meaninglessness, Reductionism, World View.

N 6
Nobility and Misery of Human Beings

a.   Frankl quotes Psalm 8:4: "'What is man that you are mindful of him?' was a question which the psalmist directed to God . . . ."[648]

b.   "What . . . is man? We have learned to know him, as possibly no generation before us. We have learned to know him in camps, where everything unessential had been stripped from man, where everything which a person had—money, power, fame, luck—disappeared: while only that remained which a man does not 'have' but which he must 'be.' What remained was man himself, who in the white heat of suffering and pain melted down to the essentials, to the human in himself.
"What then is man? . . . He is a being who continuously decides what he is: a being who equally harbors the potential to descend to the level of an animal or to ascend to the life of a saint."[649]

c.   [The different reactions to suffering by the inmates in the concentration camps prove that a person] "may remain brave, dignified and unselfish. Or in the bitter fight for self-preservation he may forget his human dignity and become no more than an animal."[650]

d.   [A human being is not] "a sublimated animal . . . [rather] . . . within him there is a repressed angel."[651]

e.   Frankl quotes Goethe: "There is no condition which cannot be ennobled either by a deed or by suffering."[652]

f.   Frankl quotes Plutarch: "The measure of a man is the way he bears up under misfortune."[653]

g.   Frankl quotes Dostoevski: "There is only one thing that I dread: not to be worthy of my sufferings."[654]

h.   "[T]he right kind of suffering is in itself a deed, nay, the highest achievement which has been granted to man."[655]

i.   "Our generation has come to know man as he really is: the being that has invented the gas chambers of Auschwitz, and also the being who entered those gas chambers upright, the Lord's Prayer or the *Shema Yisrael* on his lips."[656]

j.   "If we are to bring out the human potential at its best, we must first believe in its existence and presence. Otherwise man . . . will deteriorate. For there is a human potential at its worst as well!"[657]

See Attitudinal Values, Auschwitz, Concentration Camps, Goethe, Human Potential, Suffering.

N 7
Noogenic Neurosis

"[T]he noogenic neurosis . . . is caused by a spiritual problem, a moral or ethical conflict . . . . Last but not least, however, the noogenic etiology is formed by the existential vacuum, by existential frustration or by the frustration of the will to meaning."[658]

See Existential Frustration, Existential Vacuum.

O 1
Obsessive-Compulsive Neurotic

a.   "[T]he very tension of the patient's fight against his compulsive ideas only tends to strengthen the 'compulsion.' Pressure generates counterpressure;

the more the patient dashes his head against the wall of his obsessional ideas, the stronger they become and the more unbreakable they appear to him."[659]

b.   "[A] patient . . . suffered for fifteen years from a severe form of obsessional neurosis . . . .
      "[He went to see a psychiatrist.] This doctor . . . had to . . . concentrate on the problem of revising the patient's attitude toward his obsessional illness. He tried . . . to reconcile the patient to his illness, basing his efforts on the fact that the patient was a deeply religious person. The doctor asked the patient to accept his illness as 'the will of God,' something imposed upon him by destiny against which he must stop contending. Rather, he ought to try to live a life pleasing to God in spite of his illness . . . . After the second therapeutic session the patient stated that for the first time in ten years he had just spent a full hour free of his obsessional ideas."[660]

c.   "In correcting our patients' misguided efforts to fight desperately and tensely against their obsessions we . . . make two points: . . . on the one hand the patient is not responsible for his obsessional ideas, and on the other . . . he certainly is responsible for his attitude toward these ideas."[661]

d.   [The obsessional neurotic's goal is to] "learn to ignore his obsessional neurosis and lead a meaningful life in spite of it . . . . [H]is turning toward his concrete life task facilitates his turning away from his obsessional thoughts."[662]

See Attitudinal Values, Certainty, Meaning, Security.

O 2
Optimism
(A Positive Approach to Life)

a.   "[L]ogotherapy is an optimistic approach to life, for it teaches that there are no tragic and negative aspects which could not be by the stand one takes to them transmuted into positive accomplishments."[663]

b.   Positive Imagining[664]

Frankl recalls the example of one of the prisoners in the concentration camp: "One camp inmate . . . instinctively chose a good method for getting through the worst situations in camp life by imagining each time that he was standing on the podium before a large audience and lecturing on the things he was at the moment experiencing."[665]

See Attitudinal Values, Concentration Camps, Negative Attitude.

P 1
Paradoxical Intention

a.   "[P]aradoxical intention . . . may be defined as a process by which *the patient is encouraged to do, or to wish to happen, the very thing he fears* . . . ."[666]

b.   On the Case of a Student Who Fears Taking an Exam

   1. [Before taking the exam,] "I said to myself, 'Since I am going to fail anyway, I may as well *do my best at failing!* I'll show this professor a test *so* bad, that it will confuse him for days! I will write

down total garbage, answers that have nothing to do with the questions at all! I'll show him how a student really fails a test! This will be the most ridiculous test he grades in his entire career!' With this in mind, I was actually giggling when the test came. Believe it or not, each question made perfect sense to me—I was relaxed, at ease, and as strange as it may sound, actually in a terrific mood! I passed the test and received an A."[667]

2. "The role of humor in the practice of paradoxical intention . . . [is] . . . obvious . . . ."[668]

3. "[T]he spirit of our technique [of paradoxical intention] . . . rests on man's capacity for self-detachment."[669]

c.   On the Case of a Student's Fear of Perspiring Before Others:

1. "During the first meeting of a seminar class on Martin Buber, I spoke up saying I felt diametrically opposed to the views so far expressed . . . . I . . . resolved to deliberately show those people how much I could sweat, chanting in my thoughts as I continued to express my feeling on the subject: 'More! More! More! Show these people how much you can sweat, really show them!' Within two or three seconds after applying paradoxical intention I laughed inwardly and could feel the sweat beginning to dry on my skin. I was amazed and surprised at the result, for I did not believe logotherapy would work . . . . 'Regardless of my skeptical feelings, logotherapy actually worked in my case.'"[670]

2. "Such cases are not intended to suggest that
    paradoxical intention is effective in every case, or
    that its effect is easy to obtain. Neither paradoxical
    intention in particular nor logotherapy in general
    is a panacea—panaceas simply do not exist in
    the field of psychotherapy."[671]

See Distinctively Human Phenomena, Humor, Self-
Detachment.

P 2
Pascal, Blaise
(Scientist, Mathematician, and Philosopher)
(1623-1662)

a. Frankl quotes Balise Pascal, prefaced by the
    question, "What is man that you are mindful of him?:
    "'He is a reed,' said Pascal, 'but a reed which
    thinks!'"[672]

b. Frank again quotes Pascal: "The heart has reasons
    which are unknown to reason."[673]

c. Frankl interprets Pascal: "Sometimes the wisdom
    of our hearts proves to be deeper than the insight
    of our brains."[674]

P 3
Pastoral Counseling
(Pastoral Ministry or Pastoral Care)

a. "[D]octors today are approached by many
    patients who in former days would have seen a
    pastor, priest or rabbi . . . . What is more, the
    patients often refuse to be handed over to a
    clergyman."[675]

b.   "There is no reason why the clinical psychologist, the social worker, the pastor, priest, and rabbi should not offer advice and assistance to people who are seeking a meaning of life, or questioning the meaning of life: in other words, people in the grip of the existential vacuum."[676]

See Existential Vacuum, Medical Ministry.

P 4
Patients
(Under the Care of Medical Doctors, Psychiatrists or Psychologists)

"[W]e are not merely treating diseases but dealing with human beings."[677]

See Personalism.

P 5
Personalism[678]
(The Subjectivity of the Human Person)

a.   "[A] human being is no thing. This *no-thingness, rather than nothingness, is the lesson to learn from existentialism.*"[679]

b.   [Logotherapy affirms] "the unconditional value of each and every person. It is that which warrants the indelible quality of the dignity of man."[680]

c.   "Each human being is unique . . . and thus neither expendable nor replaceable. In other words, he is a particular individual with his unique personal characteristics who experiences a unique historical context in a world which has special opportunities and obligations reserved for him alone."[681]

d.   "On the human level, I do not use another human being but I encounter him, which means that I fully recognize his humanness; and if I take another step by fully recognizing . . . his uniqueness as a person, it is even more than an encounter—what then takes place is love."[682]

e.   "[T]he dignity of man forbids his being himself a means, his becoming a mere instrument of the labor process, being degraded to a means of production."[683]

See Buber, Encounter, Euthanasia, Existentialism, Human Uniqueness, Sex, Techniques, Work.

P 6
Phenomenology[684]

a.   "[T]he man in the street . . . has not been exposed to *reductionist indoctrination*, be it on American campuses or on analytical couches . . . . And the unbiased man in the street . . . does not see himself as the pawn and plaything of conditioning processes or drives and instincts."[685]

b.   "[T]he unbiased analysis of the unbiased man in the street reveals how he actually experiences values. Such an analysis is phenomenological, and as such it refrains from preconceived patterns of interpretation . . . .
      "The phenomenological analysis of the man in the street yields . . . three chief groups of values. I have classified them in terms of 'creative, experiential, and attitudinal values.'"[686]

c.   *"We psychiatrists . . .* have to learn from the man
      in the street, from his prereflective ontological self-
      understanding, what being human is all about. We
      have to learn from his *sapientia cordis,* from the
      wisdom of his heart, that being human means being
      confronted continually with situations, each of
      which is at once a chance and a challenge, giving
      us a 'chance' to fulfill ourselves by meeting the
      'challenge' to fulfill its meaning. Each situation is a
      call, first to listen, and then to respond."[687]

d.   [Logotherapy] "leans on the phenomenological
      analysis of pre-reflective ontological self-
      understanding. It borrows from what the patient
      knows by the wisdom of his heart and in the depth
      of his unconscious. Through logotherapy this
      knowledge is brought to the surface of
      consciousness. And if . . . *phenomenology* means
      translating this wisdom of the heart into scientific
      terms, . . . *Logotherapy* means *retranslating* this
      wisdom of the heart into plain words, into the
      language of the man in the street, so that he may
      benefit from it."[688]

e.   "Are we not . . . taught by 'inner experience,' by
      ordinary living unbiased by theories, that our natural
      pleasure in a beautiful sunset is in a way 'more
      real' than, say, astronomical calculations of the time
      when the earth will crash into the sun? Can anything
      be given to us more directly than our own personal
      experience . . . ? 'The most certain science is
      conscience,' someone once remarked, and no
      theory of the physiological nature of life, nor the
      assertion that joy is a strictly organized dance of
      molecules or atoms or electrons within the gray
      matter of the brain, has ever been so compelling
      and convincing."[689]

f.   "The freedom of decision, so-called freedom of the will, is for the unbiased person a matter of course; he has an immediate experience of himself as free. The person who seriously doubts freedom of the will must either be hopelessly prejudiced by a deterministic philosophy or suffering from a paranoid schizophrenia, in which case he experiences his will as having been 'made' unfree."[690]

See Free-Will, Human, Logotherapy, Values, World View.

P 7
Philosophical Questions[691]

a.   "The psychotherapist is . . ., in the regular course of his practice, . . . confronted with philosophical questions."[692]

b.   "Every psychotherapist knows how often in the course of his psychiatric work the question of the meaning of life comes up."[693]

c.   "A philosophical question cannot be dealt with by . . . hinting at the morbid consequences of philosophical pondering. That is only evasion."[694]

d.   "[O]ur 'psychotherapy in spiritual terms' is specially designed to handle those suffering over the philosophical problems with which life confronts human beings."[695]

See Psychotherapist, Psychotherapy.

P 8
Philosophizing

"[T]he way in which a person . . . [understands] . . . how to suffer, or . . . [knows] . . . how to die . . . . [:] "This . . . is the quintessence of all philosophizing."[696]

See Death, Suffering.

P 9
Plastic Surgery

"A patient . . . was considering plastic surgery to beautify ugly breasts, hoping thereby to assure her husband's love. She asked her doctor for advice. The doctor warned against the projected operation; he remarked that since her husband really loved her, he loved her body just as it was. An evening dress, he pointed out, does not affect a man 'in itself'; he thinks it beautiful only when the woman he loves is wearing it."[697]

P 10
Pleasure

a.   "[M]an's main concern is not to gain pleasure or to avoid pain but rather to see a meaning in his life."[698]

b.   "[P]leasure cannot be attained by directly intending it."[699]

c.   [The will to pleasure] "defeats itself. For pleasure and happiness are by-products."[700]

d.   "[P]leasure is primarily and normally not an aim but

an effect, . . . a side effect, of the achievement of a task. In other words, pleasure establishes itself automatically as soon as one has fulfilled a meaning or realized a value. Moreover, if a man really attempted to gain pleasure by making it his target, he would necessarily fail, for he would miss what he had aimed at. This can be easily demonstrated in those cases of sexual neurosis in which our patients are thwarted in obtaining sexual pleasure precisely because they attempt to attain it directly. The more a man sets out to demonstrate his potency or a woman her ability to experience orgasm, the less they will be able to do so."[701]

e.   "What is behind the emphasis on sexual achievement and power, what is behind this will to sexual pleasure and happiness, is . . . the frustrated will to meaning."[702]

f.   "[P]leasure, rather than being an end of man's striving, is actually the effect of meaning fulfillment."[703]

g.   "Pleasure is not the goal of our aspirations, but the consequence of attaining them."[704]

See Happiness, Hyperintention, Meaning, Self-Transcendence, Sex.

P 11
Plutarch
(Ancient Greek Historian)
(*ca.* 45-125 C. E.)

Frankl quotes Plutarch: "The measure of a man is the way he bears up under misfortune."[705]

See Attitudinal Values, Nobility and Misery of Human Beings, Suffering.

P 12
Pornography

"As to pornography, I detest the invocation of 'freedom from censorship' when what is really meant is simply the freedom to make money."[706]

P 13
Potzl, Otto
(Psychiatrist and Neurologist)[707]
(1877-1962)

"Besides Freud and Adler, Potzl was for me the personification of genius . . . ."[708]

See Adler, Freud.

P 14
Present
(The Present, Living in the Moment)

a.   "Since my years in the concentration camps . . . I have learned to . . . make every minute count."[709]

b.   "If man were immortal, he would be justified in delaying everything; there would be no need to do anything right now. Only under the urge and pressure of life's transience does it make sense to use the passing time."[710]

See Time, Transitoriness of Life.

P 15
Prostitution

a.   [Economic necessity] "would not force a psychologically and morally normal woman to prostitution. On the contrary, . . . frequently women resist the temptation to prostitution in spite of economic necessity."[711]

b.   [The prostitute's client] "is seeking precisely the sort of impersonal and non-binding form of love life which the relationship to a commodity will give him . . . . This is the attitude that takes sex to be a mere means to the end of pleasure—a thoroughly decadent sensualism. Sexuality, which should be the means of expression for love, is made subservient to the pleasure principle, and gratification of the instincts, sexual pleasure, becomes an end in itself."[712]

See Love, Personalism, Sex.

P 16
Psychiatric Sectarians[713]

"[T]he lack of psychiatric training, that is to say, the lack of an opportunity to compare one [psychological] school with another, accounts for much of the proselytizing among psychiatric sectarians."[714]

P 17
Psychiatrists
(or Psychiatry)

a.   "Some of the people who nowadays call on a psychiatrist would have seen a pastor, priest or rabbi in former days. Now they often refuse to be handed over to a clergyman . . . ."[715]

b.   "[T]he irreligious psychiatrist should let the religious patient have his belief . . . ."[716]

c.   "An irreligious psychiatrist never has the right to manipulate the patient's religious feelings . . . ."[717]

d.   "[R]eligious patients often do not want to deliver their intimate experiences into the hands of people who would perhaps lack understanding and thus misinterpret them. Such patients may be afraid that a psychiatrist will try to 'unmask' their religiousness as 'nothing but' the manifestation of unconscious . . . conflicts or complexes."[718]

e.   Frankl quotes one of his patients: "I know . . . why I feel so ashamed about my religious longings: Underlying all the psychotherapeutic treatment I have had these last 27 years was the more or less tacit conviction on the part of my doctors that such longings are nothing but unrealistic, baseless speculation. As they put it, only the tangible is real, and everything else is nonsense, caused by trauma or by the wish to escape life . . . ."[719]

f.   "We psychiatrists simply don't have the answer for each and every question. Lest of all do we have a prescription to hand out when it comes to the question of how to cure all the ills that afflict our society. *Let us* . . . stop ascribing divine attributes to psychiatrists."[720]

g.   "[F]or immature people the lure of psychiatry lies in its promise to *gain power over others*, to dominate and manipulate them. Knowledge is power, and so knowledge of some mechanisms possessed by us and not by others gives us power."[721]

See Materialism, Reductionism.

P 18
Psychoanalysis
(The Psychological School of Thought Founded by Sigmund Freud)

a. "[P]sychoanalysis is, and will remain forever, the indispensable foundation of every psychotherapy . . . ."[722]

b. "[P]sychoanalysis not only adopted objectivity—it succumbed to it. Objectivity eventually led to objectification, or reification. That is, psychoanalysis made the human person into an object, the human being into a thing. Psychoanalysis regards the patient as ruled by 'mechanisms,' and it conceives of the therapist as the one who knows the technique by which disturbed mechanisms may be repaired.
"[W]e can see the therapist as a technician only if we have first viewed the patient as some sort of mechanism."[723]

c. "Freud's psychoanalysis teaches how to *unmask the neurotic*, how to determine the hidden, unconscious dynamics underlying his behavior. This behavior is analyzed, and 'analyzing' . . . means interpreting . . . .
"In contradistinction, and counteraction, to the psychoanalytic system, Carl Roger's approach to counseling is characterized by restraint from being directive and abstention from interpretations . . . .
[Such interpretations] . . . are influenced by the analysts, and the patients are indoctrinated in a very specific *Weltanschauung* or ideology."[724]

d. "The theories of psychoanalysis are 'beliefs' with which 'psychiatrists in training are . . . frequently indoctrinated.'"[725]

e.   "[T]he patients' dreams can no longer be relied upon by their interpreter [that is, the psychoanalyst]. They too have been given a slant, so as to be welcomed by the doctor and fit his type of interpretation."[726]

f.   Frankl quotes Sigmund Freud who spoke about psychoanalysis, his own kind of therapy: "This technique has proved to be the only method suited to my individuality; I do not venture to deny that a physician quite differently constituted might feel impelled to adopt a different attitude to his patients and the task before him."[727]

See Adlerian Psychology, Freud, Materialism, Personalism, Unmasking, Viennese Schools of Psychotherapy, World View.

P 19
Psychology

a.   "The human quality of a human being is disregarded and neglected . . . by those psychologists who adhere to either 'the machine model' or 'the rat model,' as Gordon W. Allport termed them."[728]

b.   Different Schools of Psychology

"[S]ound findings of research in the lower dimensions, however they may neglect the humanness of man, need not contradict it. This is equally true of . . . Watsonian behaviorism, Pavlovian reflexology, Freudian psychoanalysis, and Adlerian psychology. They are not nullified by logotherapy but rather overarched by it. They are seen in the light of a higher dimension—or, . . . the findings of these schools are reinterpreted and reevaluated by logotherapy—and rehumanized by it."[729]

See Distinctively Human Phenomenon, Logotherapy, Reductionism.

P 20
Psychosomatic Illness

a.   Frankl talks about a prisoner in the concentration camp whose unfulfilled expectation may be causally connected to his sickness and death: "One day a prisoner told his fellows he had a strange dream. He dreamed that a voice spoke to him and asked whether he wanted to know anything at all—it could foretell the future. He answered: 'I should like to know when this Second World War will end for me.' Whereupon the dream voice replied: 'On March 30, 1945.' It was the beginning of March when the prisoner narrated this dream. At the time he was very hopeful and in good spirits.

"But as the thirtieth of March came closer, it began to seem less and less probable that the 'voice' would be right. In the last days before the prophesied deadline the man gave way more and more to discouragement. On March 29 he was taken to the infirmary with a high fever and in a state of delirium. On the crucial thirtieth of March—the day when the Second World War was to end 'for him'—he lost consciousness. Next day he was dead of typhus.

"[H]ow extremely dependent the organism's immunity is upon affective states! Courage for living or weariness with life, disillusionment or blighted hopes gravely influence immunity. We can therefore assume in all seriousness that the prisoner's disappointment over his dream voice's 'false' prophecy brought about a rapid decline of his organism's defenses, thus permitting the organism to succumb to a dormant infection."[730]

b. "Our view [of how the mind influences the body] is supported by an observation on a larger scale reported by a camp doctor. The prisoners in his camp, he said, had generally subscribed to the hope that they would be back home by Christmas of 1944. Christmas came, and newspaper were anything but encouraging to the camp inmates. The consequence? During the week between Christmas and New Year's Day there was unprecedented mass mortality in this concentration camp."[731]

See Anthropology (Psychosomatic Unity of the Human Person), Concentration Camps.

P 21
Psychotherapist

a. "[A] psychotherapist must not impose a value on the patient. The patient must be referred to his own conscience."[732]

b. "[I]n emergency cases the psychotherapist need not stick to his neutralism. In the face of a suicidal risk it is perfectly legitimate to intervene because only a[n] erroneous conscience will ever command a person to commit suicide."[733]

See Conscience, Hippocratic Oath, Suicide.

P 22
Psychotherapy

a. "We cannot discuss psychotherapy without taking for our starting-points psychoanalysis and individual psychology, the two great psychotherapeutic systems created by Freud and Adler respectively."[734]

b.   "[W]hat about Freud and Adler? Is logotherapy less indebted to them? By no means."[735]

c.   "The therapist must beware of interpreting his own role as that of a technician . . . . This would amount to reducing the patient . . . to *l'homme machine*."[736]

d.   "Psychotherapy is more than mere technique in that it is art, and it goes beyond pure science in that it is wisdom."[737] "But even wisdom is not the last word . . . . Wisdom is lacking without the human touch."[738]

e.   "[T]he crucial agency in psychotherapy is not so much the method, but rather the relationship between the patient and his doctor or . . . the 'encounter' between the therapist and his patient. This relationship between two persons seems to be the most significant aspect of the psychotherapeutic process, a more important factor than any method or technique."[739]

f.   "It is the rule that psychotherapy—every method of psychotherapy, that is—is not applicable to every patient with the same degree of success."[740]

g.   "Every school of psychotherapy has a concept of man, although this concept is not always held consciously."[741]

h.   "If psychotherapy is to remain therapy . . ., then it needs a correct picture of man."[742]

i.   "Psychotherapy . . . must appeal to the capacity for decision, to freedom of attitude. Thus, it must appeal . . . to the freedom of man's will."[743]

See Adler, Anthropology, Existential Psychiatry, Free-Will, Freud, Logotherapy, Psychoanalysis, Reductionism, Techniques, World View.

P 23
Purpose in Life[744]
(Goals in Life, Orientation toward the Future or Reasons to Stay Alive)

a. "To direct one's life toward a goal is of vital importance."[745]

b. Frankl quotes from the atheistic philosopher Friedrich Nietzsche: "He who has a *why* to live for can bear almost any *how*."[746]

c. "[M]an needs 'something' for the sake of which to live."[747]

d. [A basic or fundamental fact of being human, a distinctively human characteristic, is that a human being] "normally . . . is striving to find, and fulfill, meaning and purpose in life."[748]

e. Frankl talks to a patient named Anna who suffered from a psychological and emotional crisis and tells her that she now must go on with her life: "[Y]ou are in a stage where reconstruction of your life is the task awaiting you! But one cannot reconstruct one's life without a life goal, without anything challenging him."[749]

f. "Goethe worked seven years on the completion of the second part of *Faust*. Finally, in January 1832, he sealed the manuscript; two months later he died. I dare say that during the final seven years of his life he biologically lived beyond his means. His death was overdue, but he remained alive up to the moment his work was completed and meaning fulfilled."[750]

g. To illustrate the human person's need for a purpose in life, Frankl recalls the experiences of the prisoners in the concentration camps: "Any attempt at fighting the camp's psychopathological influence on the prisoner . . . has to aim at giving him inner strength by pointing out to him a future goal to which he could look forward."[751]

h. "The moment a person cannot see the end of a provisional stage in his life, he is unable to set himself any further goals, is unable to assign himself a task. Life consequently loses all content and meaning in his eyes. And, vice versa, envisioning the 'end' and a goal in the future constitutes that very spiritual support which the camp prisoner so badly needs because such spiritual support alone can keep him from succumbing to the character-marring and type-forming forces of the social environment—can save him, that is, from utterly giving in."[752]

i. Referring to the behavior of prisoners in general at Auschwitz, Dachau and Theresienstad during the Holocaust, Frankl observes: "He who can cling to no end point, to no time in the future, to no point of support, is in danger of allowing himself to collapse inwardly."[753]

j. "The prisoner who had lost faith in the future—his future—was doomed. With his loss of belief in the future, he also lost his spiritual hold; he let himself decline and became subject to mental and physical decay."[754]

k.   "[P]hysical-psychic collapse . . . results when the normal direction of human existence toward the future is blocked . . . ."[755]

l.   "It should be clear, then, that even under concentration camp conditions, psychotherapy or mental hygiene could not possibly be effective unless directed toward the crucial factor of helping the mind find some goal in the future to hold on to. For healthy living is living with an eye to the future."[756]

m.   [Frankl says that in the concentration camps, the prisoners had to be shown] "a *why*—an aim—for their lives, in order to strengthen them to bear the terrible *how* of their existence. Woe to him who saw no more sense in his life, no aim, no purpose, and therefore no point in carrying on. He was soon lost."[757]

n.   "I . . . had as students three American officers who had served long terms—up to seven years—in North Vietnamese POW camps; they too had found that the prisoners who felt there was something or someone waiting for them were the ones most likely to survive. The message . . . is that survival depended on the direction to a 'what for,' or a 'whom for.' In a word, existence was dependent on 'self-transcendence' . . . ."[758]

o.   [In the former communist country Czechoslovakia, many Czech students had fought] "for political liberalization and for the humanization of communism. They had been given a cause for which to fight, for which to live, and unfortunately, for which to die."[759]

p.   "It is a peculiarity of man that he can only live by looking to the future . . . . And this is his salvation in the most difficult moments of his existence, although he sometimes has to force his mind to the task."[760]

q.   "[A]s the *struggle for survival* has subsided, the question has emerged: *survival for what?* Ever more people today have the means to live, but no meaning to live for."[761]

r.   "[T]he struggle for existence is a struggle 'for' something; it is purposeful, and only in so being is it meaningful and able to bring meaning into life."[762]

s.   "In the Nazi concentration camps, one could have witnessed that those who knew that there was a task waiting from them to fulfill were most apt to survive."[763]

See Buhler, Concentration Camps, Hope, Meaning, Mission in Life, Nietzsche, Psychosomatic Illness, Purposelessness, Self-Transcendence, Suicide, Survival.

P 24
Purposelessness

"Karol Marshal of the East Side Mental Health Center in Bellevue, Washington, . . . 'characterized the feeling among those in the pre-30 age group who come in for help as a sense of purposelessness.'"[764]

See Purpose, Youth.

Q
Questioning the Meaning of Life[765]

a. [Human beings who despair over an answer to the question, "What is the meaning of life?"] "should know that despair over the apparent meaninglessness of life constitutes a human achievement rather than a neurosis. After all, no animal cares whether or not its existence has a meaning. It is the prerogative of man to quest for a meaning to his life, and also to question whether such meaning exists. This quest is a manifestation of intellectual sincerity and honesty . . . . However, the courage to question should be matched by patience. People should be patient enough to wait until, sooner or later, meaning dawns on them. This is what they should do, rather than taking their lives—or taking refuge in drugs."[766]

b. "[E]ach life situation confronting us places a demand on us, presents a question to us—a question to which we have to answer by doing something about the given situation."[767]

c. "The guide which guides man in his response to the question life puts, in his taking the responsibility for his life, is conscience. Conscience has its 'still small voice' and 'speaks' to us—that is an undeniable phenomenological fact."[768]

"While the urgent questioning of the meaning of life is most apt to occur during adolescence, it may also come later, precipitated by some shaking experience."[769]

See Attitudinal Values, Conscience, Existential Vacuum, Meaning, Responsibility.

R 1
Reality
(Objective Reality)[770]

"[A] cloud passes over the sun, hiding the sun from our eyes . . . . [T]he sun continues to exist, even if we do not see it for the moment. Similarly, values continue even though a person blinded to values by depression is momentarily unable to observe them."[771]

See Meaning, Truth.

R 2
Reductionism[772]

a.   "What is dangerous is the attempt of a man who is an expert, say, in the field of biology, to understand and explain human beings, exclusively in terms of biology. The same is true of psychology and sociology as well. At the moment at which totality is claimed, biology becomes biologism, psychology becomes psychologism, and sociology becomes sociologism. In other words, at that moment science is turned into ideology."[773]

b.   "Reductionists recognize no qualitative difference between . . . [human beings and animals] . . . . They deny that any uniquely human phenomenon exists, and this they do, not on empirical grounds . . . but on an *a priori* basis. They insist that there is nothing in man that cannot be found in other animals."[774]

c.   "If we present a man with a concept of man which is not true, we may well corrupt him. When we present man as an automation of reflexes, as a mind-machine, as a bundle of instincts, as a pawn of drives and reactions, as a mere product of instinct, heredity, and environment, we feed the nihilism to which modern man is, in any case, prone.

"I became acquainted with the last stage of that corruption in my second concentration camp, Auschwitz. The gas chambers of Auschwitz were the ultimate consequence of the theory that man is nothing but the product of heredity and environment—or, as the Nazi liked to say, of 'Blood and Soil.' I am absolutely convinced that the gas chambers of Auschwitz, Treblinka, and Maidanek were ultimately prepared not in some Ministry or other in Berlin, but rather at the desks and in the lecture halls of nihilistic scientists and philosophers."[775]

d.   "Reductionism is today's nihilism. It reduces a human being, by no less than an entire dimension, namely the specific human dimension . . . . In other words, reductionism is subhumanism."[776]

e.   A Reductionist View of Joy

"[T]he assertion that joy is a strictly organized dance of molecules or atoms or electrons within the gray matter of the brain . . . has [not] . . . been so compelling and convincing."[777]

See Education, Frankl (The Neurologist), Nihilism, Thompson, World View.

R 3
Religion

a. Frankl quotes Albert Einstein: "What is the meaning of human life, or for that matter of the life of any creature? To find a satisfying answer to this question means to be religious."[778]

b. "If we subscribe to his [Einstein's] definition of religion we are justified in claiming that man is basically religious."[779]

c. "[O]ne may . . . be justified in defining religion as man's search for *ultimate* meaning."[780]

d. "Logotherapy . . . leaves the door to religion open and it leaves it to the patient whether or not to pass the door."[781]

e. "[R]eligion provides man with a spiritual anchor, with a feeling of security such as he can find nowhere else." [782]

f. "[W]hen a patient stands on the firm ground of religious belief, there can be no objection to making use of the therapeutic effect of his religious convictions and thereby drawing upon his spiritual resources."[783]

g. "[R]eligion is not dying, and insofar as this is true, God is not dead either, not even 'after Auschwitz' . . . ."[784]

h. "[R]eligion involves the most personal decisions man makes . . . ."[785]

i. "[C]linical evidence suggests that atrophy of the

religious sense in man results in a distortion of his religious concepts."[786]

j.   "To all appearances religion is indestructible and indelible. Even psychosis cannot destroy it."[787]

k.   Distorted Religious Beliefs

"Joseph Wolpe and Arnold A. Lazarus 'do not shrink from attacking on rational grounds a patient's religious beliefs if they are a source of suffering.'"[788]

l.   The World beyond This World

"Just as the animal can scarcely reach out of his environment to understand the superior world of man, so perhaps man can scarcely ever grasp the super-world, though he can reach out toward it in religion—or perhaps encounter it in revelation."[789]

See also Atheism, Concentration Camps, Faith, God, *Imago Dei*, Meaning, Supermeaning, Theology and Psychiatry, Unconscious, Werfel.

R 4
Repression[790]

a.   "The concept of repression is of central importance within the psychoanalytic scheme."[791]

b.   "In the act of repression something conscious becomes unconscious; vice versa, in the removing of repression something unconscious is made conscious again."[792]

See Psychoanalysis.

R 5
Responsibility[793]

a.   "[F]reedom threatens to degenerate into mere license and arbitrariness unless it is lived in terms of responsibleness."[794]

b.   "Man is free to be responsible . . . ."[795]

c.   "[F]reedom . . . is the subjective aspect of a total phenomenon and . . . is . . . to be completed by its objective aspect, responsibility. The freedom to take a stand . . . is never completed if it has not been converted and rendered into the freedom to take responsibility"[796]

d.   "[E]ach man is questioned by life; and he can only answer to life by *answering for* his own life; to life he can only respond by being responsible."[797]

e.   "Life ultimately means taking the responsibility to find the right answer to its problems and to fulfill the tasks which it constantly sets for each individual."[798]

f.   "[B]eing human is being responsible—existentially responsible, responsible for one's own existence."[799]

g.   "[L]ogotherapy sees in responsibleness the very essence of human existence."[800]

h.   "[F]reedom and responsibility together make man a spiritual being."[801]

i.   Frankl talks of his own sense of responsibility in

writing the book *Man's Search for Meaning*: "I . . . felt responsible for writing down what I had gone through, for I thought it might be helpful to people who are prone to despair."[802]

j. "Responsibility implies something for which we are responsible—namely, the accomplishment of concrete, personal tasks and demands, the realization of that unique and individual meaning which every one of us has to fulfill."[803]

k. [A human being is] "responsible *before* something, or *to* something, be it society, or humanity, or mankind, or his own conscience. However, there is a significant number of people who interpret their own existence not just in terms of being responsible to something but rather to some*one*, namely, to God."[804]

l. "The unique achievement of Mosaic monotheism may well consist in its conveying to the human race the permanent consciousness of a divine authority. Man is seen as a being standing before God, thereby intensifying man's consciousness of responsibility by presenting his life task to him as an assignment from the Divine."[805]

m. "[T]he Statue of Liberty on the East Coast should be supplemented by a Statue of Responsibility on the West Coast."[806]

See Anthropology, Conscience, Determinism, Existential Analysis, Fatalism, Free-Will, God, Logotherapy, Religion, Suicide, Spirit.

R 6
Rogers, Carl R.
(American Psychologist)[807]
(1902-1987)

a. Frankl quotes Carl R. Rogers: "The warm, subjective, human encounter of two persons . . . is more effective in facilitating change than is the most precise set of techniques growing out of learning theory or operant conditioning."[808]

b. "Personality change is initiated by attitudes which exist in the therapist, rather than primarily by his knowledge, his theories, or his techniques . . . ."[809]

See Encounter, Kant, Love, Personalism, Sex.

S 1
Sartre, Jean Paul
(French Atheistic Existentialist Philosopher)
(1905-1980)

"Jean Paul Sartre believed that man can choose and design himself by creating his own standards . . . . Is it not . . . comparable to the fakir trick? The fakir claims to throw a rope into the air, into the empty space, and claims a boy will climb up the rope. It is not different with Sartre when he tries to make us believe that man 'projects' himself—throws himself forward and upward—into nothingness."[810]

See Meaninglessness, Nihilism.

S 2
Schweitzer, Albert
(German Theologian, Physician, and Christian Medical Missionary in Africa)
(1875-1965)

Frankl quotes Schweitzer: "The only ones among you who will be really happy are those who have sought and found how to serve."[811]

See Happiness, Self-Transcendence.

S 3
Security

a.   "Man . . . cannot achieve perfect security—not in living, not in knowing, not in making decisions.[812]

b.   "[T]he normal person desires a half-way-secure world, whereas the neurotic seeks absolute security."[813]

See Certainty, Obsessive-Compulsive Neurotic.

S 4
Science

a.   "The nature of our education, heavily weighted as it is on the side of materialism, has left most of us with an exaggerated respect for the findings of the so-called exact sciences."[814]

b.   "A scientist may stick to his science and stay in one dimension, but he should also remain open, keep his science open, at least to the *possibility* of another, higher dimension."[815]

c.   "[S]cience is *blind* to ultimate meaning . . . . However, this state of affairs does in no way entitle a scientist to deny that ultimate meaning possibly does exist."[816]

See Materialism (Philosophical), Ultimate Meaning.

S 5
Self-Actualization

a.   "[T]he true meaning of life is to be found in the world rather than within man or his own *psyche*, as though it were a closed system. By the same token, the real aim of human existence cannot be found in what is called self-actualization. Human existence is essentially self-transcendence rather than self-actualization. Self-actualization is not a possible aim at all, for the simple reason that the more a man would strive for it, the more he would miss it . . . . In other words, self-actualization cannot be attained if it is made an end in itself, but only as a side effect of self-transcendence."[817]

b.   "Self-actualization is not man's ultimate destination. It is not even his primary intention. Self-actualization, if made an end in itself, contradicts the self-transcendent quality of human existence. Like happiness, self-actualization is an effect, the effect of meaning fulfillment. Only to the extent to which man fulfills a meaning out there in the world, does he fulfill himself."[818]

c.   "Ultimately, . . . man can actualize himself only by fulfilling a meaning out in the world, rather than within himself, and self-actualization is available only as an effect of self-transcendence."[819]

d. "What is called 'self-actualization' is ultimately an effect, the unintentional by-product, of self-transcendence."[820]

See Happiness, Hyperintention, Maslow, Meaning, Pleasure, Self-Transcendence.

S 6
Self-Creation[821]

a. "Man is never fully conditioned in the sense of being determined by any facts or forces. Rather man is ultimately self-determining. He determines not only his fate but also his own self, for man is not only forming and shaping the course of his life but also his very self. To this extent man is not only responsible for what he does but also for what he is, inasmuch as man does not only behave according to what he is but also becomes what he is according to how he behaves. In the last analysis, man has become what he has made out of himself. Instead of being fully conditioned by any conditions, he is constructing himself. Facts and factors are nothing but the raw material for such self-constructing acts, and a human life is an unbroken chain of such acts. They present the tools, the means, to an end set by man himself."[822]

b. "Man . . . may very well change himself, otherwise he would not be man. It is a prerogative of being human, and a constituent of human existence, to be capable of shaping and reshaping oneself."[823]

c. "[O]ur assertion of human existence as a self-creating act corresponds to the basic assumption that man does not simply 'be,' but always decides what he will be in the next moment. At each moment the human person is steadily molding and forging his own character. Thus, every human being has a chance of changing at any instant. There is the freedom to change . . . ."[824]

d. "[M]an resembles a sculptor who chisels and hammers the unshaped stone so that the material takes on more and more form."[825]

e. "[M]an not only behaves according to what he is, he also becomes what he is according to how he behaves."[826]

f. "What . . . is man? . . . He is a being who continuously decides what he is: a being who equally harbors the potential to descend to the level of an animal or to ascend to the life of a saint."[827]

g. "There is a multitude of different possibilities in his being [that is, in man's being or being human], of which he actualizes only a single one and in so doing determines his existence as such. (The human mode of being . . . might also be termed 'the being that I am.')."[828]

h. "At any moment, man must decide, for better of for worse, what will be the monument of his existence."[829]

See Arnold, Magda B., Conditioning, Death, Decisions, Determinism, Free-Will, Identity.

S 7
Self-Detachment

a. "[H]umor is . . . a manifestation of that peculiarly human ability which in logotherapy is called self-detachment . . . ."[830]

b. "By virtue of self-detachment man is capable of joking about himself, laughing at himself, and ridiculing his own fears."[831]

See Distinctively Human Phenomena, Humor, Paradoxical Intention

S 8
Self-Transcendence

a. "It is a tenet of logotherapy that self-transcendence is the essence of existence."[832]

b. "[H]uman existence—at least as long as it has not been neurotically distorted—is always directed to something, or someone, other than itself, be it a meaning to fulfill or another human being to encounter lovingly. I have termed this constitutive characteristic of human existence 'self-transcendence.'"[833]

c. "Being human is being always directed, and pointing, to something or someone other than oneself: to a meaning to fulfill or another human being to encounter, a cause to serve or a person to love. Only to the extent that someone is living out this self-transcendence of human existence, is he truly human or does he become his true self. He becomes so, not by concerning himself with his self's actualization, but by forgetting himself and giving himself, overlooking himself and focusing outward."[834]

d.   [A human being] "finds himself only to the extent to which he loses himself in the first place, be it for the sake of something or somebody, for the sake of a cause or a fellowman, or 'for God's sake.'"[835]

e.   "[S]elf-transcendence is one of the basic features of human existence. Only as man withdraws from himself in the sense of releasing self-centered interest and attention will he gain an authentic mode of existence."[836]

f.   [A boomerang is] "a symbol of human existence. Generally, one assumes that a boomerang returns to the hunter; but actually, . . . a boomerang only comes back to the hunter when it has missed its target . . . Well, man also . . . returns to himself, to be concerned with his self, after he has missed his mission, has failed to find a meaning in his life."[837]

g.   "Consider the eye. The eye . . . is self-transcendent in a way. The moment it perceives something of itself, its function . . . has deteriorated. If it is afflicted with a cataract, it may 'perceive' its own cataract as a cloud; and if it is suffering from glaucoma, it might 'see' it[s] own glaucoma as a rainbow halo around lights. Normally, however, the eye doesn't see anything of itself. Equally, by virtue of the self-transcendent quality of the human reality, the humanness of man is most tangible when he forgets himself—and overlooks himself!"[838]

h.   Frankl quotes from the Indian Vedas: "That which does the seeing, cannot be seen; that which does the hearing, cannot be heard; and that which does the thinking, cannot be thought."[839]

i.   "The meaning which a being has to fulfill is something beyond himself, it is never just himself."[840]

j.   Frankl quotes the astronaut Lt. Col. John H. Glenn, Jr.: "[W]hat is needed [today] is a 'basis of convictions and beliefs so strong that they [lift] individuals clear out of themselves and [cause] them to live, and die, for some aim nobler and better than themselves' . . . ." [841]

See Happiness, Human, Hyperreflection, Logotherapy, Love, Maslow, Self-Actualization.

S 9
Selye, Hans Hugo Bruno
(Austrian-Hungarian Endocrinologist, Father of the Stress Concept) (1907-1982)

Frankl quotes Selye: "'[S]tress is the salt of life.'"[842]

See Tension.

S 10
Sex
(Sexual Intercourse or Sexual Intimacy)

a.   As a Means of Escaping from One's Problems

"[S]ex often serves as a cheap escape from

precisely those philosophical and existential problems which beset man."[843]

b.   Devaluation of Sex

1. "[A] woman . . . [a man] . . . can 'have' and therefore need not love. She is property, . . . without personal value . . . .
"This kind of eroticism represents a crippled form of love. The use of such a phrase as 'I have had this woman' fully exposes the nature of such eroticism. What you 'have' you can swap; what you possess you can change. If a man has 'possessed a woman, he can exchange her . . . ."[844]

2). "[S]exual promiscuity is not . . . sensitivity, or encounter."[845]

c.   Frigidity and Impotence

Referring to frigidity and impotence, Frankl says: "Sexual performance or experience is strangled to the extent to which it is made either an object of attention or an object of intention . . . . [T]he first . . . [is] . . . 'hyperreflection' and the second 'hyperintention.'"[846]

d.   Not a Distinctively Human Phenomenon

"[T]he sexual instinct cannot in itself be distinctively human. After all, it is not only a property of human beings but is shared by animals as well."[847]

e.   Spiritual Expression of Love

1. The difference between sex and love is

demonstrated in the following analysis: "I am driven to a partner by my sex drive. On the other hand, on the human level, I love the partner because, as I feel, I have a lot of reasons to do so; and sexual intercourse with her is an expression of love, its 'incarnation,' so to speak. On the subhuman level, to be sure, I would see her as no more than just an object . . .—a more or less fit means to get rid of surplus sperma. Sexual activity with such an attitude is often described by our patients as 'masturbating on a woman.' In so speaking, they implicitly contrast it with the normal approach to the partner, with sexual behavior on the human and personal level. There they no longer would see the partner as an 'object' but rather as another subject. This would preclude their regarding the other human being as a mere means to an end—any end. On the human level, one no longer 'uses' the partner but encounters him . . . . On the personal level, he meets the partner on a person-to-person basis, and this means that he loves the partner. Encounter preserves the humanness of the partner; love discovers his uniqueness as a person "[848]

2. "[T]he sexual act is the physical expression of a psycho-physical union."[849]

3. "Human sex is always more than mere sex. And it is more than mere sex precisely to the extent that it serves as *the physicals expression of something metasexual*—the physical expression of love."[850]

4. "[F]or the real lover the physical, sexual

relationship remains a mode of expression for the spiritual relationship which his love really is, and as a mode of expression it is love, the spiritual love act, which gives it human dignity."[851]

5. "Sex is human if it is experienced as a vehicle of love . . . ."[852]

See Abstinence, Encounter, Existential Vacuum, Hyperintention, Hyperreflection, Love, Marriage, Masturbation, Monogamous Marital Love, Personalism, Pleasure.

S 11
Shallow Persons

"While the 'shallow' person sees only the partner's surface and cannot grasp the depths, the 'deeper' person sees the surface itself as an expression of the depths, not as an essential and decisive expression, but as a significant one."[853]

S 12
Shame

"[S]hame has a distinctive function in love. Its task is to prevent something from becoming a mere object—an object for onlookers."[854]

See Personalism.

S 13
Skepticism

a.   Obsessive-Compulsive, Neurotic Skepticism.

1. [Frankl relates a case in which a young man wanted] "to know the roots of everything . . . . 'I want to be able to prove everything; I want to prove everything that is immediately obvious—for example, whether I am living.'"[855]

2. "Our patient . . . wanted to 'prove' intuitive data. He had to be shown that it is impossible to 'prove' such data—but that it is also unnecessary, since as intuitive data they are obvious. For the logical impossibility of doubting intuitively evident, immediate data of existence is reflected in psychological reality: such doubting represents empty talk."[856]

3. "Logotherapeutic treatment of our obsessional-neurotic patient . . . had to aim at overthrowing his exaggerated rationalism (which is what underlies all skepticism) by rational means."[857]

b.   Philosophical Skepticism

1. "The ultimate—or, . . . the first—question of radical skepticism is about the meaning of existence. But to ask the meaning of existence is meaningless in that existence precedes meaning. For the existence of meaning is assumed when we question the meaning of existence. Existence is, so to speak, the wall we are backed up against whenever we question it."[858]

2. "In his book on psychotherapy Arthur Kronfeld has remarked that skepticism negates itself . . . . For the dictum 'I doubt everything' implies always: 'everything except this particular dictum.'"[859]

S 14
Society
(Today's Society)

a.   "[T]oday's society is characterized by achievement orientation, and consequently it adores people who are successful and happy and, in particular, it adores the young. It virtually ignores the value of all those who are otherwise . . . ."[860]

b.   [Frankl quotes Edith Weisskopf-Joelson who observes] "the discomfort of middle-aged or old people in cultures, such as that of the United States, which stress the value of youth."[861]

See Euthanasia, Weisskopf-Joelson.

S 15
Solomon
(King of Israel During Biblical Times)
(*ca.* 970-931 B. C. E.)

"Speaking of the self-defeating quality inherent in the pursuit of pleasure, happiness, self-actualization, . . . brings to . . . mind that story according to which Solomon was invited by God to utter a wish. After pondering for a while, Solomon said that he wished to become a wise judge for his people. Thereupon God said: 'Solomon, I will . . . make you the wisest man who ever existed. But precisely because you did not care for long life, health, wealth, and power, I will grant them to you . . . and along with making you the wisest man, I will also make you the mightiest king who ever existed.' Thus Solomon received the very gifts which he had not intended."[862]

See Happiness, Hyperintention, Pleasure, Self-Actualization.

S 16
Soul
(The Human Soul)

"In the setting of a discussion a young man s asked whether it was justified to speak of a soul if it cannot be seen. Even if we explore the brain tissue in a microscope, he said, we will never find anything such as a soul. Now the moderator asked me to handle the issue. And I started by asking the young man what motivated him in raising the question. 'My intellectual honesty,' he answered. 'Well,' I continued challenging him, '[I]s it bodily? Is it tangible? Will it be visible in a microscope?' 'Of course, it won't,' he admitted, 'because it is mental.' 'Aha,' I said, 'in other words, what you are searching for in vain in the microscope is a condition for your search, and presupposed by you all along, isn't it?'"[863]

See Empiricism, God, Religion.

S 17
Spirit
(Spiritual, Spirituality)

a. Frankl uses a German word to describe the spiritual aspects or spiritual reality of the human person: "By . . . *Geist* . . . we mean the core or nucleus of the personality."[864]

b. "[M]an is more than psyche: Man is spirit. By the very act of his own self-transcendence he leaves the plane of the merely biopsychological and enters the sphere of the specifically human, the noological dimension."[865]

c. "'Spiritual' is used [in logotherapy] . . . to indicate . . .

a specifically human phenomenon, in contrast to the phenomena that we share with other animals. In other words, the 'spiritual' is what is human in man."[866]

d.   "The spirituality of man is a thing-in-itself. It cannot be explained by something not spiritual; it is irreducible."[867]

e.   "[H]umanity has demonstrated *ad nauseam* in recent years that it has instincts, drives. Today it appears more important to remind man that he has a spirit, that he is a spiritual being."[868]

See Anthropology, Distinctively Human Phenomena, Noological Dimension, Self-Transcendence.

S 18
Sports

"In the midst of a sea of affluence, islands of asceticism emerge! . . . I regard sports as the modern, the secular, form of asceticism."[869]

S 19
Starvation

a.   [My father, Gabriel] "was seen scraping potato peelings from a nearly empty trash can. Later I was transferred from Theresienstadt to the camp Kaufering, where we suffered terribly from starvation, and it was there that I came to understand my father better. Now it was I who scraped a tiny piece of carrot from the icy soil—with my fingernails."[870]

b.   Frankl's describes the starvation of the inmates in the concentration camp: "When the last layers of subcutaneous fat had vanished, and we looked like skeletons disguised with skin and rags, we could watch our bodies beginning to devour themselves. The organism digested its own protein, and the muscles disappeared. Then the body had no powers of resistance left. One after another the members of the little community in our hut died."[871]

See Concentration Camps.

S 20
Subjectivism

"Man's original and natural concern with meaning and values is endangered by the prevalent subjectivism and relativism. Both are liable to erode idealism and enthusiasm."[872]

See Meaning, Truth.

S 21
Success[873]

a.   "Attitudinal values . . . are actualized wherever the individual is faced with something unalterable, something imposed by destiny. From the manner in which a person takes these things upon himself, assimilates these difficulties into his own psyche, there flows an incalculable multitude of value-potentialities. This means that *human life can be fulfilled not only in creating and enjoying, but also in suffering!*
"Those who worship the superficial cult of success obviously will not understand such conclusions."[874]

b.   "[W]e . . . meet people who in spite of success are caught in despair— . . . who [attempt] suicide in spite of their affluence . . . ."[875]

c.   [Many suicidal persons] "have good jobs and are successful but want to kill themselves because they find life meaningless."[876]

d.   "Success and *happiness* must *happen*, and the less one cares for them, the more they can."[877]

See Attitudinal Values, College (or University) Graduates, College (or University) Students, Despair, Happiness, Meaninglessness, Suicide.

S 22
Suffering[878]

a.   Attitude toward Suffering.

   1.   "*[D]espair is suffering without meaning.*"[879]

   2.   [The difference between despair and meaning is the] "attitude we choose toward suffering."[880]

   3.   "Sometimes the patient . . . finds additional meaning in suffering. He may even succeed in making suffering into a triumph . . . . [H]owever, meaning rests on the attitude the patient chooses toward suffering."[881]

   4.   "Life can be made meaningful . . . through *the stand we take* toward a fate we no longer can change (an incurable disease, an inoperable cancer, or the like)."[882]

5. "What is significant is the person's attitude toward an unalterable fate. The opportunity to realize such attitudinal values is therefore always present whenever a person finds himself confronted by a destiny toward which he can act only by acceptance. The way in which he accepts, the way in which he bears his cross, what courage he manifests in suffering, what dignity he displays in doom and disaster, is the measure of his human fulfillment."[883]

6. "[T]he right kind of suffering . . . [is] . . . courageous suffering!"[884]

7. "[S]uffering may well be a human achievement . . . ."[885]

8. Frankl quotes Yehuda Bacon: "[S]uffering . . . can have a meaning if it changes *you* for the better."[886]

b.   Finding Meaning in Suffering.

1. "If there is a meaning in life at all, then there must be a meaning in suffering."[887]

2. "Man is ready and willing to shoulder any suffering as soon and as long as he can see a meaning in it."[888]

3. Anastasia Kotek, a woman with terminal cancer, struggling to find a meaning to her suffering and, thus, her life, speaks to Frankl:
    "I have had a great deal to suffer; but I also tried to be courageous and steadfast in enduring what I must. You see, Doctor, I regard my suffering as a punishment. I believe in God."

On this Frankl replies: "But cannot suffering also be a challenge? Is it not conceivable that God wanted to see how Anastasia Kotek would bear it? . . ."
Frankl later continues: "What matters in life is to achieve something. And this is precisely what you have done. You have made the best of your suffering. You have become an example to our patients because of the way you take your suffering upon yourself. I congratulate you for this achievement, and I also congratulate the other patients who have the opportunity to witness such an example . . . . [Y]our life . . . has been a great achievement. You may be proud of it, Frau Kotek. And how few people may be proud of their lives . . . I should say, your life is a monument. And no one can remove it from the world."[889]

4. Frankl quotes Professor Joyce Travelbee: "[W]hat can be more demoralizing to an ill individual than to believe that his illness and suffering are meaningless?"[890]

c.   Not Indispensable to the Meaning of One's Life.

"Is . . . suffering . . . indispensable to the discovery of meaning? In no way. I only insist that meaning is available in spite of—nay, even through—suffering, provided . . . that the suffering is unavoidable. If it is avoidable, the meaningful thing to do is to remove its cause, for unnecessary suffering is masochistic rather than heroic."[891]

d.   Purpose of Suffering.

"Suffering is intended to guard man from apathy, from

psychic *rigor mortis*. As long as we suffer we remain psychically alive. In fact, we mature in suffering, grow because of it—it makes us richer and stronger."[892]

See Attitudinal Values, Masochism, Meaning, Meaninglessness, Suicide, Tragic Triad, Weisskopf-Joelson.

S 23
Suicide[893]

a. Frankl quotes the French atheist and existentialist philosopher Albert Camus (1913-1960): "There is but one truly serious problem, and that is . . . judging whether life is or is not worth living . . . ."[894]

b. "[L]ogotherapy . . . teaches that suicide may be caused by a feeling of meaninglessness and that its prevention accordingly presupposes that the patient discover a meaning to life."[895]

c. "Not a few cases of suicide can be traced back to . . . [the] . . . existential vacuum."[896]

d. "[N]ot each and every case of depression is to be traced back to a feeling of meaninglessness, nor does suicide—in which depression sometimes eventuates—always result from an existential vacuum. But . . . it may well be that an individual's impulse to take his life would have been *overcome* had he been aware of some meaning and purpose worth living for."[897]

e. "'[S]uicide . . . in the United States, . . . is [the] third [leading cause of death] now among youth fifteen to nineteen years old, and second among college students.'"[898]

f.   Frankl recalls two specific cases of would-be suicide in a concentration camp: "I remember two cases of would-be suicides, which bore a striking similarity to each other. Both men had talked of their intentions to commit suicide. Both used the typical argument—they had nothing more to expect from life. In both cases it was a question of getting them to realize that life was still expecting something from them; something in the future was expected of them. We found, in fact, that for one it was his child whom he adored and who was waiting for him . . . . For the other it was a thing, not a person. This man was a scientist and had written a series of book[s] which still needed to be finished."[899]

g.   "A man who becomes conscious of the responsibility he bears toward a human being . . ., or to an unfinished work, will never be able to throw away his life [that is, commit suicide]. He knows the 'why' for his existence, and will be able to bear almost any 'how.'"[900]

h.   "[W]e know of a psychotherapeutically trained neurologist who was himself a prisoner [of a concentration camp]. In the evenings, when his fellow inmates lay in the dark in their crowded huts, exhausted from work, he would give little [encouraging] talks . . . which restored to a good may of his fellow prisoners the courage and will they needed to go on."[901]

i.   [Many suicidal persons] "have good jobs and are successful but want to kill themselves because they find life meaningless."[902]

j.   "[S]uicide is never ethically justified . . . . For suicide not only makes it impossible for a person to grow and to mature as a result of his own suffering (thus realizing attitudinal values), but it also makes it impossible for him ever to make up for the suffering he may have inflicted on someone else.

"[I]t is our duty to convince the would-be suicide that taking one's own life is categorically contrary to reason, that life is meaningful to every human being under any circumstances."[903]

k.   Frankl quotes Walter Freeman: "Doctors of medicine are more prone to suicide than are men in other occupations" [and] "psychiatrists appear to be at the top of the list."[904]

l.   Frankl quotes from the diary of a Carmelite nun who was suffering from depression: "The depression is my steady companion. It weighs my soul down . . . . I am living as if I were thrown into a vacuum. For there are times at which . . . even God is silent. I then wish to die. As soon as possible. And if I did not possess the belief that I am not the master over my life, I would have taken it."[905]

m.   [If a person has found meaning in life] "he is prepared to suffer, to offer sacrifices, even, if need be, to give his life for the sake of it. Contrariwise, if there is no meaning he is inclined to take his life, and he is prepared to do so even if all his needs, to all appearances, have been satisfied."[906]

n.   Discovering a Meaning to One's Life After a Failed Attempt at Suicide

"[P]atients have repeatedly told me how happy they were that the suicide attempt had not been successful; weeks, months, years later, they told me that there *was* a solution to their problem, an answer to their question, a meaning to their life."[907]

See Concentration Camps, Depression, Despair, Distinctively Human Phenomena, Doctor, Euthanasia, Existential Vacuum, Hippocratic Oath, Meaninglessness, Purpose in Life, Responsibility, Success, Will.

S 24
Sunday Neurosis

a.   [One of the signs or manifestations of the existential vacuum is the] "Sunday neurosis . . ."[908]

b.   [The Sunday neurosis is] "a depression which afflicts people who become conscious of the lack of content in their lives—the existential vacuum—when the rush of the busy week stops on Sunday and the void within them suddenly becomes manifest."[909]

c.   "We get the impression that these people [the Sunday neurotics] who know no goal in life are running the course of life at the highest possible speed so that they will not notice the aimlessness of it. They are at the same time trying to run away from themselves—but in vain. On Sunday, when the frantic race pauses for twenty-four hours, all the aimlessness, meaninglessness, and emptiness of their existence rises up before them once more.
      "What lengths they go to then to escape this experience. They flee to a dance hall. There the music is loud and boisterous . . . . And there is no necessity to think, either, since all attention can be directed toward the dancing."[910]

d.   "Victims of 'Sunday neurosis' . . . get drunk in order
         to flee from their spiritual horror of emptiness."[911]

See Diversions, Existential Vacuum, Meaninglessness.

S 25
Survival[912]
(Human Survival)

a.   "[S]urvival is dependent on direction. However,
         survival cannot be the supreme value. Unless life
         points to something beyond itself, survival is
         pointless and meaningless. It is not even possible.
         This is the very lesson I learned in three years spent
         in Auschwitz and Dachau, and has . . . been
         confirmed by psychiatrists in prisoner-of-war
         camps: Only those who were oriented toward the
         future, toward a goal in the future, toward a meaning
         to fulfill in the future, were likely to survive."[913]

b.   "There is nothing in the world, I venture to say, that
         would so effectively help one to survive even the
         worst conditions as the knowledge that there is a
         meaning in one's life."[914]

See Concentration Camps, Hope, Purpose in Life.

T 1
Techniques
(Used in Psychotherapy)

a.   "[W]e should not be disdainful of technique, for in
         therapy a certain degree of detachment on the part
         of the therapist is indispensable."[915]

b.   "Logotherapy . . . has succeeded in developing . . .

a technique. However, this is not to say that we logotherapists overrate the importance of techniques . . . . [W]hat matters in therapy is not techniques but rather the human relations between doctor and patient, or the personal and existential encounter."[916]

c.   "Approaching human beings merely in terms of techniques necessarily implies manipulating them, and approaching them merely in terms of dynamics implies reifying them, making human beings into mere things. And these human beings immediately feel and notice the manipulative quality of our approach and our tendency to reify them . . . . [R]eification has become the original sin of psychotherapy. But a human being is no thing. This *no-thingness, rather than nothingness, is the lesson to learn from existentialism.*"[917]

See Existentialism, Logotherapy, Personalism, Psychotherapy.

T 2
Tension
(or Frankl's Term "Noodynamics")[918]

a.   "[W]hat we have to fear in an age of existential frustration is not so much tension per se as it is the lack of tension that is created by the loss of meaning."[919]

b.   "[M]an's search for meaning may arouse inner tension . . . ."[920]

c.   "[A]n architect once said to me: 'The best way to buttress and strengthen a dilapidated structure is to increase the load it has to carry.' In fact, mental and somatic strains and burdens—what in modern times is known as 'stress'—are by no means always and necessarily pathogenic or disease producing."[921]

d.   "A sound amount of tension, such as that tension which is aroused by a meaning to fulfill, is inherent in being human and is indispensable for mental well-being. What man needs first of all is that tension which is created by direction. Freud once said that 'men are strong as long as they stand for a strong idea.' In fact, this has been put to the test both in Japanese and North Korean prisoner-of-war-camps . . . as well as concentration camps. Even under normal conditions, a strong meaning orientation is a health-promoting and a life-prolonging, if not a life-preserving, agent. It not only makes for physical but also for mental health . . . ."[922]

e.   "[M]an should not be subjected to too much tension. What he needs is rather a moderate amount, a sound amount, a sound dosage, of tension. Not only too-great demands, but also the contrary, the lack of challenges, may cause disease."[923]

f.   "Pathology results not only from stress, but also from relief of stress which ends in emptiness. A lack of tension created by the loss of meaning is as dangerous a threat in terms of mental health as is too high a tension."[924]

g.   "[M]an needs a specific tension, namely, the kind of tension that is established between being a human being, on the one hand, and, on the other hand, a meaning he has to fulfill."[925]

h.   "This tension is inherent in being human and hence indispensable for mental well-being."[926]

i.   "Even Selye, the father of the stress concept, . . . admitted that 'stress is the salt of life.'"[927]

See Existential Frustration, Existential Vacuum, Human (On Being Human), Mental Health, Moses.

T 3
Terminal Illness

"[T]he patient [with an incurable, terminal illness] has become a hero who is meeting his fate and holding his own by accepting it in tranquil suffering. That is, upon a metaphysical plane, a true achievement . . . ."[928]

See Attitudinal Values, Suffering.

T 4
Theology and Psychiatry
(or Religion and Psychiatry)

a.   "[P]sychotherapy and religion . . . [are] . . . two different dimensions, the dimensions of anthropology and theology. As compared with the dimension of anthropology, that of theology is the higher one in that it is more inclusive."[929]

b.   "I . . . draw the line of demarcation between religion and psychiatry . . . sharply . . . . [T]he difference between them is no more nor less than a difference between various dimensions . . . . [T]hese realms are by no means mutually exclusive. A higher dimension, by definition, is a more *inclusive* one. The lower dimension is included in the higher one; it is subsumed in it and encompassed by it."[930]

c.   "[T]he dignity of a science is based on that unconditional freedom that guarantees its independent search for truth."[931]

"As for faith, . . . it depends in what manner I speak of faith—as psychiatrist, philosopher, or simply as a human being . . . . [W]e need to consider the audience to whom we speak. I would not dream of confessing my personal faith when speaking about logotherapeutic methods and techniques to psychiatrists."[932]

See Faith, Religion, Truth.

T 5
Thompson, William Irwin
(Interdisciplinary Scholar)[933]
(1938-)

Frankl quotes Thompson: "'Humans are not objects that exist as chairs or tables; they live, and if they find that their lives are reduced to the mere existence of chairs and tables, they commit suicide.'"[934]

See Reductionism, Suicide.

T 6
Time

"[A]t any time each of the moments of which life consists is dying, and that moment will never recur."[935]

See Present, Transitoriness of Life.

T 7
Tolerance

a. Swanee Hunt, the United States ambassador to Austria, says, regarding Frankl, "There is . . . an extraordinary sense of tolerance in his thinking . . . . The concentration camps in which he suffered and in which his loved ones died were, after all, created to annihilate those who were different.

"But for Frankl, such tolerance does not imply a lack of judgment. For there is evil in the world, and his life bears the scars."[936]

b. "Being tolerant does not mean that I share another one's belief. But it does mean that I acknowledge another one's right to believe, and obey, his own conscience."[937]

c. "Tolerance does not mean that one accepts the belief of the other; but it does mean that one respects him as a human being, with the right and freedom of choosing his own way of believing and living."[938]

d. "[I]t is precisely the religious man who should respect the freedom of . . . choice, because he is the one who believes man to be created free. And this freedom includes the possibility of saying no, for instance, by deliberately refusing to accept any religious *Weltanschauung* [world view]."[939]

See Free-Will.

T 8
Tragic Triad

a. "[T]he three components of the 'tragic triad' . . . [are] . . . pain, guilt, and death . . . ."[940]

b. "Suffering is only one aspect of what I call 'the tragic triad' of human existence. This triad is made up of pain, guilt, and death. There is no human being who may say that he has not failed, that he does not suffer, and that he will not die."[941]

c. [A human being] "is a finite and mortal being who inevitably has to face dying, and . . . suffering."[942]

d. "'[A] tragic optimism' . . . means that one is, and remains, optimistic in spite of the 'tragic triad' . . . : 1) pain; 2) guilt; and 3) death."[943]

e. [In spite of the tragic triad, there is still meaning to life] "inasmuch as we may turn *suffering* into a human achievement and accomplishment; derive from *guilt* the opportunity to change for the better; and see in *life's transitoriness* an incentive to take responsible action . . . ."[944]

See Death, Guilt, Suffering.

T 9
Transcendence[945]

"I cannot be the servant of my conscience unless I understand conscience as a phenomenon transcendent of man."[946]

See Conscience.

T 10
Transitoriness of Life[947]

a.   "Face to face with life's transitoriness we may say that the future does not yet exist; the past does not exist any more; and the only thing that really exists is the present. Or we may say that the future is nothing; the past too is nothing; and man is a being coming out of nothingness; 'thrown' into being; and threatened by nothingness. How, then, in view of the essential transitoriness of human existence, can man finding meaning in life?"[948]

b.   "As to the undeniable transitoriness of life, logotherapy contends that this really applies only to the possibilities to fulfill a meaning, the opportunities to create, to experience, and to suffer meaningfully."[949]

c.   Frankl contrasts two views about the passing of time and, thus, the process of aging—the pessimistic view and the optimistic view: "The pessimist . . . observes with fear and sadness that his wall calendar, from which he daily tears a sheet, grows thinner with each passing day. On the other hand, the [other] person . . . removes each successive leaf from his calendar and files it neatly and carefully away with its predecessors, after first having jotted down a few diary notes on the back. He can reflect with pride and joy on all the richness set down in these notes, on all the life he has lived . . . . What will it matter to him if he notices that he is growing old? . . . What reasons has he to envy a young person? For the possibilities open to a young person, the future that is in store for him? 'No, thank you,' he will think. 'Instead of possibilities, I have realities in my past, not only the reality of work done and of love loved, but of sufferings bravely suffered."'[950]

See Death, Present, Suffering, Time.

T 11
Truth[951]

a.   Objective Truth

1. [To find the meaning of one's life] "implies that this meaning is to be discovered and not invented. It implies that the meaning of one's life is, in a certain sense, objective."[952]

2. "[E]very true cognitive act implies the objectivity of the object. So, what is called the object, or . . . more generally, the world, is essentially more than a mere self-expression of the subject . . . . It is true that man cannot grasp more than a subjective segment as it is cognitively cut out of the world, or in other words, he can only make a subjective selection from the full spectrum of the world; nevertheless, he is always making a subjective selection from an objective world."[953]

3. "[W]hat we mean by this term 'objective' is that values are necessarily more than a mere self-expression of the subject himself. They are more than a mere expression of one's inner life . . . ."[954]

4. Frankl quotes Sigmund Freud: "[B]ear in mind Freud's own admonition that 'reverence before the greatness of a genius is certainly a great thing. But our reverence before facts should exceed it.'"[955]

b.   Subjective Truth[956]

"[T]he . . . thing which is subjective is the perspective through which we approach reality, and this subjectiveness does not in the least detract from the objectiveness of reality itself. . . .
"[I]f you look through a telescope you can see something which is outside of the telescope itself. And if you look at the world, or a thing in the world, you also see more than, say, the perspective. What is *seen through* the perspective, however subjective the perspective may be, is the objective world. In fact, 'seen through' is the literal meaning of the Latin word, *perspectum.*"[957]

See Existentialism, Meaning, Reality.

U 1
Ultimate Meaning
(Super-Meaning or Supra-Meaning)[958]

a.   "[I]t is my contention that faith in the ultimate meaning is preceded by trust in an ultimate being, by trust in God."[959]

b.   [Religion is] "an expression, a manifestation, of not only man's will to meaning, but of man's longing for ultimate meaning, that is to say a meaning that is so comprehensive that it is no longer comprehensible . . . . But it becomes a matter of believing rather than thinking, of faith rather than intellect. The positing of a super-meaning that evades mere rational grasp is one of the main tenets of logotherapy, after all. And a religious person may identify Super-meaning as something paralleling a Super-being, and this Super-being we would call God."[960]

c.   [There is a meaning] "that is 'up to heaven,' . . . some
        sort of ultimate meaning, that is; a meaning of the
        whole, of the 'universe,' or at least a meaning of one's
        life as a whole; . . . a long-range meaning . . . . To
        invoke an analogy, consider a movie: It consists of
        thousands upon thousands of individual pictures, and
        each of them makes sense and carries a meaning,
        yet the meaning of the whole film cannot be seen
        before its last sequence is shown. On the other hand,
        we cannot understand the whole film without having
        first understood each of its components, each of the
        individual pictures. Isn't it the same with life?"[961]
        "Is it not conceivable that there is still another
        dimension, a world beyond man's world; a world
        in which the question of an ultimate meaning of
        human suffering would find an answer?"[962]

See God, Logos, Meaning, Religion, Suffering.

U 2
Unconscious
(The Unconscious)[963]

a.   "[W]here the spirit is . . . fully itself, precisely there
        it is also unconscious of itself."[964]

b.   "[E]xistence is *essentially* unconscious, because
        the foundation of existence cannot be fully reflected
        upon and thus cannot be fully aware of itself."[965]

c.   "[T]he center of the human person in his very depth
        is unconscious."[966]

d.   "[Many people] enjoy life in a wholly unreflective
        manner . . . ."[967]

See Anticipatory Anxiety, Hyperreflection, Self-
Transcendence.

U 3
Unemployment[968]

a.   "The jobless man experiences the emptiness of
his time as an inner emptiness, as an emptiness
of his consciousness. He feels useless because
he is unoccupied. Having no work, he thinks life
has no meaning. Just as idle organs in the body
may become the hosts for rampant growths, so
idleness in the psychological realm leads to morbid
inner developments."[969]

b.   "[W]hat ultimately underlies unemployment neurosis,
is the erroneous view that working is the only meaning
in life . . . . This incorrect equating of the two
necessarily makes the unemployed person suffer
from the sense of being useless and superfluous."[970]

c.   "The jobless . . . need not necessarily succumb to
unemployment neurosis . . . . [T]hey can decide
whether or not to surrender psychically to the forces
of social destiny . . . . [They] put themselves to work
elsewhere when they do not have their regular jobs.
For example, they are busy as voluntary assistants in
various organizations . . . . They have formed the habit
of . . . hearing good music. They are reading a good
deal and discussing what they have read with their
friends . . . . Such persons give meaningful form to
their surplus of leisure time and stock their
consciousness, their time, their life with content . . . .
[T]hey take an affirmative attitude toward life and are
far from hopeless. They know how to lend interest to
life and wrest meaning from it.[971]

d.   "[T]he meaning of human life is not completely

contained within paid work, . . . unemployment
need not compel one to live meaninglessly.[972]

See Attitudinal Values, Meaning, Meaninglessness, Work.

U 4
Unmasking[973]

a. Frankl gives an example of the absurdity of
    unmasking: "A young American couple who had
    served in the Peace Corps volunteered in Africa
    returned completely fed up and disgusted. At the
    outset they had to participate in a mandatory group
    session led by a psychologist [who conducted the
    following interview with them]:

    'Why did you join the Peace Corps?'
    'We wanted to help people less privileged.'
    'So you must be superior to the.'
    'In a way.'
    'So there must be in you, in your unconscious, a
        need to prove to yourself that you are superior.'
    'Well, we never thought of it that way, but you are a
        psychologist, you certainly know better.'

    "And so it went on. They were indoctrinated in the
    interpretation of their idealism and altruism as mere
    personal hang-ups. Even worse, they were
    constantly on each other's backs, playing the
    'what's *your* hidden motive game,' . . . ."[974]

b. "Unmasking . . . should stop as soon as one is
    confronted with what is authentic and genuine in
    man . . . . If it does not stop then, the only thing that
    the 'unmasking psychologist' really unmasks is his

own 'hidden motive'—namely, his unconscious need to debase and depreciate what is genuine, what is genuinely human, in man."[975]

See Freud, Motives, Psychoanalysis, Reductionism.

V 1
Values
(Three Chief Groups of Values or Three General Ways in Which Meaning May be Found)

a.   "As early as 1929 I developed the concept of three groups of values, or three possibilities to find meaning in life—even up to the last moment, the last breath. These three possibilities are: 1) a deed we do, a work we create; 2) an experience, a human encounter, a love; and 3) when confronted with an unchangeable fate (such as an incurable disease), a change of attitude toward that fate. In such cases we still can wrest meaning from life by giving testimony to the most human of all human capacities: the ability to turn suffering into a human triumph."[976]

b.   "An active life serves the purpose of giving man the opportunity to realize values in creative work, while a passive life of enjoyment affords him the opportunity to obtain fulfillment in experiencing beauty, art, or nature. But there is also purpose in that life which is almost barren of both creation and enjoyment and which admits of but one possibility . . ., namely, in man's attitude to his existence, an existence restricted by external forces. A creative life and a life of experience are banned to him. But not only creativeness and enjoyment are meaningful. If there is a meaning in life at all, then there must be a meaning in suffering."[977]

c.   "[T]he man in the street knows that meaning may be found not only in creating a work and doing a deed, not only in encountering someone and experiencing something, but also, if need be, in the way in which he stands up to suffering."[978]

See Attitudinal Values, Encounter, Identity, Love, Meaning, Phenomenology, Suffering, Work.

V 2
Viennese Schools of Psychotherapy

"In contrast to the findings of Sigmund Freud, man is no longer sexually frustrated, in the first place, but rather 'existentially frustrated.' And in contrast to the findings of Alfred Adler, his main complaint is no longer a feeling of inferiority but rather a feeling of futility, a feeling of meaninglessness and emptiness, which I have termed the 'existential vacuum.'"[979]

See Adler, Existential Vacuum, Freud, Logotherapy.

V 3
Violence
(or Aggression)

a.   "[P]eople are most likely to become aggressive when they are caught in the feeling of emptiness and meaninglessness."[980]

b.   "Robert Jay Lifton seems to agree with me when

he states that 'men are most apt to kill when they feel overcome by meaninglessness,' and statistical evidence is favorable to this hypothesis."[981]

c.   "'Clinical studies have revealed the adverse effects on children and youth of television violence, brutality, and sadism. TV violence was found in hundreds of cases to have harmful effects.' The President's Commission on the Causes and Prevention of Violence stated that the 'constant diet of violent behavior on television has had an adverse effect on human character and attitudes.'"[982]

See Existential Vacuum, Meaninglessness, Youth.

W 1
Weisskopf-Joelson, Edith
(Psychologist and Professor of Psychology)
(1910-1983)

a.   Frankl quotes Edith Weisskopf-Joelson: [Logotherapy] "may help counteract certain unhealthy trends in the present-day culture of the United States, where the incurable sufferer is given very little opportunity to be proud of his suffering and to consider it ennobling rather than degrading."[983]

b.   "[C]ultures, such as . . . [that of] the United States . . . stress the value of youth."[984]

See Logotherapy, Society, Suffering.

W 2
Werfel, Franz
(Jewish-Austrian Poet, Playwright, and Novelist)
(1890-1945)

a.   Frankl quotes Franz Werfel: "The Eternal's thought comes to fulfillment through order, and through order alone man lives up to his being the image of God."[985]

b.   Frankl again quotes Werfel: "Thirst is the surest proof for the existence of water."[986]

See God, *Imago Dei*, Meaning, Religion.

W 3
Widower
(Finding a Meaning in the Death of One's Wife)

"[A] physician . . . suffered from severe depression after his wife died. I embarked on a short Socratic dialogue by asking him what would have happened if he had died first. 'How much she would have suffered,' he answered. What was now left to me was simply to respond, 'Your wife has been spared this suffering, and after all, it is you who are sparing her this suffering—to be sure, at the price that now you have to survive and mourn her.' At the same moment, he could see a meaning in his suffering, the meaning of a sacrifice."[987]

See Suffering.

W 4
Will
(The Will to Live)

Frankl refers to the prisoners in the concentration camps during the Holocaust: "[W]e had to be concerned with the prevention of suicides . . . . We had to appeal to the will to live, to go on living, to outlive the prison. But the life-courage, or the life-weariness turned out in every case to depend solely upon whether the person possessed faith in the *meaning* of life, of his life."[988]

Concentration Camps, Faith, Free-Will, Meaning, Suicide.

W 5
Wittgenstein, Ludwig
(Austrian Philosopher)
(1889-1951)

Frankl quotes Ludwig Wittgenstein: "To believe in God is to see that life has a meaning."[989]

See Faith, God, Meaning, Religion.

W 6
Work
(Human Labor)

a.   "[T]he job at which one works is not what counts, but rather the manner in which one does the work. It does not lie with the occupation, but always with us . . . ."[990]

b.   "[W]hen a nurse does some little thing beyond her more or less regimented duties, when, say, she finds a personal word to say to a critically ill person—then and only then is she giving meaning to her life through her work . . . . The indispensability and irreplaceability, the singularity and uniqueness from the person, depend on who is doing the work and on the manner in which he is doing it, not on the job itself."[991]

c.   "The capacity to work is not everything; it is neither a sufficient nor essential basis for a meaningful life. A man can be capable of working and nevertheless not lead a meaningful life; and another can be incapable of working and nevertheless give his life meaning."[992]

See Existential Vacuum, Unemployment.

W 7
Workaholic

a.   "The real emptiness and ultimate poverty of meaning of his existence come to the fore . . . as soon as his vocational activity is halted for a certain period: on Sundays."[993]

b.   [For the] "person who is wholly wrapped up in his work, who has nothing else . . . Sunday is the saddest day of the week."[994]

See Diversions.

W 8
World View
(Weltanschauung)[995]

a.   "There is no psychotherapy without a theory of man and a philosophy of life underlying it.

Wittingly or unwittingly, psychotherapy is based on them."[996]

b.   "As is the case in any type of therapy, there is a theory underlying its practice—a *theoria*, i.e., a vision, a *Weltanschauung* . . . . [L]ogotherapy is based on an explicit philosophy life. More specifically, it is based on three fundamental assumptions which form a chain of interconnected links:

      1.   Freedom of Will;
      2.   Will to Meaning;
      3.   Meaning of Life."[997]

c.   "[I]t is important to make the concept of man by which we approach our patients conscious to ourselves, and to make the metaclinical implications of psychotherapy explicit."[998]

See Anthropology, Logotherapy, Nihilism, Psychoanalysis, Psychotherapy, Reductionism, *Zeitgeist*.

Y
Youth

a.   "[I]n the young generation . . . there is ample empirical evidence that . . . depression, aggression, [and] addiction . . . are due to what is called in logotherapy 'the existential vacuum,' the feeling of emptiness and meaninglessness."[999]

b.   "[I]t is the challenge of youth to question the meaning the meaning of life. However, the courage to question should be matched by patience. People should be patient enough to wait until, sooner or later, meaning dawns on them. This is what they should do, rather than taking their lives—or taking refuge in drugs."[1000]

See Addiction, Existential Vacuum, Purposelessness, Violence.

Z
Zeitgeist[1001]

"Even a genius cannot completely resist his *Zeitgeist*, the spirit of his era."[1002]

See Freud, World View.

Appendix

Real and Apparent Meaning in Life

What is meant by meaning? One of the frequent answers is "that which is fulfilling to each individual." What does it mean to fulfill a person? The word *fulfill* is derived from the Old English word *fullfyllan*, meaning "fill up, make full." However, real fulfillment must be distinguished from apparent fulfillment. What about the person who believes that stealing money is fulfilling to him or her? That is apparent, not real, fulfillment. A particular thing or endeavor which seems to be fulfilling but is short-lived—it lasts for a while and then it wears off—is apparent fulfillment.

The object of fulfillment must be morally right or at least morally neutral. It cannot be morally wrong. What about the masochist who feels fulfilled in inflicting suffering or pain on others? That is apparent, not real, fulfillment. What about the drug dealer who feels fulfilled in selling cocaine and crack to kids and teenagers, who, in turn, kill themselves or others? That is apparent, not real, fulfillment. A person who is addicted to drugs may feel fulfilled in taking them. So may an alcoholic feel fulfilled in drinking. But it is not real fulfillment. There is a true fulfillment or meaning in life, which is really good for a person, and a false or apparent fulfillment or meaning in life, which seems to be good for an individual but really is not.

Nihilism

Does meaning in life really exist? The philosophy of nihilism says that life is really meaningless, but one must choose for it to be meaningful anyway. Each person must imagine that life has meaning even though it really does not. Meaning is an illusion, a deeply held wish for something to be so that actually is not.

However, nihilism is contrary to common human experience. It is evident from common human experience that human beings desire something to fulfill them, something to keep their lives going, even if what they thought would fulfill them actually did not.

Problems in Perceiving Life's Meaning

Problems in perceiving life's meaning do not mean that life is meaningless. Meaning is a given, a starting point, a first principle. It is a fundamental premise or something basic to life itself. One may question the meaning of life. One may even despair over the meaning of life. But it does not mean that meaning is not really there. Rather, it only means that the person fails to perceive it or is blind to it, because of existential problems (problems relating to human existence) in his or her life.

Existential problems include personal frustration, mental confusion, depression, various kinds of addictions, such as alcohol, sex, drugs, etc., emotional problems related to personal failures or grief related to the death of a loved one or a personal tragedy, etc. One's psychological or spiritual condition may prevent him or her from seeing the meaning of his or her life for either a short or long period of time. But that does not preclude the truth that there really is meaning in life. The sun really exists even though it may be covered by clouds for a while. Eventually, however, the clouds pass, and the sun can again be seen. Likewise, the clouds of life, such as drug addition, suffering physical or emotional abuse, loss of hope or despair, may cover or obscure the reality of meaning, but that does not mean the meaning of life is not there. It is there whether one perceives it or not.

Objective or Real Meaning in Life

Meaning is objective. It is real, that is, outside or independent of the human person, whether or not he or she even perceives life to be meaningful. Meaning is "out there" in the world to be found by each individual. Meaning is discovered, because it is real. It is not invented by each person. The outside dimension of reality fulfills something inside the human person. There is a direct or one-to-one correspondence between the subject, that is, each human person, and the objective, that is, the person or thing out in the world, which fulfills him or her.

A Real Need for Meaning in Life

Human beings really need meaning in their lives. In other words, there is a "hunger" or "thirst" in the human heart for meaning in life. Human beings desire food and water, which do indeed exist. Human beings also desire meaning in their lives. Hence, it is reasonable that meaning really exists in order to fulfill the object of their desire. One may miss one's search for water and food and die from dehydration or starvation, but that does not prove that food and water do not exist. Rather, it only demonstrates that the person missed the object of his search. The food and water were not in the place that the person had sought for them.

Likewise, if a person does not find meaning in life, that does not mean it does not exist. Rather, it means that the individual missed the object of his search. He or she may have been mistaken or misguided in the search for meaning. Therefore, human beings really need meaning in order to sense that their lives are worthwhile, that they have value, that life is worth living. Meaning gives a person a reason to stay alive, to live for someone, or some worthwhile cause or something. It is because a human being has meaning in life that he or she can truly say, "Life is worth living."

Human beings find meaning when they transcend themselves, that is, go out of themselves or beyond themselves to someone or some thing. When the focus is off of themselves and on to someone or something else, they can find true fulfillment. There is always something, someone, some cause to serve or some thing to do that makes life worth living.

Human beings can live without meaning, but their lives are not fulfilled. They may not immediately sense that something is missing in their lives. However, because meaning is a necessity in life, they sooner or later sense that something is lacking in their lives. It is an inner emptiness or what Frankl calls the "existential vacuum."

Discovering the meaning of one's life may require persistence. One must keep on asking in order to find the answer to life's meaning. One must keep on seeking in order to find a meaning to life. One must keep on knocking until the door of the meaning of life opens for him or her.

Ultimate Meaning

There is an existential or day-today meaning in one's

life to sustain a person in the here and now, in this life. But there is also an ultimate meaning, which gives meaning not only to a person's overall life but also his or her moment-by-moment life. This ultimate meaning infuses the day-to-day meaning of a person's life. Theologian Paul Tillich writes:

> The anxiety of meaninglessness is anxiety about the loss of an ultimate concern, of a meaning which gives meaning to all meanings. This anxiety is aroused by the loss of a spiritual center, of an answer, however symbolic and indirect, to the question of the meaning of existence.[1003]

For religious persons, the ultimate meaning of life is grounded in the Eternal, "the Ground of Being." Such meaning comes from knowing, loving and serving God. In short, ultimate meaning comes from believing in God. Only an ultimate being is worthy of a person's ultimate commitment in life.

Atheists and agnostics evidence a need for meaning in their lives just as much as Christians, Jews, Muslims or any other religious group that believes in God. However, atheists fulfill their need for transcendence in different ways, such as being filled with a sense of wonder at the vastness of the universe, a sense of enjoyment derived from music or beautiful works of art or a sense of the sublime at a sunrise or sunset.

Select Bibliography of Books and Articles by Viktor E. Frankl in English[1004]

Books

Frankl, Viktor E. *Man's Search for Meaning.* 3rd ed. New York, N.Y.: Simon and Schuster/ Pocket Books, 1984.

_____. *Man's Search for Ultimate Meaning.* New York and London: Insight Books/Plenum Press, 1997.

_____. *Psychotherapy and Existentialism: Selected Papers on Logotherapy.* New York, N.Y.: Simon and Schuster, Inc., 1967.

_____. *The Doctor and the Soul: From Psychotherapy to Logotherapy.* 3rd rev. ed. Translated by Richard and Clara Winston. New York, N.Y.: Vintage Books/ Random House, 1955, 1986.

_____. *The Unconscious God.* New York, N.Y.: Washington Square Press/ Pocket Books/ Simon and Schuster, Inc., 1985.

_____. *The Unheard Cry for Meaning: Psychotherapy and Humanism.* rev. ed. New York, N.Y.: Washington Square Press, 1985.

_____. *The Will of Meaning: Foundations and Applications of Logotherapy.* New York, N.Y.: New American Library, 1969.

_____. *Viktor Frankl Recollections: An Autobiography.* Translated by Joseph Fabry and Judith Fabry. New York, N.Y.: Plenum Press, 1997.

Chapters in Books

Frankl, Viktor E. *Contributions to Critical Incidents in Psychotherapy*, eds. S. W. Standel, Prentice-Hall. Englecliffs, N.J., 1959.

_____. "Logotherapy and the Collective Neurosis," in *Progress in Psychotherapy*, eds. J. H. Masserman and J. L. Moreno. N.Y.: Grune and Stratton, 1959.

_____. "Philosophical Foundations of Logotherapy," in *Phenomenology: Pure and Applied*, ed. Erwin W. Straus. Pittsburgh, PA.: Duquesne University Press, 1964.

_____. "Fragments from the Logotherapeutic Treatment of Four Cases," in *Modern Psychotherapeutic Practice: Introduction in Technique*, ed. Arthur Burton. Palo Alto, Science and Behavior Books,1965.

_____. "The Will to Meaning," in *Are You Nobody?* P. Tournier, V. Frankl, H. Thielicke, P. Lehmann, H. Levinson, S. Miller. John Knox Press, 1966; Chime Paperbacks, 1973.

_____. "Accepting Responsibility and Overcoming Circumstances," in *Man`s Search for Meaningful Faith*, ed. Judith Weidman. Nashville, TN.: Graded Press, 1967.

_____. "Comment on Vatican II`s Pastoral Constitution on the Church in Modern World," in *World*. Chicago, IL.: Catholic Action Federation, 1967.

_____. "Paradoxical Intention: A Logotherapeutic Technique," in *Active Psychotherapy*, ed. Harold Greenwald. N.Y.: Atherton Press, 1967.

_____. "The Significance of Meaning for Health," in *Religion and Medicine*, ed. David Belgum. Ames, IA: Iowa State University Press, 1967.

_____. "The Task of Education in an Age of Meaninglessness," in *New Prospects for the Small Liberal Arts College*, ed. Sidney S. Letter. N.Y.: Teachers College Press, 1968.

_____. "Self-Transcendence as a Human Phenomenon," in *Readings in Humanistic Psychology*, ed. Anthony Sutich. N.Y.: Free Press, 1969.

_____. "Beyond Self-Actualization and Self-Expression," in *Perspectives in the Group Process: A Foundation for Counseling with Groups*, ed. C. Gratton Kemp. Boston, MA.: Houghton Mifflin Co., 1970.

_____. "Reductionism and Nihilism," in *Beyond Reductionism: New Perspectives in the Life Sciences*, ed. Arthur Koestler. N.Y.: Macmillan, 1970.

_____. "Universities and the Quest for Peace," in *Report of the First World Conference on the Role of the University in the Quest for Peace*. Binghamton, N.Y.: New York State University, 1970.

_____. "What is Meant by Meaning?" in *Values in an Age of Confrontation*, ed. Jeremiah Canning. Columbus, OH.: Charles Merrill, 1970.

_____. "Dynamics, Existence and Values and the Concept of Man in Logotherapy," in *Personality Theory: Source Book*, eds. H. Vetter and Barry Smith. New York: Appleton-Century-Crofts, 1971.

_____. "Youth in Search of Meaning," in *Students Search for Meaning*, ed. James Doty, Kansas City, MO.: Lowell Press, 1971.

_____. "Address Before the Third Annual Meeting of the Academy of Religion and Health," in *Discovering Man in Psychology: A Humanistic Approach*, ed. Frank T. Severin. New York: McGraw-Hill, 1973.

_____. "Meaninglessness: A Challenge to Psychologists," in *Theories of Psychopathology and Personality*, ed. Theodore Millon. Philadelphia, PA.: W. B. Saunders Company, 1973.

_____. "Encounter: The Concept and Its Vulgarization," in Psychotherapy and Behavior Change, eds. Hans H. Strupp, et. al. Chicago, IL.: Aldine Publishing Co., 1974.

_____. "Paradoxical Intention and Dereflection: Two Logotherapeutic Techniques," in *New Dimensions in Psychiatry: A World View*, ed. Silvano Arieti. New York: John Wiley and Sons, 1975.

_____. "Logotherapy," in *Encyclopaedic Handbook of Medical Psychology*, ed. Stephen Krauss. London and Boston: Butterworths, 1976.

_____. "Man's Search for Ultimate Meaning," in *On the Way to Self Knowledge*, ed. Jacob Needleman. New York: Alfred A Knopf, Inc., 1976.

_____. "The Depersonalization of Sex," in *Humanistic Psychology: A Source Book*, ed. David Welch, et. al. Buffalo, N.Y.: Prometheus Books, 1978.

_____. "Meaninglessness: A Challenge to Psychiatry," in *Value and Values in Evolution*, ed. Edward A. Maziarz. New York: Gordon and Breach, 1979.

_____. "Logotherapy," in *The Psychotherapy Handbook*, ed. Richie Herink. New York: New American Library, 1980.

_____. "Logotherapy," in *Encyclopedia of Psychology*, ed. Raymond J. Corsini. New York: John Wiley, 1984.

_____. "Logos, Paradox, and the Search for Meaning," in *Cognition and Psychology*, eds. M. J. Mahoney and A. Freeman. New York: Plenum, 1985.

_____. "Paradoxical Intention," in *Promoting Change through Paradoxical Therapy,* ed. Gerald Weeks. Homewood, IL.: Dow Jones-Irwin, 1985.

_____. "Afterword," in *Father, Have I Kept My Promise? Madness as Seen from Within*, Edith Weisskopf-Joelson. West Lafayette, IN.: Purdue University Press, 1988.

Journal Articles and Miscellaneous

Frankl, Viktor E. "In Memoriam" (Memorial Speech). *The Jewish Echo*, V, No. 6 (March 25, 1949).

_____. "The Pleasure Principle and Sexual Neurosis." *International Journal of Sexology*, Vol. 5 (1952), 128-130.

_____. "Logos and Existence in Psychotherapy." *American Journal of Psychotherapy*, VII (1953), 8-15.

_____. "Group Psychotherapeutic Experiences in Concentration Camps." *Group Psychotherapy*, VII (1954), 81-90.

_____. "The Concept of Man in Psychotherapy." *Pastoral Psychology*, VI (1955), 16-26.

_____. "From Psychotherapy to Logotherapy." *Pastoral Psychology*, VII (1956), 56-60.

_____. "Guest Editorial." *Academy Reporter*, III, No. 5 (May 1958), 1-4.

_____. "On Logotherapy and Existential Analysis." *American Journal of Psychoanalysis*, Vol. XVIII, No. 1 (1958).

_____. "The Search for Meaning." *Saturday Review* (September 13, 1958).

_____. "The Will to Meaning." *Journal of Pastoral Care*, XII (1958), 82-88.

_____. "Spiritual Dimension in Existential Analysis and Logotherapy." *Journal of Individual Psychology*, XV (November 1959), 157-165.

_____. "Beyond Self-Actualization and Self-Expression." *Journal of Existential Psychiatry*, I (1960), 5-20.

_____. "Paradoxical Intention: A Logotherapeutic Technique." *American Journal of Psychotherapy*, Vol. XIV (1960), 520-535.

_____. "Dynamics, Existence and Values." *Journal of Existential Psychiatry*, II (1961), 5-16.

_____. "Psychotherapy and Philosophy." *Philosophy Today*, Vol. V (1961), 59- 64.

_____. "Religion and Existential Psychotherapy." *Gordon Review*, VI (1961), 2- 10.

_____. "Basic Concepts of Logotherapy." *Journal of Existential Psychiatry*, III (1962), 111-118.

_____. "Logotherapy and the Challenge of Suffering." *Pastoral Psychology*, XIII (1962), 25-28.

_____. "Restoring Psychotherapy to Its Place in Medicine." *The Physician's Panorama*, Sandoz Publication (March 1962).

_____. "Psychiatry and Man's Quest for Meaning." *Journal of Religion and Health*, I (1962), 93-103.

_____. "The Will to Meaning." *Living Church*, Vol. 24, No. 24 (June 24, 1962), 8-14.

_____. "Angel as Much as Beast: Man Transcends Himself." *Unitarian Universalist Register-Leader*, CXLIV (February 1963), 8-9.

_____. "Existential Dynamics and Neurotic Escapism." *Journal of Existential Psychiatry*, IV (1963), 27-42.

_____. "Value Dimensions in Teaching and Further Comments on Values" (a transcript of a TV interview). *Value Colloquium* I (October 10-13, 1963).

_____. "Dialogue Concerning Existential School of Thought." San Quentin Prison (November 20, 1964).

_____. "In Steady Search for Meaning." *Liberal Dimension*, II, No. 2 (1964), 3- 8.

_____. "Existential Escapism." *Motive*, XXIV (January-February 1964), 11-14.

_____. "The Will to Meaning." *Christian Century*, LXXI (April 22, 1964), 515- 517.

_____. "How a Sense of Task in Life Can Help You Overcome the Bumps." *The National Observer* (July 12, 1964), 22.

_____. "The Concept of Man in Logotherapy." *Journal of Existentialism*, VI (1965), 53-58.

_____. "Logotherapy: A New Psychology of Man." *The Gadfly*, Vol. 17, No. 1 (December 1965-January 1966).

_____. "Logotherapy and Existential Analysis: A Review." *American Journal of Psychotherapy*, Vol. XX, No. 2 (April 1966), 252-260.

_____. "Self-Transcendence as Human Phenomenon." *Journal of Humanistic Psychology*, VI, No. 2 (Fall 1966), 97-106.

_____. "Time and Responsibility." *Existential Psychiatry*, Vol. 1, No. 3 (Fall 1966), 361-366.

_____. "What is Meant by Meaning?" *Journal of Existentialism*, VII, No. 25 (Fall 1966), 21-28.

_____. "Logotherapy." *The Israel Annals of Psychiatry and Related Disciplines*, VII (1967), 142-155.

_____. "Logotherapy and Existentialism." *Psychotherapy: Theory, Research and Practice*, IV, No. 3 (August 1967), 138-142.

_____. "What is a Man?" *Life Association News*, LXII, No. 9 (September 1967), 151-157.

_____. "Experiences in a Concentration Camp." *Jewish Heritage*, XI (1968), 5- 7.

_____. "The Search for Meaning." *Jewish Heritage*, XI (1968), 8-11.

_____. "Youth in Search of Meaning." *The Baker World*, I, No. 4 (January 1969), 2-5.

_____. "Eternity is the Here and Now." *Pace*, V, No. 4 (April 1969), 2.

_____. "The Cosmos and the Mind." *Pace*, V, No. 8 (August 1969), 34-39.

_____. "Entering the Human Dimension." *Attitude*, I, No. 5 (July/August 1970), 2-6.

_____. "Fore-Runner of Existential Psychiatry." Journal of Individual Psychiatry, XXVI (1970), 12.

_____. "Logotherapy." *Roche Courier*, XXIII (1970).

_____. "Determinism and Humanism." *Humanitas: Journal of the Institute of Man*, VII (1971), 23-26.

_____. "Existential Escapism." *Omega*, Vol. 2, No. 4 (November 1971), 307-311.

_____. "The Feeling of Meaninglessness: A Challenge to Psychotherapy." *The American Journal of Psychoanalysis*, Vol. XXXII, No. 1 (1972), 85-89.

_____. "Man in Search of Meaning." *Widening Horizons* (Rockford College), Vol. 8, No. 5 (August 1972).

_____. "Encounter: The Concept and its Vulgarization." *The Journal of the American Academy of Psychoanalysis*, I, No. 1 (1973), 73-83.

_____. "The Depersonalization of Sex." *Synthesis*, Vol. 1, No. 1 (Spring 1974), 7-11.

_____. "Paradoxical Intention and Dereflection." *Psychotherapy: Theory, Research and Practice*, Vol. XII, No. 3 (Fall 1975), 226-237.

_____. "A Psychiatrist Looks at Love." *Uniquest* (The First Unitarian Church of Berkeley), Vol. 5 (1976), 6-9.

_____. "Some Thoughts on the Painful Wisdom." *Uniquest*, Vol. 6 (1976), 3.

_____. "Survival for What?" *Uniquest*, Vol. 6 (1976), 38.

_____. "Logotherapy." *The International Forum for Logotherapy*, Vol. 1, No. 1 (Winter 1978-Spring 1979), 22-23.

_____. "Endogenous Depression and Noogenic Neurosis (Case Histories and Comments)." *The International Forum for Logotherapy*, Vol. 2, No. 2 (Summer-Fall 1979), 38-40.

_____. "Psychotherapy on Its Way to Rehumanization." *The International Forum for Logotherapy*, Vol. 3, No. 2 (Fall 1980), 3-9.

_____. "The Future of Logotherapy." *The International Forum for Logotherapy*, Vol. 4, No. 2 (Fall/Winter 1981), 71-78.

_____. "The Meaning Crisis in the Third World and Hunger in the Third World." *The International Forum* for *Logotherapy*, Vol. 7, No. 1 (Spring/Summer 1984), 5-7.

_____. "There is No Collective Guilt." *Austrian Information*, Vol. 41, No. 6/7 (1988).

_____. "Facing the Transitoriness of Human Existence." *Generations: Aging and the Human Spirit*, Vol. XIV, No. 4 (Fall 1990).

_____. "On the Meaning of Love." *The Educational Forum*, Vol. 54, No. 3 (Spring 1990).

_____. "Vienna's Grand Old Man of Psychotherapy." *Image*, No. 2 (1992).

Endnotes

1. *VFR*, p. 29.
2. *WM*, p. 86.
3. *VFR*, p. 56.
4. *PE*, p. 129.
5. Ibid. Italics are mine.
6. *VFR*, p. 87.
7. *UCM*, inside the front of the book.
8. *VFR*, pp. 84, 88-91.
9. Ibid., p. 91.
10. Ibid. Cf. p. 99.
11. Ibid., pp. 95, 98.
12. *DS*, inside the front of the book.
13. *VFR*, p. 21.
14. *MSM*, inside the front of the book.
15. *VFR*, pp. 23, 26.
16. Ibid., pp. 30, 100.
17. Ibid.
18. Ibid., p. 98.
19. Ibid., p. 95. The bracketed capital [H] is mine.
20. In *UCM*, p. 38, Frankl explains self-transcendence: "Being human is being always directed, and pointing, to something or someone other than oneself: to a meaning to fulfill or another human being to encounter, a cause to serve or a person to love. Only to the extent that someone is living out this self-transcendence of human

existence, is he truly human or does he become his true self. He becomes so . . . by forgetting himself and giving himself, overlooking himself and focusing outward."

21.   *VFR,* pp. 91, 99.

22.   Ibid., p. 98.

23.   *MSM,* pp. 49-50. An explanation of the above abbreviation is in order: A period before the end of a sentence, followed by four periods (e.g., ...), followed by a new line beginning with another quotation mark, followed by four more periods (e.g., " . . .) means that one or more paragraphs have been skipped and the thought continues later in another paragraph.

24.   *VFR,* p. 98. In his mind, Frankl tried to leave his physical suffering—even if for a brief period of time—by thinking about something better than his present situation. Frankl's vision was fulfilled when he spoke at the First International Congress for Psychotherapy in Leiden, Holland.

25.   Ibid., p. 104.

26.   Ibid., p. 91.

27.   *DS,* p. *ix.* Italics are the publisher's.

28.   Ibid., p. *x.*

29.   *VFR,* p. 97.

30.   Ibid.

31.   Ibid., p. 68.

32.   Ibid.

33.   Ibid., p. 73. Cf. the entry for "Steinhof Mental Hospital" on p. 141.

34.   Ibid., p. 73.

35.   *DS,* p. 262. The single quotation marks are mine and clearly indicate each of Frankl's questions. I have also created three paragraphs for the sake of clarity from Frankl's original paragraph in the English edition.

36.   *VFR,* pp. 76, 78.

37.   *MSM,* pp. 89-91.

38. Ibid., p. 91.
39. Ibid.
40. *VFR*, p. 79.
41. Ibid. Only once did he break that principle, as he explained in his autobiography (cf. ibid, par. 4).
42. Ibid., pp. 128-129.
43. Gerald F. Kreyche, quoted on the back cover of *MSM*.
44. *VFR*, p. 101.
45. Ibid., p. 116. Cf. *MSUM*, p. 187.
46. *VFR, Viktor Frankl Recollections*, p. 143.
47. Ibid.
48. See the pamphlet entitled *Education and Credentialing Program in Logotherapy* published by the Viktor Frankl Institute of Logotherapy in Abilene, Texas, issued in January 2001, p. 1.
49. *MSUM*, pp. 187-188.
50. *American Journal of Psychiatry*, quoted on the back cover of *DS*.
51. *VFR*, p. 143.
52. *WM*, p. 49.
53. Ibid., p. 33.
54. Ibid., pp. 34-35.
55. *MSUM*, p. 136.
56. World Wide Web: "Viktor Frankl—Life and Work: Chronology," in *Viktor Frankl Institute* (http://logotherapy.univie.ac.at/cvzeitt.html), accessed 14 June, 2002. I owe a special thanks to the Viktor Frankl Institute in Vienna and Dr. Franz J. Vesely for granting me permission to publish Frankl's chronology with modifications.
57. *VFR*, p. 46.
58. Ibid., p. 56
59. Ibid., p. 59.
60. Ibid., p. 48.
61. Ibid., pp. 48, 50.
62. Ibid., p. 51.

63. Ibid., pp. 51, 60.
64. Ibid., p. 55.
65. Ibid., p. 60.
66. Ibid., p. 64.
67. Ibid., pp. 60-62.
68. Ibid., p. 63.
69. Ibid., p. 68.
70. Ibid., pp. 68-69.
71. Ibid., p. 71.
72. Ibid., p. 73.
73. Ibid., p. 73.
74. Ibid., p. 75.
75. Ibid., p. 76.
76. Ibid., p. 64.
77. Ibid., pp. 82-83.
78. Ibid., p. 76.
79. Ibid., pp. 81-82.
80. Ibid., p. 87.
81. Ibid., pp. 89-90. Cf. pp. 20-21.
82. Ibid., pp. 23, 26.
83. Ibid., pp. 21, 90-91.
84. Ibid., p. 95.
85. Ibid., p. 97.
86. Ibid., pp. 95, 98.
87. Ibid., pp. 91, 100.
88. Ibid., p. 104.
89. Ibid., pp. 105-109.
90. Ibid., p. 129.
91. Ibid., p. 66.
92. The books have not yet been translated into English.
     The German titles of Frankl's books were translated
     into English for me by Dr. Franz J. Vesely through an
     email correspondence on 14 June, 2002.
93. The book has not yet been translated into English.
94. VFR, pp. 108-109.
95. Ibid., p. 129. Adapted from a student from Berkeley. In

the context, Frankl was asked by *Who's Who in America* to summarize the meaning of his life in one sentence. The student from Berkeley summarized what he believed that Frankl had written, saying, "The meaning of your life is to help others find the meaning of theirs." Frankl approved of the student's words, saying, "That was it, exactly. Those are the very words I had written" (ibid).

96.   *DS,* p. 84. The bracketed uppercase [T] is mine. In the context of the passage, Frankl refers to certain persons "overcoming the original handicaps and barriers to freedom that biological factors have imposed, who have surmounted the initial obstacles to their spiritual development" (*DS,* p. 83). The challenge to such individuals is what they will do with their physical or even psychological disabilities. Today, such conditions are called being "physically challenged" or "mentally challenged."

97.   *DS,* p. 153. Frankl often refers to "fate" in his writings, by which he means an unfortunate condition that is thrust upon a human being, which includes but is not limited to cancer, some kind of tragic accident rendering an individual as paraplegic or quadriplegic, the sudden death of a loved one; it may refer to a person who is born with some kind of debilitating mental or physical condition or born into a social environment of poverty, drug abuse or physical abuse.

For Frankl, the kinds of fate which can be overcome should be; the other kinds of fate which cannot be overcome either physically or mentally should be accepted as an opportunity to grow as a human being, a challenge to grow spiritually, to "overcome" oneself by the right kind of attitude one adopts toward his or her predicament. By using the term "fate," Frankl does not imply that there is no God. See Attitudinal Values.

98.   *DS,* p. 170. Sexual propaganda is promoted so often in

the Hollywood community and on the television (in commercials, sitcoms, and movies) that a virgin, for example, may feel "abnormal" because she has not had sexual intercourse by the time she is fifteen. She thinks that something must be wrong with her, because she stands out from among her friends in that she is the only one who is a virgin. If she is still a virgin, say, by the time she is seventeen, then she feels guilty of committing a "sin" against her peers who have blindly accepted the propaganda of many television producers and directors in Hollywood. Such is an example of what Frankl calls "neurotic sexual anxiety." Sexual propaganda has a similar affect on males who choose to abstain from sexual intercourse.

99.   *DS*, p. 170.

100. *MSM*, p. 144. As a physician, Frankl was surely aware of the fact that not every case of drug addiction may be traced back to the existential vacuum. However, there are a few cases that may be traced back to it. Cf. *UG*, pp. 97-100; *UCM*, pp. 26-28.

Stanley Krippner, PhD, is an American psychologist. He is a professor of psychology at Saybrook Graduate School in San Francisco, CA. Annemarie von Forstmeyer wrote "The Will to Meaning as a Prerequisite for Self-Actualization," a thesis presented to the faculty of California Western University, San Diego, in partial fulfillment of the requirements for the degree, Master of Arts, 1968.

101. *MSUM*, p. 138. Adlerian psychology, of course, is named after its founder Alfred Adler. He, however, called his own psychology "individual psychology." In his early years, Frankl rejected Freudian psychoanalysis and accepted many of the teachings of Adler or individual psychology.

102. *UCM*, p. 108. Italics are mine.

103. In general, aggression may result from continual frustration. It may be directed outwardly against others

(in either verbal or physical attacks) or inwardly against oneself. Cf. R. L. Timpe, "Aggression," in *Baker Encyclopedia of Psychology*, ed. David G. Benner (Grand Rapids, MI.: Baker Book House, 1985), pp. 33-35.

104.   *MSM*, p. 144. Cf;. *UG*, p. 140; *UCM*, p. 39. Carolyn Wood Sherif (1922-1982) was an American psychologist or, more specifically, a social psychologist studying the interactions of human beings in various kinds of group settings.

105.   *UCM*, p. 84. Emotional alienation involves the fear to say what one is feeling. A person who is emotionally alienated is "not in touch" with his or her own emotions, not allowed—either by others or by society in general— to acknowledge or express them. Hence, one suppresses his or her feelings.

106.   Preface to *MSM*, p. 10.

107.   Frankl's logotherapy has a world view—that is, a vision or understanding of who the human person is. This does not mean that logotherapy is not objective as a philosophy or therapy. Every person has some viewpoint and approaches reality from that viewpoint. Everyone has a vantage point from which to "see" or understand the world, whether one is aware of it or not. The naive thinker is not one who is aware of his convictions and commitments, but one who is unaware of them. Different world views or starting points may lead to different conclusions about anthropology, ethics, religion, etc.

108.   *PE*, p. 137. The single quotation marks are mine to indicate a special term that Frankl uses.

109.   The phrase "embodied human person" means that the human body conveys something of the human spirit, that the external is a manifestation of the internal, that the body is the external manifestation of the human spirit, that a human person is not only a body but also a spirit-

body component, that the human body is the human spirit's bridge to come into contact with the physical world, especially the world of other human persons.

110. *DS,* p. 139.

111. *PE,* p. 35. The bracketed [the] is mine.

112. *PE,* p. 13.

113. *MSUM,* p. 161, note 58. Cf. *Documents of Vatican II: Pastoral Constitution on the Church in the Modern World, Gaudium et Spes,* 7 December, 1965 (Boston, MA.: St. Paul Editions/ Daughters of St. Paul, n.d.), no. 55: "Thus we are witnesses of the birth of a new humanism, one in which man is defined first of all by this responsibility to his brothers and to history."

114. *PE,* p. 75.

115. *PE,* p. 121.

116. *PE,* p. 137. The bracketed words are mine.

117. For Frankl, the noological dimension of the human person is a distinctively human characteristic. Animals lack that dimension, because it is spiritual. It may also be called the "noetic" (meaning "spiritual") dimension. The noological dimension of the human person means that a human being has a spirit, a mind (from the Greek word *nous*), which is capable of reflecting on oneself. In other words, a human being is more than matter, a body; a human being also has a spirit. Cf. *PE,* pp. 63, 74.

118. *WM,* p. 17. The bracketed [dimensions] is mine and clarifies "ones."

119. *PE,* p. 3.

120. *PE,* p. 142.

121. *DS,* p. 82. Frankl, of course, was not a philosophical materialist and, thus, a reductionist. In other words, Frankl did not reduce the mind to the brain. The mind may include the brain, but the mind is much more than the brain. The mind is not strictly material. Rather, the mind is an immaterial or spiritual reality. Although the

mind is a part of the body, the mind also transcends the body. That is why human beings are capable of rising above the adverse conditions (whether they be biological, psychological or sociological) which influence their lives.

122. *MSM,* p. 84.

123. *MSUM,* p. 34.

124. *PE,* pp. 74-75.

125. *MSUM,* p. 34. The bracketed [I] is mine.

126. *WM,* p. 20.

127. *DS,* p. 135. In the context, "psyche" refers to the human mind.

128. *DS,* p. *xvi.* The *somatic* dimension refers to the human body. It is derived from the Greek word *soma,* meaning "body." The *mental* dimension refers to the human mind—reason, the intellect. The *spiritual* refers to the invisible or immaterial dimension of the human person, that which is distinctively human, which separates a human being from animals, machines and computers.

129. *DS,* p. *xvii,* footnote.

130. *DS,* p. 158.

131. *DS,* p. 159.

132. *DS,* pp. 158-159.

133. *UCM,* p. 52. Cf. Magda B. Arnold, *The Human Person* (New York, N.Y., 1954), p. 40.

134. *DS,* p. 134. I have changed the verb tenses from the original "happens to be" to the subjunctive mood [may have], which is the realm of possibility, because in the context of the quotation, Frankl is referring to three levels which unite men and women to each other: the sexual, the erotic and the deepest level, love.

135. *WM,* p. 42. The bracketed [is] and uppercase [I] are mine.

136. It is incorrect to say, "Because atheists do not believe in God, they have no meaning in life." After all, Frankl was fond of often quoting the atheistic philosopher Friedrich Nietzsche in order to teach one of the principles

of logotherapy, namely, that a goal or purpose in a person's life is to give it meaning.

137. *MSM,* p. 109. Italics are the publisher's. Cf., p. 84. In other words, if a person has a goal or purpose in life, then he will find the courage and patience to endure any obstacle in order to achieve it.

138. *MSUM,* p. 55. Human beings are incurably religious. Repress the sense of religion from consciousness and it will manifest itself in other ways. Even the non-religious person has, in the words of theologian Paul Tillich, an "ultimate concern." In other words, in the hierarchy of human values, usually something is at the top, that is, most important to an individual. Every person is concerned about something passionately, something that is most important to him or her. Every person values something or someone above all other things or persons. In the sense that every person has an ultimate concern, every person is religious at the core of his or her being.

139. *MSUM,* p. 151. Frankl's comment is essentially the thesis of his book *UG.*

140. *WM,* p. 153.

141. The term "attitudinal values" means "having the right kind of attitude about life," especially its difficult or negative situations such as unavoidable sufferings and unexpected tragedies, chronic illnesses and terminal illnesses. Frankl contends that in unchangeable, negative situations, even in the most hellish conditions in which a person may find himself or herself, one is still free to choose how he or she will respond to them, either positively or negatively. This he calls "attitudinal values," which presuppose free-will.

142. *UG,* pp.125-126.

143. *MSM,* p. 139.

144. *PE,* p. 83. Cf. *DS,* p. 113: "[T]here is achievement in suffering." It depends, of course, on the right kind of

attitude of the one who is suffering. In unavoidable suffering, one may choose to become bitter about it or become better because of it—that is, mature or grow spiritually.

145. *MSUM*, p. 142.
146. *DS*, p. 282.
147. *WM*, p. 75.
148. *WM*, p. 131.
149. *DS*, p. 282.
150. *DS*, p. 80. Italics are the publisher's. [M] is mine.
151. *DS*, p. 44.
152. *WM*, pp. 70-71. Rabbi Earl Grollman, chairman of the National Center of Death Education, is a lecturer and grief counselor. He has written extensively about grief and bereavement. The uppercase bracketed [S] is mine.
153. *MSUM*, p. 124. Psychologists "S. Kratochvil and I. Planova were from the Department of Psychology, University of Brno, Czechoslovakia" (ibid.). Frankl explains what Kratochvil and Planova mean by the phrase "one's value system": "[I]t is dependent on whether or not one is aware of attitudinal values as a meaning potential to fulfill, if need be." (ibid.).
154. *MSM*, p. 75.
155. *DS*, p. 30. Frankl does not cite the source of the survey.
156. *WM*, p. 55. Augustine said to God, "[Y]ou made us for yourself and our hearts find no peace until they rest in you." Cf. Saint Augustine, *Confessions*, trans. R. S. Pine-Coffin (New York, N.Y.: Penguin Books, 1961, reprinted 1986), p. 21.
157. *MSM*, p. 22.
158. *MSUM*, p. 19.
159. *MSUM*, p. 19. The quotation marks within the quotation refer to "the title of a book," as Frankl says. The book was written by a rabbi.
160. *MSM*, p. 154.
161. Yehuda Bacon, quoted in *WM*, p. 79. In 1941, at the age

of thirteen, he was sent to the Theresienstadt concentration camp. In 1943, he was deported to a concentration camp in Auschwitz. A couple of years later, Auschwitz was evacuated, and the prisoners marched to Mauthausen, an Austrian concentration camp. In 1945, the camp was liberated by American soldiers.

162. *PE,* p. 12.
163. *WM,* p. 128. In other words, human beings need to be presented with challenges in order to move beyond themselves, out of themselves, to someone or something and, thus, find personal fulfillment, meaning in life. The normal tension created by the sense of "ought" in life gives meaning to the "is," to being human.
164. *MSM,* p. 111.
165. *PE,* p. 122.
166. *PE,* p. 104. The bracketed word [prisoner] is mine and establishes the context of Frankl's quotation. Buber is well known in philosophy for his book *I and Thou* (1923). It is his philosophy of dialogue. In the book, Buber distinguishes between two kinds of relationships: an I-Thou relationship and an I-It relationship. For Buber, the ultimate I-Thou relationship is between a human being and God, the ultimate Thou.
167. *VFR,* p. 136, endnote 32. She, along with a group of scientists in the 1930s, did "research on child and youth psychology . . ." (ibid).
168. Charlotte Buhler, "Some Observations on the Psychology of the Third Force," *Journal of Humanistic Psychology* 5: 54, 1965, quoted in *WM,* p. 33. The uppercase bracketed [M] is mine and is used to begin the sentence. The bracketed word [lives] is mine and is used to change the verb from "living" in the original wording to the simple present tense.
169. Certainty refers to the normal process of knowing something, which most people ordinarily know or experience, the common knowledge human beings.

170. *DS*, p. 189. The so-called normal person is the lay person, the person of everyday common human experience, not an academic specialist, such as a philosopher, who deeply probes into the validity of rational thought and its logical conclusions.

171. *DS*, p. 78.

172. *WM*, p. 73.

173. *DS*, footnote on pp. 59-60. Cf. I Peter 2:21. The first single quotation marks are mine and indicate a term which is used in logotherapy. The second single quotation marks are Frankl's. The English term "passion" comes from the Latin word *passio*, meaning "suffering, enduring," which, in turn, is derived from the Latin stem *pati*, meaning "to suffer, endure."

   By the way or manner in which Christians suffer, they may display an attitude of courage, patience or love for God instead of bitterness toward him. They may bear witness to the strength of Christ who enables them to accept their suffering. They also may become more holy through their suffering, thus becoming more like Jesus (cf. I Peter 4:1). A Christian's suffering, then, is not meaningless. On the contrary, it has meaning for the sufferer himself or herself and for those who witness such suffering. That is why it is called "redemptive suffering" in Christian theology.

174. *DS*, xv. Frankl paraphrases two quotes from psychiatrists whom he does not name. The bracketed uppercase [N] is mine.

175. *PE*, p. 115.

176. *UCM*, p. 21, footnote.

177. *UCM*, p. 21.

178. *UCM*, pp. 20-21.

179. *DS*, p. 96.

180. *MSM*, p. 74.

181. *MSM*, p. 74. Italics are the publisher's.

182. *MSM*, pp. 153-154. Italics are the publisher's.

183. *MSM,* p. 75.
184. *MSM,* p. 76.
185. *PE,* p. 35.
186. *DS,* p. 104. On the one hand, there were certain men who had faith in God before going into the concentration camp and then lost their faith as a result of the concentration camp experiences. On the other hand, many men who had lost their faith in God before going into the concentration camp actually experienced a new-found faith in God as a result of being prisoners in the camp.
187. *PE,* pp. 99-100. The bracketed uppercase [T] is mine.
188. *PE,* p. 110. The "dead colleagues" are explained by the bracketed words, which are mine.
189. *PE,* pp. 104-105. The concentration camps are a microcosm (literally, "small world"), reflecting the everyday lives of human beings in the cosmos, the world at large, the world of humankind. That is why reading Frankl's book *Man's Search for Meaning* is just as relevant today's as it was when it was first published in America forty years ago, in 1963. In the first section of the book, the autobiographical account of his experiences and the experiences of the other prisoners in the concentration camps teach psychological truths, which are applicable to human beings in general.
190. *MSM,* p. 89. Frankl, of course, is not making light of the evils of being in a concentration camp. On the contrary, the prisoners endured tremendous evil at the hands of the Nazis; but as a result of enduring those experiences, the prisoners, through their own examples of bravery and survival, would be in a position to help others who must endure the various hardships and tragedies in life. Evil in itself, then, is not good, but good may come from evil, depending on the attitude of the person who endured it. See Attitudinal Values.
191. *UCM,* p. 51.

192. *PE,* pp. 59-60.
193. *WM,* p. 18. The bracketed [to] is mine. The noological dimension refers to the human spirit. In other words, a human being is a body but something more than a body; that "something more" is the spirit or spiritual dimension of the human person.
194. *MSUM,* p. 60.
195. *MSUM,* p. 59. Transcendent is derived from the Latin word *transcendere* (from *trans,* meaning "across," "over," "beyond," and *scandere,* meaning "to climb." See *Dictionary of Philosophy,* ed. Peter A. Angeles [New York, N.Y.: Harper and Row, Publishers, 1981], p. 296.) The origin of conscience is outside, above or beyond, the human person. Transcendent means that there is a spiritual (immaterial) center of awareness or knowledge in a human being, which is greater or more than the human brain. Conscience, the center of human self-awareness, cannot be reduced to the brain or any other organ in the human body. Conscience, in other words, comes from a spiritual, trans-personal agent, a supreme being or god.
196. *MSUM,* p. 63.
197. *MSUM,* p. 60. The bracketed words are mine.
198. *WM,* p. 66. Italics are the publisher's.
199. *DS,* p. *xxvi.*
200. *WM,* p. 65.
201. *PE,* p. 3.
202. *WM,* p. 63.
203. *WM,* pp. 66-67. The bracketed uppercase [O] is mine.
204. *UCM,* p. 126. In saying that a person has "no mind" in death, I presume that Frankl means "no brain." Because the mind is a spiritual phenomenon, a property of the human spirit, it survives death.
205. *UCM,* p. 127.
206. *UCM,* p. 128. Death is compared to sleep, and waking up from the sleep of death is to enter into a new reality. One's real self is revealed in death. Cf. Psalm 17:15.

207. *DS*, p. 110. In other words, even if a person refuses to think about his or her own death, even if a person pushes it out of his or her consciousness or awareness, it does not deny the inevitable reality of death. It is better to cope with the meaning of one's death than to avoid the issue. The former is accepting reality while the latter is a flight from it.

208. *WM*, p. 72.

209. *PE*, p. 128. Just as a story must come to an end, so too must life. The ending of that life may be either meaningful or meaningless, depending on the kind of decisions a person makes throughout his or her life.

210. *DS*, pp. 129-130. I call this "death in the third person" either singular or plural. "He died" or "She died," "John died" or "Jane died" is death in the third person singular, talking about the death of another person. "They died" or "They were killed by a plane crash" is death in the third person plural. In constantly speaking and thinking this way about the deaths of others, a person not only can distance himself from death but can also subconsciously delude himself into believing that death only happens to others. That is Frankl's point.

211. *PE*, p. 35. The decision character of life is inevitable. In other words, not to decide is to decide, namely to decide against making a decision; or not to choose is to make a choice, namely a choice against making a choice.

212. A letter from Jerry Long to Viktor Frankl, quoted in *MSM*, p. 148. Jerry died at the age of forty-two.

213. *WM*, p. 49. With the gift of freedom comes responsibility. Frankl's concern is to address an overemphasis on the claim to personal freedom to the exclusion of responsibility to oneself and to other human beings. Especially in America, for example, there is almost an overemphasis on the claim of individual rights to the neglect of individual responsibilities.

214. *WM*, pp. 131-132. The bracketed explanatory phrase

is mine. Unfortunately, not only in some Roman Catholic circles but also in Christian circles in general, there is an a priori refusal to believe that Christians can be depressed or mentally ill, because they believe in God. For example, a Christian woman suffering from depression approached a minister for spiritual help, but he rebuffed her, saying, "I won't pray for you, because depressed people feel sorry for themselves and God doesn't condone that." Another erroneous saying is "If you are a committed Christian you shouldn't need a psychiatrist." A Christian man with severe panic attacks was told by a Christian woman: "It's all emotional—just get a hold of yourself." Still another erroneous saying is "No one who is right with the Lord has a nervous breakdown." Some Christians automatically and erroneously link the cause of emotional problems with sin. Those kinds of attitudes reflect a false spirituality, making faith and reason enemies of each other, placing faith and medicine in opposition to each other. Science and faith can be friends instead of foes. Cf. Dwight L Carson, MD, *Why Do Christians Shoot Their Wounded?: Helping (Not Hurting) Those with Emotional Difficulties* (Downers Grove, IL.: Inter-Varsity Press, 1994), pp. 13-16.

215. *MSUM,* p. 99.
216. *MSM,* p. 143. Italics are the publisher's.
217. *UCM,* p. 54.
218. *MSM,* 3rd ed., p. 12.
219. *WM,* p. 137. In other words, one who has experienced despair and overcome it may, because of his own experience, be able to help those who are in despair.
220. *WM,* p. 91. The bracketed explanatory phrase is mine.
221. *WM,* p. 95.
222. *UG,* p. 137. Italics are the publisher's.
223. *DS,* p. 14. The bracketed words are mine. Despair may be a spiritual problem, which results from a frustrated

search for meaning, an as yet unsatisfactory answer to the question: "What is the meaning of life?" It may require a rather long period of time in order to answer the question satisfactorily. Thus, the search requires patience—perhaps great patience. Therefore, even if a person has not yet found meaning but is searching for it, the search itself is not absurd, meaningless. There is a moment-by-moment meaning in the search for a greater or fuller meaning to one's life. "Seek and ye shall find."

224. *DS*, p. 20.

225. *UCM*, p. 56.

226. Distinctively, human phenomena are those traits or characteristics of human beings which separate them from animals. The human traits indicate that there is not only a quantitative but also a qualitative difference between human beings and animals. In other words, human beings are different from animals not only in degree but also in kind.

227. *UCM*, pp. 30-31.

228. *UCM*, p. 137.

229. *MSUM*, p. 111. Frankl is responding to reductionistic interpretations of the human person. For example, "A human being is nothing but a highly advanced animal" or "A human being is nothing but a highly complicated machine, such as a computer."

230. *UCM*, p. 138. The bracketed word is mine.

231. *DS*, p. 26.

232. *DS*, p. 77.

233. *MSUM*, p. 115.

234. Diversions are various forms of human activities in which human beings attempt to escape from facing the emptiness or void within themselves. Human beings cannot really get away from themselves no matter how fast they are moving in their day-to-day activities. Conscience or consciousness will eventually rear its

head, will creep up from inside to confront one's self. This is expressed well in a line from Jackson Browne's classic rock song which has the line, "No matter how fast I run, I can never seem to get away from me." Cf. Jackson Browne, "Your Bright, Baby," *The Pretender*, Released November 10, 1976, Elektra/ Asylum Records.

235. *PE*, p. 125.

236. *WM*, p. 97.

237. *PE*, p. 126.

238. *WM*, p. 97.

239. *DS*, p. 49.

240. *DS*, pp. 49-50.

241. Frankl took the first draft of the manuscript of his book *The Doctor and the Soul* (which was written in German) into the concentration camp at Auschwitz. The German title *Die Arztliche Seelsorge* literally means "The Medical Ministry." Cf. *VFR*, p. 58.

242. *VFR*, p. 91. The bracketed words are mine and explain "the manuscript" to which Frankl was referring. The bracketed uppercase [I] is mine. The manuscript was lost in Auschwitz and eventually destroyed there. Cf. *VFR*, p. 99.

243. *VFR*, p. 98. Frankl became sick with typhus in the concentration camp at Turkheim. Cf. *VFR*, p. 95.

244. *DS, xi*. The single quotation marks are mine and indicate that Frankl is quoting Psalm 126:6.

245. The Spanish legend of Don Juan, the "Seducer of Seville," originated in the 17th century. In the legend, Don Juan was a "womanizer." He made more than a thousand sexual conquests. One day, as he passed by a tomb, a voice came from the statue on the tomb. It warned Don Juan that he would be punished for his immoral deeds. Don Juan, however, would not change his behavior. The statue eventually came to life, went to Don Juan's house, grabbed him and forcibly took him into hell.

246. *DS,* p. 168.
247. *MSM,* p. 75.
248. *DS,* p. 141. Frankl paraphrases the words of a medical doctor.
249. R. L. Koteskey, "Drive," in *Baker Encyclopedia of Psychology,* ed. David G. Benner (Grand Rapids, MI.: Baker Book House, 1985), p. 332, defines a drive as "An aroused state resulting from a biological need. The concept of drive is a major one in the field of motivation. When an animal or a person is deprived of essentials, such as food, water, or air, it is said to be in a state of arousal known as the drive state. The energized drive state then pushes the organism to do something to reduce the need. After the need is satisfied, the drive subsides."
250. *WM,* p. 43.
251. *MSM,* p. 141.
252. *MSUM,* p. 100. Italics are the publisher's. Instead of LSD, which was widely used back in the 1960s and '70s, many people today turn to crack or cocaine to fill their inner emptiness. But Frankl's principle is essentially the same: when human beings sense that something is missing from their lives, when they experience an inner emptiness or existential vacuum, many times they try to fill it with the wrong things.
253. Frankl quotes Betty Lou Padelford, "The Influence of Ethnic Background, Sex, and Father Image upon the Relationship between Drug Involvement and Purpose in Life" (United States International University, San Diego, January 1973), in *MSUM,* p. 101. Presumably, the Nowlis to whom Padelford is referring is the American psychologist Helen Howard Nowlis (1913-1986).
254. *DS,* pp. 130-131. Frankl does not literally mean that a person should not take time to rest. Rather, he is talking about finding new challenges in life. Personal dullness refers to failing to perceive messages from the various

external stimuli in life, which challenges one to fulfill a new meaning in life, to grow or mature more deeply as a human being. Personal dullness, in the words of a rock song by Pink Floyd, means "I have become comfortably numb."

255. *PE,* p. 27. Frankl does not make light of dying young; rather, it is tragic. But "it is not necessarily the years in life that count but the life in years." The phrase "years in life" refers to duration, how long one has lived. The phrase "life in years" refers to a meaningful life. This is not to say that it is not good to live a long life. But duration alone—that is, living a long life without a sense of meaning and purpose, without knowing why one is here and without any hope of life after death, is not good, even though life itself is good. But for a young person who dies with a sense of meaning and purpose in life, his life may actually be more meaningful than a person who has lived a long life.

256. *DS,* p. 66.

257. James C. Crumbaugh, "Cross-Validation of Purpose-in-Life Test Based on Frankl's Concepts," *Journal of Individual Psychology* 24:74, 1968, quoted in *WM,* p. 89.

258. *WM,* pp. 46-47. This is certainly true, in general, of Americans in the twenty-first century. For example, to say, "You can't impose your ideas on me," is a self-defeating, contradictory statement, because that statement itself imposes the idea that one's ideas cannot be imposed on others. Again, to say, "You can't tell others what to do," is a self-defeating, contradictory statement, because that statement itself is telling another person that he or she cannot tell others what to do. Still again, the statement, "There is no such thing as objective truth," purports to be an objective truth (that is, a real truth) that there is no objective truth. The statement defeats itself. It is self-contradictory and, therefore, false.

259. *WM,* p. 85.

260. *WM,* p. 86.
261. Albert Einstein, quoted in *PE,* p. 93, note 4.
262. *DS,* p. 111. The single quotation marks are mine.
263. *DS,* p. 111. To be alive psychically means to be "in touch" with one's emotions—both "up" and "down" emotions. One is aware of his or her own emotions instead of denying them or repressing them. Apathy, on the other hand, is from the Greek word *apatheia,* which, in turn, is from the negative prefix *a,* meaning "without" and *pathos,* meaning "emotion, feeling, suffering." It is difficult for an apathetic person to get excited about anything. Sometimes, it is even hard for such a person to feel sad. Psychologically, it is better to let oneself feel emotional pain than to be in emotional pain and not feel it. The person who can feel his or her emotional pain is at least alive enough psychically and, thus, spiritually, acknowledges it. However, an apathetic person may not even know that he or she is in emotional pain.
264. *WM,* p. 151.
265. *WM,* p. 152.
266. *UCM,* pp. 72-73. The bracketed words [Existentialists interpret] are mine. The concept of encounter was introduced by Martin Buber, Ferdinand Ebner, and Jacob L. Moreno. An interpersonal relationship, the proper relationship by which two human beings treat each other, is called "I and thou." In a specific sense, it involves a relationship of love between two persons. In a general sense, it involves a relationship of respect between two persons. An I-and-thou relationship then is treating another human being as *someone,* not *something,* as a *what,* not a *who* It is acknowledging that another person is a subject, not an object. Not respecting another human being reduces that person to an object, a thing. Using another person for one's own benefit and not the other person's benefit reduces that person to an object. It is described as an "I and it" relationship.

267. *PE*, p. 120.

268. As a physician, Frankl's medical ethic is reflected in the Hippocratic Oath. He opposed euthanasia on the basis of his ontological view of human value or worth. Frankl's view of human worth is not utilitarian. In other words, it does not depend on how useful a person is to others or to society. This may also be called the "quality of life" ethic.

The Greek word *ontos,* from which the English word "ontological' is derived, means "being." Hence, for Frankl, a person's unconditional value stems first and foremost from who (or whom) he or she is, not what he or she does or how much he or she can contribute to the good of society. Ontological dignity is the basis for unconditional meaning in life, a meaning regardless of one's condition of health. Logotherapy teaches the unconditional meaningfulness of life. In other words, every human being, regardless of his or her physical or mental condition, regardless of the severity or intensity of one's sufferings, regardless of whether one is terminally ill or chronically ill, has a meaning in life and retains that meaning to the very end of his or her life.

269. *MSM,* pp. 151-152.

270. *MSM,* p. 152.

271. *MSM,* p. 152. What is particularly significant about Frankl's critique of the usefulness or quality of life philosophy, and thus euthanasia, is that they are written not only by a physician and a philosopher but also by a man who was a prisoner in concentration camps for three years during the Holocaust. Dr. Leo Alexander, American medical science consultant to the Nuremberg War Crimes Trails, said, "Whatever proportions these crimes finally assumed, it became evident to all who investigated them that they had started from small beginnings. The beginnings at first were merely a shift in emphasis in the basic attitude of the physicians. It

started with the acceptance of the attitude, basic in the euthanasia movement, that there is such a thing as life not worthy to be lived. This attitude in its early stages concerned itself merely with the severely and chronically sick. Gradually the sphere of those to be included in this category was enlarged to encompass the socially unproductive, the ideologically unwanted, the racially unwanted and finally all non-Germans." Cf. Leo Alexander, "Medical Science Under Dictatorship," *New England Journal of Medicine* 241 (July 14, 1949): 44.

272. *DS,* p. 47.

273. *DS,* p. 48.

274. *DS,* p. 47. One of the first principles of the practice of medicine is expressed in an old Latin phrase, *primum, non nocere,* meaning "first, do no harm." A physician's primary role is to heal, not harm, a sick or dying patient. The Latin phrase is not explicitly stated in the Hippocratic Oath since it was originally written; nevertheless, the idea was expressed in the oath in such ethical guidelines as "I will use treatment to help the sick according to my ability and judgment, but never with a view to injury and wrong-doing. Neither will I administer a poison to anybody when asked to do so, nor will I suggest such a course . . . . Into whatsoever houses I enter, I will enter to help the sick, and I will abstain from all intentional wrong-doing and harm, especially from abusing the bodies of man or woman . . . ." Cf. *Hippocrates,* 4 Vols., trans. W. H. S. Jones (Cambridge, MA.: Harvard University Press/The Loeb Classical Library, 1923), Vol. 1, pp. 299-301.

275. *DS,* p. 47. Italics are mine.

276. *PE,* p. 129. Italics are mine.

277. *DS,* p. 49.

278. *VFR,* p. 41.

279. *PE,* p. 125. Frankl does not mean that the hectic pace of every executive of a company or corporation is

indicative of the existential vacuum. Nevertheless, there are certain executives who may be experiencing the existential vacuum, and one of the ways in which they may escape from facing it is to stay busy, to divert their attention from themselves by constantly moving from one activity to the next.

280. *PE*, pp. 126-127.

281. Existential analysis stresses the spiritual or distinctively human dimensions of a person such as free-will and responsibility. Existential analysis is logotherapy's response to psychoanalysis.

282. *MSUM*, p. 28.

283. *MSUM*, p. 29. The bracketed [T] is mine. Self-consciousness means that I become conscious or aware of myself as a self.

284. *DS*, p. 55.

285. Preface to *MSM*, p. 9.

286. *PE*, p. 44. Italics are the publisher's.

287. *PE*, p. 50.

288. *UCM*, p. 115.

289. *WM*, p. 6. Italics are the publisher's.

290. *WM*, p. 3.

291. *PE*, p. 42. Because human beings have a will to meaning and are in search of meaning, existential frustration is a feeling or sense of not attaining what should be attained namely, true meaning in life. In one's search for meaning, one may have gone about it in the wrong way, such as intending or deliberately seeking pleasure or happiness; or one may have been searching for meaning in the wrong object or the wrong thing, such as power, wealth or drugs. The result of existential frustration is the existential vacuum. At times, however, Frankl uses the term "existential frustration" as a synonym for "the existential vacuum" (see ibid.).

292. *PE*, p. 124. The bracketed words are mine.

293. *PE*, p. 42.

294. *PE*, pp. 66-67. The bracketed [is] is mine.
295. *PE*, p. *vi*. The bracketed [s] is mine.
296. *UCM*, p. 15. Cf. *American Psychological Association Monitor*, May 1976.
297. *UCM*, pp. 20-21.
298. *WM*, pp. 75-76. Rolf H. Von Eckartsberg, PhD, is a psychologist who accepts the existential understanding of the human person over the behaviorist understanding, which interprets human behavior in the light of laboratory experiments with animals.
299. *MSM*, pp. 110-111. The bracketed explanatory word is mine.
300. *PE*, p. 71.
301. *PE*, p. 71.
302. *MSUM*, p. 95.
303. *MSM*, p. 112. Libido is the energy of the sexual drive.
304. *PE*, p. 27.
305. *UCM*, pp. 92-93.
306. *MSUM*, p. 128. Italics are the publisher's. The bracketed explanatory terms are mine.
307. *UCM*, p. 107. Frankl is speaking in general terms, which means that there are still specific cases of sexual frustration and feelings of inferiority.
308. *MSUM*, p. 134. In other words, the feeling of meaninglessness, the experience of the existential vacuum, means that something has gone wrong with the human spirit, but it does not mean that a person is mentally ill. What is the meaning of human life? For Sigmund Freud, to ask such a question is a sign of mental illness. He wrote, "The moment a man questions the meaning and value of life he is sick." See Sigmund Freud, *Letters of Sigmund Freud*, ed. Ernst L. Freud (New York, N.Y.: Basic Books, Inc., 1960), quoted in *PE*, p. 20. Freud wrote his opinion in a letter to Princess Bonaparte.
309. *MSUM*, p. 112. The bracketed [T] is mine.
310. *MSUM*, p. 99. Italics are the publisher's. The bracketed

[said] is mine. The term "dope" was widely used in the 1960s through 1970s and meant "taking drugs illegally;" "getting high."

311. *UCM,* p. 28.

312. *MSUM,* p. 17. Italics are the publisher's.

313. *WM,* pp. 145-146. The "ultimate being" is Frankl's term for God.

314. *WM,* pp. 156-157. The Scripture quotation is from Habakkuk 3:17-18.

315. *MSUM,* p. 19.

316. *DS,* p. 81. The fatalist says, "I can't change; that's just the way that I am." If one believes that one's destiny is predetermined by one's biology or chemical make-up or by one's social environment or upbringing, then that belief may paralyze one's will to change, to improve his or her life for the better. Logotherapy says in effect, "To the extent that one is able to change one's life—regardless of his or her biological, psychological or sociological conditions—one should choose to change for the better. For example, "Frankl says, 'Biological destiny is the material which must be shaped by the free human spirit'" (*DS,* p. 83). My biology, then, shapes (or influences) me but it does not make me the person that I am. In short, I become what I am or I make myself through my choices.

317. *DS,* pp. 86-87.

318. *DS,* p. 87.

319. *WM,* p. 65.

320. *PE,* p. 24.

321. *PE,* p. 109. The words are incredible, especially since they also come from a man whose unborn child, wife, mother, father, and brother were killed by the Nazis and their "system" of racism and anti-Semitism.

322. *PE,* p. 111. Frankl's words are significant, especially in the light of the context in which they were spoken. He delivered a memorial speech to the Society of Physicians in Vienna on March 25, 1949, honoring the physicians who

died in the Holocaust in the years 1938-1945. Cf. *PE*, p. 107. By forgiving the living, Frankl is referring to many of the perpetrators of the Holocaust who were still alive.

323. Matthew Scully, "Viktor Frankl at Ninety: An Interview," in *First Things*, http://www.firstthings.com/ftissues/ft9504/scully.html. It can also be found in Matthew Scully, "Viktor Frankl at Ninety: An Interview." *First Things*, 52 (April, 1995): 39-43.

324. Viktor E. Frankl, *Viktor Frankl Recollections: An Autobiography*, trans. Joseph and Judith Fabry (Reading, MA.: Perseus Books, 1997), p. 124. Frankl's words were addressed to Pope Paul VI in a private audience granted to Frankl and his wife, Elly. This book by Frankl shall be abbreviated as *VFR*.

325. *VFR*, p. 28.

326. *VFR*, p. 57.

327. *VFR*, p. 56.

328. Allport's quotation is in *MSM*, p. 10. Gordon Allport was a professor of psychology at Harvard University.

329. *VFR*, pp. 43-44. Frankl received his pilot's license at the age of sixty-seven.

330. *VFR*, p. 41.

331. *UCM*, p. 52.

332. *UCM*, p. 37.

333. *VFR*, p. 124.

334. *WM*, p. 86.

335. *MSM*, p. 96. Frankl is probably referring to Psalm 118:5.

336. *WM*, pp. 155-156.

337. *VFR*, p. 129.

338. *DS*, pp. 137-138. In the context, Frankl refers to himself in the third person singular, saying, "[W]e have the following narrative by a former concentration-camp inmate . . ." (ibid., p. 137). This is supported by the video *Viktor Frankl's Choice* (Princeton, N.J.: Films for the Humanities and Sciences, 2002). In the video, the words

refer to Frankl's own experience as an inmate in the concentration camp.

339. *WM,* p. 21. I changed the spelling of "computor" in the original English quotation to the modern English spelling "computer."

340. *PE,* p. 131. In the context, Frankl is not referring to the philosophy of nihilism, which teaches that being or existence itself is meaningless. Rather, he is referring to a practical or "'lived' nihilism," as he calls it. It is one's own experience of meaninglessness. It is subjective rather than objective meaninglessness. Cf. *PE,* p. 121. A mote is a speck of dust, and a beam may be a rather long, thick, wooden object. In other words, Frankl had to be in touch with his own existential vacuum in order to help others with theirs.

341. *VFR,* p. 38.

342. *MSM,* p. 109.

343. *UCM,* pp. 51-52.

344. *WM,* p. 137, footnote 19.

345. *VFR,* p. 22. The inkblot test was developed by Hermann Rorschach (1884-1922), a Swiss psychiatrist.

346. A psychotherapist is someone who is authorized or licensed (depending on the laws of a state or nation) to practice medicine, a medical doctor, and is involved in the diagnosis and treatment of mental or emotional problems. A psychotherapist, for example, may counsel persons who have social problems and various kinds of addictions. In the United States, a psychotherapist may also be a licensed psychologist or even a social worker.

347. *VFR,* p. 73.

348. *VFR,* p. 35.

349. Free-will is a theme in existentialism. Frankl was a philosopher and philosophy, especially existentialism, had an influence on Frankl's development logotherapy,

the Third Viennese School of Psychotherapy. A human being has free-will, because he or she is not only a body but also a spirit in a body. Free-will is a property of the human spirit. A human being, then, is much more than his or her body. Because a person has free-will, a spiritual center of self-control, he or she has freedom of choice and therefore can choose between different options or courses of action. In other words, because a human being has a spirit, he or she has the power of self-transcendence, the capacity for self-detachment or self-distancing. Because a human being has a spirit, he or she can choose to take a stand toward conditions, "even the worst conditions conceivable" (*UCM*, p. 52). See Self-Transcendence.

350. *MSUM*, pp. 105-106.

351. *MSM*, p. 132. Italics are the publisher's.

352. *PE*, p. 3. The parenthetical comments are mine.

353. *DS*, footnote, p. 97.

354. Magda B. Arnold, *The Human Person* (New York, N.Y., 1954), p. 40, quoted in *UCM*, p. 52.

355. *MSUM*, p. 32.

356. *PE*, p. 63.

357. *DS*, p. 76.

358. *PE*, p. 60.

359. *WM*, p. 17.

360. *MSM*, p. 75.

361. *VFR*, pp. 47-51. In his early years, Frankl became fascinated with Sigmund Freud and the psychological school he founded, called "Psychoanalysis." Frankl corresponded with Freud via letters and postcards. Frankl even met Freud once. However, Frankl eventually rejected psychoanalysis and came under the influence of Alfred Adler and the psychological school he founded, called "individual psychology."

362. *DS*, p. 3. William Stekel was a well-known Austrian psychiatrist and psychoanalyst. For Frankl, the "giant" is Sigmund Freud.

363. *WM*, p. 12. Rabbi Loew (1520-1609) was known as "the Great Rabbi of Prague."

364. *WM*, p. 48. For empirical or scientific confirmation of Frankl's view of the therapeutic value of tension, see Sigmund Freud, *Gesammelte Werke*, Vol. 10, p. 113. The German title may be translated into English as *Collected Works*.

365. *VFR*, p. 50.

366. *PE*, p. 118. In other words, the commonly held beliefs about religion during Freud's time were accepted by him uncritically and used in understanding his patients.

367. *WM*, p. 11.

368. *WM*, p. 11.

369. *UCM*, pp. 51-52.

370. Sigmund Freud, *Letters of Sigmund Freud*, ed. Ernst L. Freud (New York, N.Y.: Basic Books, Inc., 1960), quoted in *PE*, p. 20.

371. *PE*, p. 20.

372. *WM*, p. 27. Freud addressed his words to Ludwig Binswanger in a letter, the source of which is not cited by Frankl.

373. *WM*, p. 44.

374. *WM*, p. 52. Cf. Gordon W. Allport, *Personality and Social Encounter* (Boston, MA.: Beacon Press, 1960).

375. *PE*, p. 7. The bracketed words are mine.

376. *WM*, p. 54.

377. *PE*, p. 110.

378. *MSUM*, p. 147.

379. *PE*, p. 104.

380. Ludwig Wittgenstein, quoted in *MSUM*, p. 153.

381. *WM*, p. 145. Faith in a supreme being, a higher power or god, gives meaning to life.

382. *PE*, p. 181.

383. *MSUM*, p. 19.

384. *WM*, p. 146.

385. Ludwig Wittgenstein, quoted in *WM*, p. 146. Frankl seems to accept Wittgenstein's view because Frank says, "[M]an

cannot speak of God but he may speak to God" (*WM,* p. 146). For Wittgenstein, human language is confined only to this world of empirical objects. In other words, one cannot really speak about a trans-empirical God. Wittgenstein accepts a form of religious agnosticism, which says that God cannot be known. Wittgenstein's position seems to be self-contradictory or self-defeating, because he assumes to know something about God in order to deny that God can be known. Philosopher Norman Geisler asks: "But . . . how can one know that God is inexpressible without thereby revealing something expressible about God?" Cf. Norman Geisler, *Christian Apologetics* (Grand Rapids, MI.: Baker Book House, 1976, 8th printing, 1987), p. 23. Geisler continues: "The very attempt to deny all expressions about God is an expression about God. One cannot draw the limits of language and thought unless he has transcended those very limits he would draw. It is self-defeating to express . . . the inexpressible cannot be expressed"(ibid.).

Wittgenstein says, "My propositions are elucidatory in this way: he who understands me finally recognizes them as senseless, when he has climbed out through them, on them, over them. (He must so to speak throw away the ladder, after he has climbed up on it.). He must surmount these propositions; then he sees the world rightly. Whereof one cannot speak, thereof one must be silent." Cf. Ludwig Wittgenstein, *Tractatus Logico-Philosophicus,* trans. C. K. Ogden (London: Routledge and Kegan Paul, 1971), 6.54; 7, p. 189. However, "One cannot use the scaffold of language and thought about the limits of reality only to say the scaffold cannot be so used. If the ladder was used to get on top of the house, one cannot thereupon deny the ability of the ladder to get one there" (Norman Geisler, *Christian Apologetics,* op. cit., pp. 23-24).

386.   *MSUM,* p. 68.

387. *MSUM,* p. 68. God may be known as the *Deus absconditus,* the "hidden God" or the "God who hides himself." Cf. Isaiah 45:15.

388. *MSUM,* p. 77. The bracketed words [the psychiatrist] and [in] are mine. Italics are the publisher's.

389. Johann Wolfgang Von Goethe, quoted in *PE,* p. 18, footnote 10. Goethe, of course, wrote in German; his statement may also be translated into English as, "If we take man as he is, we make him worse; if we take him as he ought to be, we help him become it" (ibid., p. 12). Elsewhere, Frankl says Goethe's words are "the finest maxim for any kind of psychotherapy" (*DS,* p. 90). Frankl often quotes Goethe in order to stress that human beings can change for the better, that they are not totally conditioned by some fate over which they have no control. It is, then, possible for a person to change.

    Frankl teaches that there needs to be an idealist in the human person. In other words, in each personal or I-thou relationship (one person to another), in order to make a human being better than he or she is now, to encourage that person to become what he or she can be, each person must overestimate the other person.

390. *DS,* p. 56. Frankl does not cite the source of his quotation of Goethe.

391. Johann Wolfgang Von Goethe, quoted in *PE,* p. 128.

392. *WM,* p. 137, footnote 19.

393. *WM,* pp. 142-143.

394. Benedict de Spinoza (1632-1677), *The Ethics,* Part V, quoted in *PE,* p. 99. The Latin *Sed omnia praeclara tam difficilia quam rara sunt* may also be translated as, "But all things excellent are as difficult as they are rare."

395. *DS,* p. 110. To "narcotize" an emotion means to take drugs, such as sleeping pills or tranquilizers, in an attempt to numb the emotion so as not to feel it or to ignore it. This is a form of denial, which is "an unconscious mental mechanism in which refusal to

perceive or admit the existence of something serves as an ego defense against some unpleasant, unacceptable aspect of reality. Thus, when some internal or external perception is judged by the unconscious ego as potentially threatening, the perception or memory of that reality is filtered out of conscious awareness." Cf. R. Larkin, "Denial," in *Baker Encyclopedia of Psychology*, ed. David G. Benner (Grand Rapids, MI.: Baker Book House, 1985), p. 299.

396. To attribute guilt to a person who is actually guilty of wrong-doing is to treat him or her as a human being, not an animal. Viktor Frankl taught that legal punishment, punishment under the law, presupposes free-will and responsibility. To convict human beings of a crime because they are, in fact, guilty, is to pay them a compliment. It is to be treated as a human being who is responsible for his or her actions, not an animal nor a machine.

397. *WM*, p. 7.

398. *WM*, p. 74. Italics are the publisher's.

399. *DS*, p. 22. The uppercase bracketed [A] is mine.

400. *PE*, p. 41.

401. *MSUM*, p. 90. The bracketed words [T] and [is] are mine. Attention (from the Latin *attendere*, meaning "give heed to") refers to mental focus on something. Intention (from the Latin *in*, meaning "toward" and *tendere*, meaning "to stretch") refers to willingness, that is, the will to deliberately choose to do something.

402. *UG*, pp. 84-85. A self-absorbed or self-centered person who lives to pursue and gratify all of his or her wants is really unhappy. Happiness cannot be pursued; rather, it must ensue, follow from focusing outwardly on others rather than focusing inwardly on one's self. The paradox of happiness is that by forgetting about one's self and serving others, one will become happy and experience a sense of self-fulfillment.

403. *UCM,* p. 21.

404. *UCM,* p. 21.

405. *MSUM,* p. 87.

406. *WM,* p. 30.

407. *MSUM,* p. 138. For Frankl, "height psychology" refers to logotherapy.

408. *MSUM,* p. 139. For Frankl, "depth psychology" refers to Sigmund Freud's pleasure principle or will to pleasure and Alfred Adler's principle of the inferior person striving for superiority.

409. Hillel was a famous scribe and rabbi who founded the School of Hillel (or *Beit Hillel,* the House of Hillel) around 20 B. C. E. Rabbi Shammai was a contemporary of Hillel and founded the School of Shammai (or *Beit Shammai,* the House of Shammai). Hillel and Shammai respectively represent two different schools of rabbinic thought.

410. Rabbi Hillel, quoted in *PE,* p. 89.

411. *PE,* p. 89. The bracketed words are mine.

412. *PE,* pp. 89-90. The bracketed words are mine

413. *PE,* p. 90. The comment in the parenthesis is Frankl's. Hillel teaches that one lives not only for one's own sake but for something or someone else's. Life is directed not only inwardly but also outwardly, toward giving oneself to others. No one, then, can take your place in the world, nor can anyone take mine. Hillel teaches that each human being is unique, precious, and unrepeatable in worth.

414. *WM,* p. 67. Some kinds of behavior are simply wrong and instead of suggesting that a patient not engage in such behavior, the doctor should be "directive." In other words, the doctor tells the patient not to commit suicide. Being directive sometimes means telling a patient or client something that he or she does not want to hear but, nevertheless, needs to hear, because it is (and always should be) for that person's own good.

Therefore, a doctor's or counselor's values cannot be imposed on a patient or client; however, sometimes they should be proposed to him or her.

415. Logotherapy teaches that human beings need hope to sustain them in the present. Hope is looking to the future with optimism. It is necessary for a meaningful life. It can even prevent depression and despair. Hope, then, is mentally and spiritually healthy.

416. *MSM*, p. 99.

417. *MSM*, p. 84. Because the human person is a psychosomatic unity, what affects the human soul (or spirit or mind) may also affect the body and *vice versa*.

418. *MSM*, p. 82.

419. *UCM*, p. 38. Self-transcendence occurs when an individual, instead of focusing exclusively on one's self, being preoccupied with one's self, focuses outwardly on another human being in the act of love or service to others, on a cause to serve and give one's life to or on a work or art, science, etc. It is living for or giving one's self to someone or something. In the process, one forgets about one's self and finds a sense of self-fulfillment.

420. *DS*, p. 5. Italics are the publisher's.

421. *UCM*, pp. 30-31.

422. *MSUM*, p. 126. Italics are the publisher's.

423. *WM*, p. 17.

424. *PE*, p. 114. The uppercase bracketed [T] is mine. Ptolemy (or Claudius Ptolemaeus), an astronomer, mathematician and geographer, lived in Alexandria, Egypt, from around 87 to 150 CE. He taught the geocentric view of the universe. In other words, the earth (from the Greek word *ge*) was the center of the universe. Thus, it was commonly accepted during the Medieval Period or the Middle Ages that human beings had dwelt as the center of the universe. However, the astronomer Nicolaus Copernicus (1473-1543 CE.) formulated the

heliocentric view of the universe. In other words, the sun (from the Greek word *helios*) was the center of the solar system. His theory was eventually confirmed by Galileo Galilei's (1564-1642 CE.) observations, using a telescope. In short, the sun did not revolve around the earth (geocentricity). Rather, the earth revolved around the sun (heliocentricity). Human beings were not, after all, the center of the universe. For Frankl, that did not mean their dignity was diminished by their location in the universe.

425.   The psalmist directed the question to God in Psalm 8:4. Blaise Pascal is quoted in *PE*, pp. 110-111.

426.   Human potential refers to what a person is capable of becoming (e.g., lazy or industrious, good or evil) through his or her own choices.

427.   *MSUM*, pp. 88-89. Italics are the publisher's.

428.   *PE*, p. 9. Socrates was born in Athens, Greece, around 469 BCE. Indeed, Socrates's "decision" "made all the difference." He was a teacher and philosopher; actually, one of the greatest of the ancient Greek philosophers. His most famous student was Plato. Through his writings, Socrates's ideas have influenced Western civilization for thousands of years.

429.   *PE*, p. 35.

430.   *PE*, pp. 13-14. The bracketed [n] is mine. Frankl who lived through the "hell" of the Holocaust is not saying that Hitler was good; rather, Frankl is saying that having the human capacity to make choices or decisions is good, even though human beings may make evil choices rather than good ones. See for example Kolbe, Father Maximilian.

431.   *PE*, p. 103.

432.   *MSM*, p. 151.

433.   *DS*, p. 72.

434.   *PE*, p. 44. Italics are the publisher's.

435.   *MSM*, p. 113.

436. *WM*, pp. 54-55. Frankl is not denying that there is life after death, for he believed in God. Rather, Frankl is saying that since each human being is unique, each has unique opportunities to fulfill before he or she dies.

437. *DS*, p. 136.

438. *WM*, p. 19.

439. p. 110.

440. *MSM*, p. 54.

441. *PE*, p. 4. The noetic dimension refers to the mind or human spirit, that is, a distinctively human characteristic.

442. *WM*, p. 17. Cf. Psalm 2:4; 37:13; 59:8.

443. *UCM*, p. 137. A laughing hyena "laughs," but it is not laughing at itself. It appears to be laughing from a human perspective, because it makes a noise similar to human laughter. But to say that a hyena is laughing is to anthropomorphize animal behavior—that is, to attribute or impose on animals human characteristics. It is to humanize animals, to interpret the lower life-form of animals in the light of the higher life-form of human life. It is the opposite error of reductionism. The reductionist interprets the higher life-forms—that is, human beings, in the light of the lower life-forms, such as rats, monkeys or other kinds of animals. For example, since animals copulate and procreate and humans do the same, then human beings are animals, but highly advance animals. Both humanizing animals and dehumanizing human beings by interpreting their behavior in the light of sub-human phenomena are errors, which fail to understand distinctively human phenomena. In other words, there is a distinct, qualitative difference between human beings and animals. Human beings are not merely highly evolved or advanced animals. Humans are not merely different from animals by degree but in kind. At the *radix*, the Latin word meaning "root," point of origin, human beings are radically different from animals.

444. *UCM*, p. 138. Unless, of course, the computer has been programmed by a human being to laugh at itself. It is the distinctively human capacity of laughter, which is put into or programmed into that which is inanimate and cannot laugh at itself, namely, a computer.

445. *WM*, p. 108.

446. *WM*, p. 109.

447. "Hyperintention" is derived from the Greek word *hyper*, meaning "over" or "beyond." "Intention" is derived from the Latin *in*, meaning "toward" and *tendere*, meaning "to stretch." Intention refers to willingness—that is, the will in deliberately choosing to do something. Hence, hyperintention is an excessive kind of mental attention or specific focus, a deliberate intention or aiming at something, which proves to be self-defeating.

448. *UCM*, p. 85. The bracketed comment is mine.

449. *WM*, p. 33. A woman before sexual intercourse who is excessively concerned with or intending or aiming at having an orgasm actually may not have it. A man who is excessively concerned with or intending or aiming at having an erection, actually may not have it. Too much attention and intention prove to be self-defeating.

450. *MSUM*, p. 98.

451. *MSUM*, p. 98.

452. "Hyperreflection" pertains to attention (from the Latin *attendere*, meaning "give heed to"). It refers to mentally focusing on something. Hyperreflection, then, is an excessive, if not inordinate, reflection on oneself. One consciously thinks about one's every thought, movement, etc. One tries to be aware of virtually everything that one does. It results in a kind of self-paralysis, stifling human creativity.

453. *UCM*, p. 87.

454. *DS*, p. 191.

455. *MSUM*, p. 43. Frankl does not oppose any kind of self-

reflection whatsoever but only a mentally unhealthy kind, the kind that stunts or hinders human growth. Frankl notes: "Reflection comes only later"(ibid.).

456. *WM*, p. 100.

457. *MSUM*, p. 155, notes, chapter 2, note 1.

458. Hyper-specialization is the compartmentalization of the sciences to the point that there is no unified view of the human person. Each science sees the person from its own specialized standpoint. But the problem is that the findings of one branch of science may contradict the findings of another. Frankl does not oppose the specialization of knowledge *per se*. In fact, he says, "Society cannot do without specialists" (*WM*, p. 20). However, to say that only one science has the true view of reality or the human person is to succumb to the philosophical error of scientism, which, in turn, leads to the philosophical error of reductionism, reducing a human being to a single factor, whether it be in biology, chemistry, psychology, etc.

459. *WM*, p. 20.

460. *WM*, p. 21. Italics are the publisher's.

461. *WM*, p. 30.

462. *WM*, p. 41.

463. *PE*, p. 9.

464. *WM*, pp. 127-128. The bracketed uppercase letters [Y] and [G] are mine.

465. The *Imago Dei* is the "image of God" in the human person.

466. *MSUM*, p. 60. Human conscience points beyond itself to a personal god, a god who has a personality. That personal god made human makes human beings persons. They are a reflection of his nature.

467. *MSUM*, p. 63.

468. *WM*, p. 16.

469. *MSUM*, p. 115. Italics are the publisher's.

470. In 1938, Hitler's troops invaded Austria. The Nazis were

deporting Jews to concentration camps. In order to escape from deportation and possibly death, Frankl applied for a visa to emigrate to the United States. In 1939, he was supposed to go to the American Consulate and pick up his visa. He had the opportunity to leave Vienna and go to the United States, but he never did. Not wanting to desert his elderly parents, he allowed the visa to lapse and remained with them and, along with them, was deported to the concentration camps.

471. *VFR,* pp. 82-83. This incident reveals Frankl's love for his parents and his loyalty to them. It also reveals his courage to remain with them and be deported to the concentration camp, knowing that he too may die there with them.

472. *DS,* p. 146.

473. *DS,* p. 151.

474. *DS,* p. 147. The bracketed linking verb is mine.

475. *DS,* p. 135. For example, John loves Jane not only because she is beautiful, for there are many other women who share that same trait. But John does not love the other women who are beautiful. John loves Jane not only because she is smart, for there are many other women who are smart, sharing the same trait. But John does not love the other women who are smart. John loves Jane not only because she is sensitive and compassionate, for there are many other women who share the same traits. But John does not love the other women who are sensitive and compassionate. John loves Jane not only because she is athletic, for there are other women who are athletic—maybe even more athletic. In the final analysis, John loves Jane because she alone is Jane in all her uniqueness and singularity. For John, no one else in the whole world is Jane. Only Jane is Jane, only she is she, even though there are other women who have the same name. Visa versa: the principle also applies to Jane's love for John.

476. *DS,* p. 156.

477. *WM*, pp. 97-98. Frankl quotes from the Latin translation of Psalm 16: 7. It is literally translated: "Even in the night my heart admonishes me." I placed single quotation marks around 'noogenic sleeplessness,' because it is Frankl's term.

478. M. P. Cosgrove, "Instinct," in *Baker Encyclopedia of Psychology*, ed. David G. Benner (Grand Rapids, MI.: Baker Book House, 1985), p. 585 says, "Freud used the term *instinct* . . . to mean an inborn primitive force or drive such as hunger, thirst, or sex." Italics are the publisher's.

479. *DS*, pp. *xxiv-xxv*. The bracketed word [however] is mine.

480. Gordon W. Allport, *Personality and Social Encounter* (Boston, MA.: Beacon Press, 1960), p. 60, quoted in *WM*, p. 39.

481. Herbert Spiegelberg, *The Phenomenological Movement* (The Hague: Martinus Nijhoff, 1960), p. 719, quoted in *WM*, p. 39. I supplied the bracketed linking verb [is]. Spiegelberg (1904-1990) was a philosopher particularly specializing in phenomenology.

482. Franz Brentano, *Psychologie vom empirischen Standpunkt* (Leipzig, Meiner, 1924), p. 125, quoted in *WM*, pp. 39-40. The German title may be translated into English as *Psychology of the Empirical Point of View*. Brentano (1838-1917) was a German philosopher. He has been generally regarded as the founder of intentionalism or act psychology, which primarily concerns itself with the acts of the mind, not the content or what is in the mind. In 1864, he was ordained a Roman Catholic priest.

483. *DS*, p. 110. There are different causes to being intoxicated or drunk. On the one hand, it may be traced back to a biochemical disorder. On the other hand, a person may be intoxicated or drunk because he or she is attempting to flee from some kind of painful reality, such as problems on the job or with family or with the failure to

cope with life in general. Drunkenness, then, may be a retreat into one's private little world instead of facing the real world with its demands and responsibilities.

484. Karl Jaspers, quoted in *WM,* p. 38. Jasper's words apply to Frankl. He had a cause to serve, namely, after his own experience of surviving the Holocaust, he taught that life holds an unconditional meaning for all persons, under all adverse situations. He lived that philosophy until his death at the age of ninety-two.

485. *DS,* p. 153. In the context of Frankl's pronoun "its," he is referring to jealousy, which is a form of "erotic materialism," to quote Frankl. Erotic materialism, for example, refers to man treating the woman whom he "loves" as if she were his exclusive possession. It is treating a person as if she were an object, a thing, to be used by the man alone. The same attitude may be vice versa. Cf. ibid., p. 152.

486. *PE,* p. 111.

487. *MSM,* p. 58.

488. *PE,* p. 80. Frankl does not cite the source, probably because Kant's words are well known. Kant wrote: "[M]an and generally any rational being exists as an end in himself, not merely as a means to be arbitrarily used by this or that will, but in all his actions, whether they concern himself or other rational beings, must be always regarded at the same time as an end . . . . Beings whose existence depends not on our will but on nature's, have nevertheless, if they are irrational beings, only a relative value as means, and are therefore called things; rational beings, on the contrary, are called persons, because their very nature points them out as ends in themselves, that is as something which must not be used merely as means, and so far therefore restricts freedom of action (and is an object of respect).

"Accordingly . . . : So act as to treat humanity, whether in thine own person or in that of any other, in every case as an end withal, never as means only." Cf. Immanuel Kant, *Fundamental Principles of the Metaphysic of Morals*, trans. Thomas Kingsmill Abbott, 1785, in World Wide Web: Philosophy Resources on the Internet, *http://www.class.uidaho.edu/mickelsen/texts/Kant%20-%20Fundamentals%20.%20.%20.txt* Copyright 2003. Retrieved on 21 July, 2003.

489. *PE*, p. 80.

490. *PE*, p. 81. Italics are the publisher's.

491. *MSM*, p. 154.

492. *MSUM*, p. 157, note 8.

493. *MSUM*, p. 29.

494. *UCM*, pp. 124-125. Italics are the publisher's.

495. The term "logotherapy" is derived from the Greek word *logos*. The word, for example, was used in the ancient world by the Jewish philosopher Philo of Alexandria and in the New Testament in the Gospel of John and the Book of Revelation (John 1:1-14; Revelation 19:13). The general meaning of the word *logos* in the ancient world was "a word, a saying, a statement; reason, the mental faculty of thinking, calculation." See Joseph Henry Thayer, *A Greek-English Lexicon of the New Testament*, 4th ed. (Milford, MI.: Mott Media, 1901, 1977, reprinted 1982), pp. 380-381. In logotherapy, *logos* denotes "meaning." Hence, human beings are in search of *logos*—that is, meaning.

496. *PE*, p. 74. The bracketed explanatory term [of the human person] is mine.

497. *MSUM*, p. 68. Italics are the publisher's.

498. *VFR*, p. 64: "It was Wolfgang Soucek who dubbed logotherapy 'the Third Viennese School of Psychotherapy.'"

499. *WM*, p. 116. The bracketed words are mine.

500. *VFR*, p. 64. The bracketed explanatory comment is mine. Cf. the context of p. 64 (ibid.) for the founding of the Academic Society for Psychology.

501. *MSUM*, p. 136.
502. The word "logotheory" was coined by Frankl. Cf. *VFR*, p. 75.
503. *VFR*, p. 75.
504. *MSM*, p. 104. Italics are the publisher's.
505. *MSUM*, p. 128.
506. *PE*, p. 72.
507. *UCM*, p. 19.
508. *UCM*, p. 22.
509. *PE*, p. 1. Frankl defines two Greek words. In his usage, *ontos* is translated "being" and *logos* is translated "meaning."
510. *PE*, p. 25.
511. *WM*, p. 143.
512. *UCM*, p. 129.
513. *PE*, p. 56, footnote 4. Brackets enclosed by a word, e.g., [Logotherapy is], or words are mine. They provide the immediate context of the quotation.
514. *WM*, p. 143. The parenthetical comment is mine.
515. *WM*, p. 143.
516. *MSUM*, p. 128. Cf. *VFR*, pp. 66-67.
517. *WM*, pp. 5-6. Italics are the publisher's.
518. *WM*, p.114. The bracketed explanatory word [psychological] is mine.
519. *VFR*, p. 61. The bracketed explanatory clarification is mine. The parenthetical comment is the publisher's.
520. *WM*, pp. 4-5.
521. *MSUM*, p. 109.
522. *WM*, p. 98.
523. *UCM*, pp. 82-83.
524. While suffering mentally and physically in the concentration camps, what gave Frankl a meaning even then, a reason to stay alive, a hope for a better tomorrow, was the love he had for his wife. He found comfort and spiritual support from the contemplation or loving thought of his wife. In short, love gives meaning to life.

Similarly, Pope John Paul II writes: "Man cannot live without love. He remains a being that is incomprehensible for himself, his life is senseless, if love is not revealed to him, if he does not encounter love, if he does not experience it and make it his own, if he does not participate intimately in it." Cf. Pope John Paul II, *The Redeemer of Man, Redemptor Hominis*, 4 March, 1979 (Boston, MA.: Daughters of St. Paul/ St. Paul Editions, n.d.), no. 10.

525. *MSUM,* p. 42.

526. *DS,* p. 137. Intentionality is related to the Latin word *intendere*, which, in turn, is from the Latin *in*, meaning "in" and *tendere*, meaning "to stretch." It is "the directional activity (plan, design) toward purposely accomplishing something." Cf. Peter A. Angeles, *Dictionary of Philosophy* (New York, N.Y.: Barnes and Noble Books/ A Division of Harper and Row, Publishers, 1981), pp. 135-136. Intentionality, then, has to do with the thoughts in one's own mind. In one's mind, one thinks or forms a plan (i.e., purpose, goal or aim) and the will carries out the plan. One intends to perform a specific act in order to attain a specific end or goal. Cf. ibid., p. 136. Human love, then, involves one's thoughts and one's will, which carries out the thoughts toward the beloved.

527. *MSM,* pp. 48-49. Italics are the publisher's.

528. *MSUM,* p. 84. A properly ordered person uses things and loves people rather than using people and loving things.

529. *UCM,* p. 110.

530. *DS,* p. 137. The Latin words *essentia* and *existentia* mean "essence" and "existence" respectively. Frankl's phrase "may be annihilated by death" means that a person's body is destroyed by death. The phrase does not mean that a person's spirit is destroyed, because when a person's physical appearance has gone or his body has died, Frankl says, "It is far from the same as

saying that the person himself no longer exists" (ibid.,
p. 139).

531.   *DS*, p. 136.

532.   *DS*, p. 133.

533.   *DS*, p. 135. In the spiritual aspect of love, the lover grasps
something of the essence of the beloved. Love is not
merely an emotion, a feeling; nor is it merely sexual
arousal, because those aspects of love are temporary—
they come and go. For the most part, love does not
involve feelings, because feelings alone cannot sustain
a relationship. Nor can sex alone keep a marriage
together. A couple can only have so much sex; after
orgasm, each must deal with the other as a human
being the remainder of the twenty-four hours in a day.
To sustain a loving relationship, to make it last, love must
issue from one's will. In other words, love is a choice, a
decision, a commitment to will that which is good for
the beloved. Love cannot be one sided. It must be
reciprocal; otherwise, it will not last. See Choosing to
Love and Unmerited Love.

534.   *DS*, pp. 145-146. The scholastics were theologians and
philosophers (Jewish, Muslim and Christian) who lived in
the Middle (Medieval) Ages, from around 1000 to 1300
BCE. They were very logical and systematic in their
presentation of theological and philosophical truths. They
sought a rational defense of their respective positions. As
Frankl rightly noted, angels are different from each other.
No two angels are the same. Each has a distinct species,
its own species. Cf. Thomas Aquinas, *Summa
Theologica*, I, Q. 50, Art. 4. Similarly, although all human
beings have the same human nature, making all of them
equal in nature, each human person is—to borrow a Latin
phrase—*sui generis*, literally, "of its own kind" or "alone of
its kind." In short, each person is unique, one of a kind. Cf.
Peter A. Angeles, op. cit., p. 283.

535.   *DS*, p. 147.

536. *DS,* p. 132.

537. *WM,* p. 19. The bracketed phrase is mine. The bracketed [M] is mine.

538. *DS,* p. 135. For example, John loves Jane not only because she is beautiful, for there are many other women who share that same trait. But John does not love the other women who are beautiful. John loves Jane not only because she is smart, for there are many other women who are smart, sharing the same trait. But John does not love the other women who are smart. John loves Jane not only because she is sensitive and compassionate, for there are many other women who share the same traits. But John does not love the other women who are sensitive and compassionate. John loves Jane not only because she is athletic, for there are other women who are athletic, maybe even more athletic. In the final analysis, John loves Jane, because she alone is Jane in all her uniqueness and singularity. For John, no one else in the whole world is Jane. Only Jane is Jane, only she is she, even though there are other women who have the same name. Visa versa: the principle also applies to Jane's love for John.

539. *DS,* p. 133. The mystery of unmerited love is that one person loves another "without having done anything to bring this about" (ibid.).

540. The English translation of the cover of the original German edition of Frankl's book was *Say Yes to Life in Spite of Everything.* Cf. *VFR,* p. 108.

541. *VFR,* p. 109.

542. Preface to *MSM,* p. 10.

543. *VFR,* p. 114. The bracketed explanatory comment is mine.

544. *VFR,* p. 128. Later, when the two met, Jerry Long said to Frankl, "The accident broke my back, but it did not break me" (ibid.).

545. Matthew Scully, "Viktor Frankl at Ninety: An Interview," *First Things,* http://www.firstthings.com/ftissues/ft9504/scully.html. It can also be found in Viktor Frankl at Ninety: An Interview. *First Things,* 52 (April, 1995): 39-43.

546. Publisher's remarks in the "About the Author" section in *VFR,* p. 143.

547. *VFR,* p. 127.

548. Marcel was a Roman Catholic and thus a theistic (believing in God) existentialist. In contrast, the French philosophers Albert Camus and Jean-Paul Sartre were known as atheistic existentialist philosophers.

549. *VFR,* p. 114.

550. *DS,* p. 69.

551. Abraham Maslow, "Comments on Dr. Frankl's Paper," *Readings in Humanistic Psychology,* eds. Anthony J. Sutich and Miles A. Vich (New York, N.Y.: The Free Press, 1969), quoted in *MSUM,* p. 86.

552. Abraham H. Maslow, *Eupsychian Management: A Journal* (Homewood, IL.: Irwin, 1965), p. 136, quoted in *WM,* p. 38.

553. *MSUM,* p. 123. The term [refer] was bracketed because the word in the original English edition was in the past tense—that is, "referred." However, the sense or meaning of Frankl's quotation has not changed by changing the verb tense from the past to the present.

554. *MSUM,* p. 142.

555. *MSM,* p. 112. Frankl's statement should be understood in general and in the light of the total context of his writings. Otherwise, one may conclude that he is being overly simplistic. Frankl does not mean that every case of depression, aggression, and addition can automatically be traced back to the existential vacuum. He was a physician and thus, recognized that such conditions may be traced back to genetic and biochemical causes.

556. *PE,* p. 39.

557. *MSUM,* p. 92. The bracketed comment is mine.

558. *DS*, p. 169. The commas are mine and serve as an appositive. In other words, "the act of masturbation" is "sexuality experienced in an undirected way." The uppercase bracketed [T] and [M] are mine. So is the bracketed linking verb [is].

559. *WM*, p. 152. The bracketed words are mine. Frankl implies that a materialist will not believe in God or a supreme being unless God can be seen with human eyes. Frankl calls this "a primitive epistemology" (ibid.).

560. *MSUM*, p. 27.

561. Practical materialism is the inordinate accumulation of wealth or money and possessions. It is one of the symptoms or signs of the existential vacuum.

562. *UCM*, p. 25.

563. *MSUM*, p. 93.

564. *UG*, p. 134. In the letter to Frankl, the author went on to say that he was being healed by logotherapy.

565. *UG*, pp. 134-135. In the letter, the author went on to say that he, too, was being healed by logotherapy.

566. *UCM*, p. 21. Italics are the publisher's.

567. *DS*, p. 126. The bracketed words are mine. The "content" to which Frankl refers is "meaning in life."

568. Meaning is to life what fuel is to a vehicle or what oxygen is to human lungs or what food and fluids are to the human body. Most cars are designed to run by means of fuel. Human lungs are designed to breathe, to receive oxygen or air. The human body is designed to receive nourishment by means of food and fluids. Without the proper kind of fuel, a vehicle will not run or, at least, not run properly. Without enough oxygen, the human body cannot function properly. Without any oxygen, a human being cannot breathe and will die. Without enough food and fluids or without the proper kind of food and fluids, the human body becomes malnourished, undernourished. Without any food and fluids, a human being cannot be nourished and will die of starvation and

dehydration. Similarly, meaning is the "fuel," "oxygen," or "nourishment" of life. Granted a human being can function without meaning in his or her life, but he cannot function properly because something is missing that should be there, namely, meaning itself. In short, all human beings need meaning. It is what keeps them going; however, not only going, but going well or, at least, reasonably well. Meaning, then, gives a person a reason to stay alive.

569. *WM*, pp. 55-56.

570. *MSM*, p. 145.

571. Finding the meaning of life is not a purely subjective process. In other words, a human being cannot simply create or concoct his or her own meaning in life. A sadist, for example, cannot create his own meaning in life by the pleasure he or she derives from inflicting pain on others. Likewise, a thief cannot create his own meaning in life by making a living from robbing others, even though he or she may enjoy stealing. Such actions are objectively wrong, not really fulfilling to a human being. A drug dealer may attempt to create his own meaning by illegally selling drugs and thus making lots of money and having lots of material comforts. Logotherapy teaches that the meaning of life is objective; it's real— it's out there in the real world to be discovered by every person.

572. *DS*, p. 44. A human being's life is intrinsically or inherently (in the very fact of being human itself) meaningful. To be a human person is to have meaning. Because each human being is *sui generis*, "only one of a kind, unique," every person has a unique reason for being alive or a unique meaning in life. However, the subjective problem often is in finding or discovering the meaning of one's own existence.

573. *MSM*, p. 115.

574. *WM*, p. 60. Italics are mine.

575. Personal meaning is an individual matter and, therefore, may differ from one person to the next.

576. *PE*, p. 44.

577. *PE*, p. 72.

578. *PE*, p. 72. A search for the meaning of life is evidence of a distinctively human trait, one which separates human beings from animals, for animals cannot ask, "What is the meaning of life?" Human beings are the only creatures who are in search of meaning. Hence, they are not mentally ill when they ask, "What is the meaning of life?" On the contrary, asking the question is mentally healthy, because it shows that a person is in touch with the spiritual dimension of his being, the soul.

579. *PE*, p. 20.

580. *WM*, pp. 68-69.

581. *MSUM*, p. 112.

582. *UCM*, p. 107.

583. *UCM*, pp. 30-31.

584. *UCM*, p. 16.

585. *WM*, p. 95.

586. Frankl quotes Nicholas Mosley, *Natalie, Natalia* (New York, N.Y.: Coward, McCann and Geoghehan, 1971), in *MSUM*, pp. 127-128. Mosley (1923—), a highly respected author from England, has written several novels, screenplays and biographies.

587. *VFR*, p. 53.

588. *MSUM*, p. 122.

589. *MSUM*, p. 122. The parenthetical comment is mine. Frankl refers to "outer as well as inner conditions" (ibid., p. 124). "Inner" conditions would include, for example, learning to live with a chronic or incurable illness or depression due to a chemical imbalance in the brain. "Outer" conditions would include learning to accept tragedy in one's life, such as the sudden death of a loved one, the loss of a job, home or even a bodily limb.

590. *PE*, p. 129. Italics are mine.

591. *MSUM,* p. 129.

592. *UCM,* p. 47.

593. *UCM,* p. 47. The parenthetical capital "M" is mine.

594. *MSM,* p. 85. The bracketed lower case [s] is mine

595. *WM,* p. 19.

596. The will to meaning can be frustrated by inordinate sexual pleasure, the desire for power, drugs, preoccupation with work, and the hectic pace of various day-to-day activities. Cf. *PE,* pp. 125-126.

597. *MSUM,* p. 85.

598. *PE,* pp. 121-122.

599. *MSM,* p. 117.

600. S. Kratochvil and I Planova, "Comments on Dr. Frankl's Paper," in *Readings in Humanistic Psychology,* eds. Anthony J. Sutich and Miles A. Vich (New York, N.Y.: The Free Press, 1969), quoted in *UG,* p. 80.

601. *PE,* p. 121.

602. *PE,* p. 17.

603. *MSM,* pp. 152-153. Italics are the publisher's. Cf. George A Sargent, "Transference and Countertransference in Logotherapy," *The International Forum for Logotherapy,* Vol. 5, No. 2 (Fall/Winter 1982), pp. 115-118.

604. *DS,* p. 67.

605. *DS,* p. 67. Frankl uses the same argument in *PE,* p. 32.

606. Medical ministry involves two phases. First, the physician or doctor determines that medicines and treatments are no longer of any avail because the patient's illness (somatic or bodily illness) is incurable. Second, the physician or doctor uses "attitudinal values," the mental process whereby the doctor tries to help the patient to see that he (or she) must "take a stand" toward his predicament, that the patient can still have meaning in life, depending on the right kind of attitude he adopts toward the illness.

607. *PE,* p. 115.

608. *DS*, p. 281.

609. *DS*, p. 283.

610. *WM*, p. 117. The bracketed uppercase [T] and [W] are mine. Each is used respectively to begin a sentence. The bracketed word [bodily] is mine. It is explains the word "somatic."

611. *WM*, p. 125.

612. *UCM*, p. 21, footnote.

613. *MSM*, p. 108. Italics are the publisher's.

614. *WM*, p. 48.

615. *WM*, p. 48.

616. *PE*, p. 83.

617. W. M. Millar, "Mental Health and Spiritual Wholeness," *Journal of Societal Issues* 1:7, 1964, quoted in *WM*, p. 140.

618. *WM*, p. 144. The bracketed uppercase [R] is mine.

619. *WM*, p. 139. Once a human being, always a human being, regardless of how well or ill a person is, regardless of a person's mental or physical condition. A human being does not cease to be human by virtue of his or her illness or debilitating condition.

620. Carl J. Rote, "Mental Retardation: The Cry of Why?" *Association of Mental Hospital Chaplains Newsletter* 2: 41, 1965, quoted in *WM*, p. 140. The twenty-first century reader may misunderstand the term "idiot child" as a put-down, a term demeaning a child. Rote is using the term in a technical tense, meaning "a retarded person who is mentally equal or inferior to a child two years old."

621. Each person has a reason for being alive—has a specific and unique mission to fulfill in life, which no one else can fulfill for him or her and it is up to that person to discover his or her reason for being. Meaning, then, is an individual matter; each person has a task to fulfill what no one else can fulfill for him or her. If one

searches long enough, he or she will eventually see that life has a meaning; life is worth living.

622. *PE*, p. 44. Italics are the publisher's.

623. *UCM*, p. 107.

624. *PE*, p. 124.

625. *PE*, p. 124. The professional task is one's job or place of employment. When one is not at work or when one retires from one's job, there are still meanings in life to be realized by that individual. Although meaning in life may include one's job, there is certainly more to a meaningful life than one's job.

626. *PE*, p. 127.

627. *WM*, p. 97.

628. *WM*, p. 96.

629. *MSUM*, p. 130.

630. For Frankl, the highest form of monogamous love is the exclusive love between a man and a woman in the bond of marriage. Such love is definitive, a once-for-all choice by a particular man to commit himself to a particular woman and to no one else. Although there may be other women that he might possibly love, all other choices of possible loves are ruled out by that one particular choice of a particular woman in marriage and vice versa.

631. *DS*, p. 148. The commas after the phrase "Erotic maturity" are mine and serve as an appositive. In other words, "Erotic maturity" is defined as "being . . . inwardly mature enough for a monogamous relationship."

632. *DS*, p. 147.

633. *PE*, p. 12. Frankl is not using the term "peacemaker" in a diplomatic sense. In other words, he is critical of neither government officials nor people in general who want peace instead of war. Frankl is not critical of peacemakers in the biblical sense of the term. Rather, he uses the term "peacemaker" in a psychological sense of a person who

is content to remain as he or she is; one who does not want to be bothered by new challenges and, thus, mature or grow as a human being.

634. *MSUM, p.* 105.

635. *MSM, p.* 104. Italics are the publisher's.

636. *WM, p.* 52. Cf. Gordon W. Allport, *Personality and Social Encounter* (Boston, MA.: Beacon Press, 1960).

637. *DS, p.* 86.

638. *PE, pp.* 138-139. Frankl's comment is especially relevant, because he was a professor of neurology and psychiatry at the University of Vienna.

639. *PE, p.* 122. The single quotation marks within the quotation are mine and indicate Alfred Adler's words. "Neuroses," of course, is the plural of neurosis. It is a frequent sense of uneasiness experienced by an individual or, in Frankl's words, a "nervous condition." Cf. *PE, p.* 113.

640. *WM, pp.* 132-133.

641. *MSM, p.* 109. Italics are the publisher's. Cf., p. 84. Frankl does not give the source for the quotation. The German may also be translated "If we have our own *why* of life, we shall get along with almost any *how.*" Cf. Friedrich Nietzsche, "Twilight of the Idols," in *The Portable Nietzsche,* ed. and trans. Walter Kaufmann (New York, N.Y.: Viking Penguin Inc., 1982), p. 468, no. 12. Italics are from the Viking Penguin edition. The point of the quotation is that if a person has a goal or purpose in life, then he will find the courage and patience to endure any obstacle in order to achieve it.

642. *MSM, p.* 89. Frankl does not give the source of the quotation, probably because it is widely known in both Europe and America. The German may also be translated "What does not destroy me, makes me stronger." Cf. Friedrich Nietzsche, "Twilight of the Idols," in *The Portable Nietzsche,* op. cit., p. 467, no. 8.

643. *MSM, p.* 152.

644. *MSM*, p. 131.

645. *WM*, p. 21.

646. *MSUM*, p. 127.

647. Frankl quotes a letter to him from a graduate student in psychology at the University of California at Berkeley, in *MSUM*, p. 127. If not with their intellects, then at least deep down inside their hearts (the seat of feeling or emotion), nihilists really believe that life has meaning; even suffering has a potential meaning. Nihilists, then, can deny meaning with their heads but not in their hearts.

648. *PE*, p. 107. Frankl certainly meant no disrespect for women in using the term "man." By the term "man," Frankl was referring to human beings in general, male and female. For Frankl, "man" was an inclusive term. Frankl wrote before the "inclusive language" debate in the Unites States of America. Especially in the 1980s and 1990s, various women's rights movements in the United States insisted that the generic term "man" be dropped, because it was too patriarchal, suggestive of the long history of oppression of women in male-dominated cultures. The new inclusive terms for both sexes are "humankind" or "human beings" or simply "men and women." Hence, when Frankl refers to "man," he means "humankind," "human beings in general," "both men and women." This note is directed more toward the inclusive language sensitivities of American readers than it is for readers in other countries.

649. *PE*, p. 110.

650. *MSM*, p. 76.

651. *MSUM*, p. 65. The bracketed words are mine.

652. Johann Wolfgang Von Goethe, quoted in *PE*, p. 128.

653. Plutarch, quoted in *UG*, p. 126.

654. *MSM*, p. 75.

655. *PE*, p. 128.

656. *PE*, p. 35.

657. *MSUM*, pp. 88-89.

658. *WM*, p. 89. Etiology (from the Greek words *aitia*, meaning "cause" and *logia*, meaning "word," "description") is the science of causes or origins of diseases or psychological problems.

659. *DS*, p. 185.

660. *DS*, pp. 187-188. In the context, Frankl explains that the obsessional neurosis was so severe that the patient planned to commit suicide. Even a psychiatrist could not help the patient. When he went to see a second psychiatrist, the patient received help in coping with his obsessions. The bracketed words [He went to see a psychiatrist] are mine and serve as a transitional sentence.

661. *DS*, p. 188.

662. *DS*, p. 188. The bracketed words [The obsessional neurotic's goal is to] and the uppercase bracketed [H] are mine.

663. *WM*, p. 73.

664. Positive imaging is thinking about something good while one is enduring something negative, some adverse condition or situation. It is an ego-defense mechanism, helping an individual cope with a present distress, a negative situation, while mentally projecting into the future something good resulting from that situation.

665. *DS*, p. 100.

666. *UCM*, p. 132. Italics are the publisher's.

667. *UCM*, pp. 133-134. Italics are the publisher's.

668. *UCM*, p. p. 136. The bracketed word [is] is mine.

669. *UCM*, p. 150. The bracketed words [of paradoxical intention] are mine and serve as an explanatory comment.

670. *UCM*, pp. 148-149.

671. *UCM*, pp. 150-151.

672. The psalmist directed the question to God in Psalm 8:4. Blaise Pascal, quoted in *PE*, pp. 110-111. Cf. Blaise

Pascal, *Pensees*, trans. A. J. Krailsheimer (New York, N.Y.: Penguin Books, 1966, reprinted 1984), no. 200, p. 95: "Man is only a reed, the weakest in nature, but he is a thinking reed . . . . Thus all our dignity consists in thought."

673. *WM*, p. 95. The French "*Le coeur a ses raisons, que la raison ne connait point*" may also be translated: "The heart has its reasons of which reason knows nothing." Cf. Blaise Pascal, *Pensees*, op. cit., no. 423, p. 154.

674. *WM*, p. 95.

675. *PE*, pp. 90-91

676. *WM*, p. 90.

677. *WM*, p. 28.

678. Personalism stresses the unrepeatable uniqueness of the human person. It means that every human being is a subject, not an object; a "thou," not an "it;" some one, not some thing; an end in one's self, not a means to an end. It protests all forms of thinking in which human beings are reduced to objects, whether sexual or scientific objects.

679. *WM*, p. 6. Italics are the publisher's.

680. *MSM*, p. 151.

681. *PE*, p. 44.

682. *MSUM*, p. 92.

683. *DS*, p. 126.

684. According to Frankl, "Phenomenology . . . speaks the language of man's prereflective self-understanding rather than interpreting a given phenomenon after preconceived patterns" (*PE*, p. 2, footnote). In the phenomenological approach to the human person, an attempt is made to describe or circumscribe a person's experience. Such an approach does not analyze a person's inner motives or causes of behavior. The phenomenological approach is primarily concerned with the *data,* the given, of a human person. It attempts to

describe a person as much as possible without imposing one's own conceptual judgments and interpretations on the other person.

685.   *MSUM*, p. 122. Italics are the publisher's.

686.   *MSUM*, pp. 122-123.

687.   *MSUM*, p. 126. Italics are the publisher's. The Latin term *sapientia cordis* literally means "wisdom of the heart."

688.   *MSUM*, p. 128. Italics are the publisher's. Logotherapy is not for an elite group of people such as psychiatrists, psychologists, therapists, professors. Rather, it is applicable to almost anyone. It is for scholars and the non-scholarly, "the man in the street." In short, it is for human beings, whether they have received any kind of higher education or not.

689.   *DS*, p. 39.

690.   *DS*, pp. 77-78.

691.   For Frankl, philosophical questions are indicative of the spiritual nature of the human person. Out of that nature issue profound questions such as "Who am I?" This is the search for one's true identity in the midst of an ever-changing world, a world of flux. "Why am I here?" or "Why am I alive?" This relates to the purpose of one's existence or the goal of life. "What should I do with my life?" or "What is the meaning of my life?" This relates to the day-to-day activities or short-range goals, which give meaning to one's life in the here and now. "What is happiness?" or "What is really fulfilling in life?" "Is life worth living?" Since I know that I must eventually die, what is the point of living?" "What happens to me after I die?" or "Is there life after death?" Most human beings ask either one or all of the questions. They are distinctively human questions, separating human beings from animals. After all, no dog asks, "Why am I alive?" No monkey asks, "What is the meaning of my life?"

692. *DS*, p. 12.
693. *DS*, p. 13.
694. *DS*, p. 13.
695. *DS*, p. 29. According to Frankl, logotherapy is "psychotherapy in spiritual terms."
696. *PE*, p. 104. I have changed Frankl's original wording in English from the past tense "understood" to the present "understand" in order to apply Frankl's words to today. For the same reason, I have also modified the punctuation.
697. *DS*, p. 141.
698. *MSM*, p. 117.
699. *WM*, p. 37.
700. *MSUM*, pp. 89-90.
701. *PE*, p. 40.
702. *MSUM*, p. 90.
703. *WM*, p. 35.
704. *DS*, p. 35.
705. Plutarch, quoted in *UG*, p. 126.
706. *MSUM*, p. 93.
707. *VFR*, p. 136, endnote 34. From 1928 to 1945, Potzl was the head of the Department of Neurology and Psychiatry at the University Clinic in Vienna, Austria (ibid., p. 70).
708. *VFR*, p. 69.
709. *VFR*, p. 34.
710. *PE*, p. 88. The human body is mortal, subject to the inevitability of death. Frankl is not denying the immortality of the human soul or spirit.
711. *DS*, p. 156.
712. *DS*, p. 157. A commodity, of course, is something that may be bought and sold. It is an object, a thing. In fact, in prostitution, a woman is sold by a pimp, the prostitute's agent, and bought, paid a price for her body by the client. This, however, is contrary to a human being's dignity or personal worth. A human being is a

person, a self-reflecting and volitional center of consciousness. In short, a person is a subject, not an object—someone, not something. In prostitution, a human being is treated like a thing, a means to an end, a pleasurable means to relieve the client's sexual desires and tensions.

713. There seem to be as many psychological schools of thought—each with is own founder—as there are Christian denominations.

714. *WM,* p. 133. The bracketed explanatory word [psychological] is mine.

715. *MSM,* pp. 119-120.

716. *MSUM,* p. 78.

717. *MSUM,* p. 80.

718. *MSUM,* p. 53. Similarly, C. S. Lewis gave his advice to a Christian who sought counseling: "Keep clear of psychiatrists unless you know that they are also Christians. Otherwise they start with the assumption that your religion is an illusion and try to 'cure' it: and this assumption they make not as professional psychologists but as amateur philosophers." See C. S. Lewis, *Letters of C. S. Lewis,* ed. W. H. Lewis (New York: Harcourt Brace Jovanovich, 1966), p. 211.

719. *MSUM,* p. 55.

720. *MSUM,* p. 136. Italics are the publisher's.

721. *VFR,* p. 53. Italics are the publisher's.

722. *WM,* p. 10.

723. *MSUM,* p. 26. The bracketed [M] is mine.

724. *MSUM,* pp. 106-107. The bracketed comment [Such interpretations] is mine. The counselor cannot completely divorce himself from his or her own world view. Interpretations of human behavior are based on the *Weltanschauung* or world view of the counselor. This is also true of the logotherapist, the counselor who views the world from the "lenses" of logotherapy. It, too, is a world view or vision of the human person. That

vision is used to interpret human behavior. The decisive question is: "Which world view corresponds most closely to reality, to what a human being is?"

725. Frankl quotes H. J. Eysenck, *Behavior Therapy and the Neuroses* (New York, N.Y.: Pergamon Press, 1960), cf. pp. *ix*, 4, 13, 82, in *MSUM*, p. 108.

726. *PE*, p. 119. The bracketed comment is mine, explaining that "the interpreter" Frankl refers to is the psychoanalyst.

727. *WM*, p. 110. Frankl does not give the source of his quotation.

728. *WM*, pp. 15-16. Cf. Gordon W. Allport, *Personality and Social Encounter* (Boston, MA.: Beacon Press, 1960).

729. *WM*, p. 26. The terms "lower dimensions" and "higher dimension" do not mean that the other psychological schools are inferior to logotherapy. Rather, "higher dimension" means that logotherapy includes the valid insights of the other schools.

730. *DS*, p. 101. The paragraphs are mine. The uppercase bracketed [H] is mine. The exclamation point is mine.

731. *DS*, pp. 101-102. The bracketed words are mine. They explain the context of the quotation.

732. *WM*, p. 66.

733. *WM*, p. 66.

734. *DS*, p. 3.

735. *WM*, p. 10.

736. *PE*, p. 144. The French term *l'homme machine* means "the man machine." In other words, a human being is only a highly complex machine. A human being then is purely material, nothing more. In other words, there is no immaterial reality or spirit that is inside the human body.

737. *WM*, p. 7.

738. *WM*, pp. 7-8.

739. *PE*, p. 144.

740. *WM*, p. 109.

741. *DS*, p. *xxiv*.

742. *PE*, p. 142.

743. *DS*, p. xxvi. The therapist should hold the patient responsible for making decisions. Otherwise, the patient may see himself or herself as a helpless victim of conditions (whether they be psychological, biological or sociological) or circumstances, with no desire to change.

744. Another synonym for purpose in life is expressed by the French term *raison d'etre*, meaning, "reason for being." People who have a purpose in life also have a reason for living, for going on courageously in this world with all of its vicissitudes. Mentally, they have goals set before them, which give them a sense of direction and, in completing them, a sense of personal satisfaction, fulfillment and thus, meaning in life.

745. *PE*, p. 124. Having a purpose or goal in life is of "vital importance." The word "vital" is derived from the Latin word *vita*, meaning "life." A goal, then, is vital—that is, necessary, for a meaningful life.

746. *MSM*, p. 109. Italics are the publisher's. Cf., p. 84. In other words, if a person has a goal or purpose in life, then he will find the courage and patience to endure any obstacle in order to achieve it.

747. *MSM*, p. 105.

748. *MSUM*, p. 85.

749. *WM*, p. 127.

750. *PE*, p. 22.

751. *MSM*, p. 81.

752. *DS*, p. 100.

753. *PE*, p. 97.

754. *MSM*, p. 82.

755. *PE*, p. 97.

756. *DS*, p. 102.

757. *MSM*, pp. 84-85. Italics are the publisher's.

758. *UCM*, p. 38.

759. *MSUM*, p. 95.

760. *MSM*, p. 81.

761. *UCM*, p. 21. Italics are the publisher's.

762. *DS*, p. 129.

763. *MSM*, p. 109.

764. *American Psychological Association Monitor*, May 1976, quoted in *UCM*, p. 27.

765. Questioning the meaning of life is either an objective process or a subjective process. It is either a person being questioned by the vicissitudes of life itself or a person questioning the meaning of life.

766. *MSUM*, p. 134.

767. *MSUM*, p. 141.

768. *DS*, p. 62.

769. *DS*, pp. 28-29. The "shaking experience" includes but is not limited to the following events: the sudden, accidental death of a friend, parent, brother or sister; the tragic death of a child, baby, or adolescent; the suicide of a friend; the unexpected news from a doctor that one has cancer, etc. These and other similar experiences may prompt one to ask, "What is the meaning of life?"

770. Subjective reality is inside the human person—that is, what he or she is feeling, thinking or perceiving. Objective reality is the world outside the human person—that is, what he or she is feeling, thinking or perceiving. Objective reality does not change with one's feelings or moods, even the "down mood" of depression.

771. *DS*, p. 89. The uppercase bracketed [T] is mine. In the context, Frankl paraphrased the words that an anonymous doctor relayed about a patient who was suffering from depression.

772. Reductionism occurs when the human person is understood exclusively in the light of one's discipline. It reduces the multifaceted nature of a human being down to a single factor, whether it be biological, chemical,

neurological, or animal. An animal may behave like a human in several respects, but a human is much more than an animal.

773. *WM,* pp. 20-21.

774. *UCM,* p. 62. The bracketed, explanatory comment is mine.

775. *DS,* p. *xxvii.*

776. *VFR,* p. 60.

777. *DS,* p. 39. The bracketed word [not] is mine.

778. Albert Einstein, quoted in *PE,* p. 93, note 4.

779. *WM,* p. 150. The bracketed explanatory word [Einstein] is mine.

780. *MSUM,* p. 17. Italics are the publisher's.

781. *WM,* p. 143.

782. *WM,* p. 144.

783. *MSM,* p. 122.

784. *MSUM,* p. 19.

785. *MSUM,* p. 70.

786. *MSUM,* p. 75. Just as there can be a distorted religious sense in the human person, so, too, can there be a distorted sense of God. After George Whitefield explained his understanding of the sovereignty of God, the Anglican priest John Wesley was reported to have written to Whitefield: "Your God is my devil."

787. *WM,* p. 138.

788. Joseph Wolpe and Arnold A. Lazarus, *Behavior Therapy Techniques* (Oxford, England: Pergamon Press, 1966), quoted in *MSUM,* pp. 121-122.

789. *DS,* p. 32.

790. Repression is a psychological defense mechanism. It is "the process by which anxiety-producing ideas or impulses are kept out of or removed from conscious awareness." Cf. R. Larkin, "Repression," in *Baker Encyclopedia of Psychology,* ed. David G. Benner (Grand Rapids, MI.: Baker Book House, 1985), p. 1009. "Although the person is not consciously aware of

repressed material or of the process of repression, this material continues to influence behavior" (ibid, p. 1010).

791. DS, p. 4.

792. MSUM, p. 32.

793. Responsibility is a theme in existentialism. Frankl was a philosopher, and philosophy, especially existentialism, had an influence on Frankl's development logotherapy, the Third Viennese School of Psychotherapy. Responsibility presupposes that a human being has free-will, that a person is a self-determining agent—meaning that he or she may freely choose a course of action. Human choices are caused by the chooser, not by someone or something else.

If there were no free-will, then there can be no responsibility for one's actions. If there were no free-will, then no person can really be blamed for morally bad actions, such as murder, stealing, raping nor can a person really be praised for morally good actions, such as a father sacrificing himself to save the life of his son, a fireman rushing into a burning building to save a child or even a young boy helping an old lady cross the street. Ultimately, praise and blame are meaningless terms. A human being makes his or her own choices in life and must accept both the good and the bad consequences which follow from those choices. To say that a person is not responsible for his actions is to reduce a human being to the status of an animal, which is determined by its genetic make-up.

794. UCM, p. 95.

795. PE, p. 64.

796. PE, pp. 63-64.

797. MSM, pp. 113-114. Italics are the publisher's.

798. MSM, p. 85.

799. MSUM, p. 32.

800. PE, p. 13.

801. PE, p. 121.

802. *MSM,* p. 12.

803. *PE,* p. 127.

804. *PE,* pp. 12-13. Italics are the publisher's. As a neurologist, psychiatrist, and philosopher, Frankl would, of course, presuppose that there are certain human beings who are not fully responsible, such as babies, children, the developmentally disabled, and the mentally ill.

805. *DS,* footnote on p. 59.

806. Viktor Frankl, *The Will of Meaning: Foundations and Applications of Logotherapy,* p. 49.

807. Carl Rogers stressed the importance of the interpersonal "connection" between the therapist and the patient. If there is "connection" between the therapist (doctor, psychiatrist or psychologist) and the patient (client), if the two are compatible, the patient may be able to deal with his or her life problems more effectively, resulting in change or personal growth in the latter.

808. Carl R. Rogers, "Two Divergent Trends," *Existential Psychology,* ed. Rollo May (New York, N.Y.: Random House, Inc., 1961), quoted in *PE,* p. 78. Frankl comments: "The personal encounter or, in Jaspers' term, the 'existential communication' seems to matter" (ibid.).

809. Carl R. Rogers, "The Process Equation of Psychotherapy," *American Journal of Psychotherapy,* 15: 27-45 (1961), quoted in *PE,* p. 78.

810. *MSUM* p. 64.

811. *UG,* p. 85, footnote 1.

812. *DS,* p. 194. For Frankl, there is a relative, not absolute, security in living, that sense of being psychologically comfortable with oneself in order to live from day to day relatively free from the fear of making wrong decisions and being skeptical about everything one thinks and believes.

813. *DS,* p. 194.

814. *DS*, p. 39. Mathematics and the physical sciences (such as physics, chemistry, and astronomy) are exact sciences. In an exact science, a hypothesis or theory can be verified or even falsified by measurement, experiment, or observation.

815. *UCM*, p. 69. Italics are the publisher's. The "one dimension" to which Frankl refers is the strictly empirical method of science, which is based experimentation and observation. It confines itself only to what can be verified empirically.

816. *MSUM*, p. 145. Italics are the publisher's. By science, Frankl means "strict physical science, empirical science," which tests reality by examining it in the light of one or more of the five human senses.

817. *MSM*, p. 175. The quotation is from Viktor E. Frankl, *Man's Search for Meaning* (New York, N.Y.: Simon and Schuster/Pocket Books, 1963). Italics are the publisher's. The wording in the 1984 edition slightly differs from the 1963 edition.

818. *WM*, p. 38.

819. *MSUM*, p. 159, note 25.

820. *MSUM*, p. 84.

821. Self-creation is a theme in existentialism. Frankl was a philosopher, and philosophy, especially existentialism, had an influence on his development of logotherapy, the Third Viennese School of Psychotherapy. Self-creation presupposes that a human being has a spirit and free-will, which is a property of the human spirit. In a sense, a human being is a sculptor, but he or she is carving, making, or forming not a clay, stone or wood, but a character. Self-creation means that by one's choices, a human being determines what kind of person he or she is going to be. A person is not determined from without (outside factors) but from within, by one's own spirit, which includes the intellect and will.

822. *PE*, pp. 60-61.

823. *WM*, p. 73.

824. *PE*, p. 61.

825. *DS*, p. 65.

826. *PE*, p. 35.

827. *PE*, p. 110.

828. *DS*, p. 76. The bracketed words are mine and serve as an explanatory phrase. The words in parenthesis are Frankl's.

829. *MSM*, p. 124.

830. *UCM*, p. 137.

831. *UCM*, p. 138.

832. *PE*, p. 82.

833. *MSUM*, p. 84.

834. *UCM*, p. 38. Self-transcendence occurs when instead of focusing exclusively on one's self, being preoccupied with one's self, one focuses outwardly on another human being in the act of love or service to others, on a cause to serve and give one's life to or on a work or art, science, etc. It is living for or giving one's self to someone or something. In the process, one forgets about one's self and finds a sense of self-fulfillment.

835. *PE*, p. 82.

836. *PE*, p. 46.

837. *PE*, pp. 8-9.

838. *MSUM*, p. 85.

839. *MSUM*, p. 37.

840. *PE*, p. 11.

841. *PE*, p. 18. The bracketed [today] is mine and serves as a present-day context for the quotation. For the same reason, I changed the past tense verbs "lifted" and "caused" in the original quotation to the present tense verbs "lift" and "cause." Frankl does not cite the original source of Glenn's quotation.

842. *UCM*, p. 107.

843. *WM*, p. 84. An overemphasis on sex may be an attempt

to escape from a deeper problem, namely, the existential vacuum, a lack of content or meaning in life.

844. *DS*, p. 144. The bracketed words [a man] are mine and take the place of the masculine pronoun "he" in the original English edition.

845. *UCM*, p. 83.

846. *MSUM*, p. 90. The bracketed words [T] and [is] are mine.

847. *MSUM*, p. 91.

848. *UCM*, pp. 81-82.

849. *DS*, p. 157.

850. *MSUM*, p. 90. Italics are the publisher's.

851. *DS*, p. 140. Frankl is right. Copulation, the sex act, is not a distinctively human phenomenon, because animals, too, copulate. But what distinguishes human copulation from animal copulation is the spiritual dimension of love. It is a spiritual expression, an expression of the human spirit, which is conveyed through the body to another human being.

852. *MSUM*, p. 93. The spiritual phenomenon of love makes sexual intercourse human.

853. *DS*, p. 140. There is more to a woman than meets the eye. Physical beauty is important but not the most important element in a relationship between a man and a woman. Because the human body is material and subject to change with the passing of time, physical beauty will eventually fade. If a man "loves" a woman only for her "beautiful" body, then he may no longer "love" her when her body changes, ages. If a man loves a woman mainly because of her body, her external beauty, then he really does not love her. Rather, he only desires to enjoy sexually one of her traits—that is, her beautiful body, which, in fact, is shared by many other beautiful women.

854. *MSUM*, p. 53.

855. *DS*, p. 196. Frankl discusses skepticism in the light of a particular case of a young man who was an obsessive-compulsive neurotic.

856. *DS*, p. 196.

857. *DS*, p. 197.

858. *DS*, p. 196. Existence—that is, reality, is undeniable to a rational or normal person, one who has common sense. In other words, there really must be some meaning, something of real value, in asking, "What is the meaning of existence?" Hence, one presupposes real meaning in asking, "What is the meaning of existence?"

859. *DS*, p. 197. Arthur Kronfeld (1886-1941), MD and PhD, was a Jewish psychiatrist and psychotherapist. He was a critic of psychoanalysis.

860. *MSM*, p. 152.

861. Edith Weisskopf-Joelson, quoted in *PE*, p. 84.

862. *WM*, p. 41. Cf. I Kings 3:6-15.

863. *WM*, p. 151.

864. *DS*, p. 8. The German word *geist* means "spirit."

865. *PE*, p. 63.

866. *MSUM*, p. 28. The bracketed [in logotherapy] is mine.

867. *DS*, p. xxiv.

868. *DS*, p. xxiv.

869. *UCM*, p. 108. Frankl does not condemn sports per se, but he is critical of the wrong attitude with which one approaches it, either as the athlete himself or herself or as the spectator who avidly follows his or her favorite team. Sports can become an idol, one's "ultimate concern" or all-consuming passion in life. Football, baseball, and basketball are not the most important things in the world. Athletes can train for them with a similar kind of dedication as, say, a monk who exclusively dedicates himself to spiritual things, the things of God. Cf. *DS*, p. 128.

870. *VFR*, p. 24. Theresienstadt and Kaufering were concentration camps.

871. *MSM*, p. 42.

872. *WM*, p. 52. Subjectivism teaches that moral truth is dependent on the subject—that is, the person. Each person decides what his or her moral truth is. What is morally true for one person may be false for another. Hence, moral truth is like private property in that it is one's own possession and not necessarily another's. However, there is a philosophical problem with the denial of objective moral truth. For example, the person who says, "All moral truth is subjective" has contradicted himself or herself, because it is stated as an objective moral truth—that is, the statement purports to be really true. On the other hand, objective moral truth is independent of the subject or person. It is "out there" whether a person perceives it or not.

Relativism teaches that there are no absolute moral truths. The relativist says, "There are no moral absolutes." However, there is a philosophical problem with moral relativism. For example, the person who says, "There are no absolutes" has contradicted himself or herself, because it is stated as an absolute moral truth that there are no absolutes. Since the statement is self-contradictory, therefore, it is false.

Another version of relativism says, "Moral principles are right at some time and in some place for some people; but no moral principle is right at all times and in all places for all people." But this kind of moral relativism itself is a principle that applies to all times and in all places for all people. In short, moral relativism is an absolute moral principle. It destroys itself. Surely, not all moral truth is objective; nor is it all subjective.

873. Success involves excelling beyond others in what one— such as an artist, a musician, actor or actress, an athlete, etc.—does. It may involve advancing beyond others in employment with a company or corporation. Financially, it may involve making lots of money or being a millionaire or billionaire. Success, then, usually

involves public recognition or praise for one's accomplishment or accomplishments.

874.   *DS*, pp. 105-106. Italics are the publisher's.

875.   *UCM*, p. 46. The bracketed word [attempt] is mine. I have changed the original past tense "attempted" with the present tense "attempt" in order to make its meaning relevant to today.

876.   *UCM*, p. 15.

877.   *WM*, p. 35. Italics are the publisher's.

878.   Frankl taught that a person should not seek to suffer in order to derive pleasure from it. That is psychologically unhealthy—that is masochism. Frankl addressed the issue of unavoidable suffering, a passive condition, something which had happened to an individual but was not deliberately sought.

879.   *UG*, p. 137. Italics are the publisher's. For example, chronically ill or terminally ill persons despair of their suffering when they do not see any meaning in it. Despair makes their suffering unbearable; as a result, they want to commit suicide. Psychologically, it is better to choose to find a meaning in suffering than to suffer in despair.

880.   *PE*, p. 24.

881.   *WM*, p. 131. The bracketed uppercase [H] is mine.

882.   *PE*, p. 15. Italics are the publisher's.

883.   *DS*, p. 44.

884.   *PE*, p. 107. The bracketed linking verb is mine.

885.   *MSM*, p. 108.

886.   Yehuda Bacon, quoted in *WM*, p. 79. Italics are the publisher's.

887.   *MSM*, p. 76.

888.   *PE*, p. 56.

889.   *UCM*, pp. 122-123. The bracketed uppercase [Y] is mine. Frankl comments on his interview with Anastasia (Frau) Kotek: "A week later she died. During the last week of her life, however, she was no longer depressed

but, on the contrary, full of faith and pride. Prior to this, she had felt agonized, ridden by the anxiety that she was useless. Our interview had made her aware that her life was meaningful and that even her suffering was no in vain" (ibid., p. 123).

890. Joyce Travelbee, *Interpersonal Aspects of Nursing* (Philadelphia, PA.: F. A. Davis Company, 1966), p. 170, quoted in *WM,* p. 124.

891. *MSM,* p. 148.

892. *DS,* p. 109.

893. Suicide is a distinctively human phenomenon. For example, animals do not commit suicide, because they are suffering from deep despair; only humans do.

894. Albert Camus, *The Myth of Sisyphus* (New York, N.Y.: Vintage Books, 1955), p. 3, quoted in *UCM,* p. 24.

895. *MSUM,* p. 132.

896. *MSM,* p. 112. The bracketed [the] is mine. Frankl's original wording in English was "this existential vacuum."

897. *MSM,* p. 143. Italics are the publisher's.

898. Frankl quotes Earl A. Grollman, *Concerning Death: A Practical Guide for the Living* (Boston, MA.: Beacon Press, 1974), quoted in *MSUM,* p. 99.

899. *MSM,* p. 87.

900. *MSM,* pp. 87-88. The bracketed words are mine. Frankl is referring to the words of Friedrich Nietzsche: "He who has a *why* to live for can bear almost any *how.*" See Purpose in Life.

901. *DS,* p. 103. The bracketed words are mine. They explain the context of the quotation. Because life is often difficult, filled with obstacles in achieving one's goals, human beings need encouragement. "Encouragement" is derived from the French word *encouragier,* which, in turn, comes from the prefix *en,* meaning "make, put in" and *corage,* meaning "courage." The French word is derived from the Latin *cor,* meaning "heart," which is a metaphor for inner strength. The would-be suicidal

person needs—to borrow a phrase from the title of Paul Tillich's book—*the courage to be.* Words that are positive, uplifting, can actually give courage to those who are discouraged, suffering from some kind of physical or psychological problem. Words can literally be a matter of life and death, depending on the psychological condition of the person who hears them. In short, the would-be suicidal person needs words and gestures to encourage him or her to go on living.

902. *UCM,* p. 15.

903. *DS,* p. 51.

904. Walter Freeman, "Psychiatrists Who Kill Themselves: A Study in Suicide," in *American Journal of Psychiatry* 124: 154, 1967, quoted in *WM,* p. 134. The bracketed [and] is mine.

905. *WM,* p. 132. People who believe in God are not immune from troubles in life. They, too, can commit suicide. But it is also true that belief in God can prevent a person from committing suicide. Many more religious people have stayed alive because of their belief in God than those who have killed themselves in spite of their belief.

906. *UCM,* p. 20.

907. *MSM,* p. 144. Italics are the publisher's.

908. *MSM,* p. 112.

909. *PE,* p. 125.

910. *DS,* pp. 127-128; cf. p. 28.

911. *DS,* p. 28.

912. The crucial questions are "Survive for what?" "Why should one survive?" In other words, there must be some reason that a person wants to stay alive, something to motivate a person to keep on living.

913. *MSUM,* pp. 134-135.

914. *MSM,* p. 109.

915. *PE,* p. 144.

916. *WM,* p. 6. The bracketed uppercase [W] is mine.

917. *WM,* p. 6. The bracketed uppercase [R] is mine.

Italics are the publisher's. The term "dynamics" refers to searching for a person's unconscious motivations. "Reification" comes from the Latin word *res*, meaning "thing." Hence, reification is treating a person as if he or she were a thing, an inanimate object.

918. Cf. *PE*, pp. 68, 10. For Frankl, there is a mentally healthy kind of tension, which is created by the gap between what *one is* (Frankl calls it "meaning orientation"—that is, a person's "will to meaning") and what one *ought to become* (Frankl calls it "meaning confrontation"). The good kind of tension, then, is between being and meaning, between oneself and that which is beyond oneself. Hence, meaning is not merely in being but also in becoming—that is, in meeting and fulfilling challenges in life.

919. *PE*, p. 83.

920. *MSM*, p. 109.

921. *PE*, p. 116. Within Frankl's quotation, the single quotation marks are mine and identify what the architect said to Frankl.

922. *WM*, p. 48. For empirical or scientific confirmation of Frankl's view of the therapeutic value of tension, see Sigmund Freud, *Gesammelte Werke*, Vol. 10, p. 113. (The German title may be translated into English as *Collected Works*); J. E. Nardini, "Survival Factors in American Prisoners of War," *American Journal of Psychiatry* 109: 244, 1952; Robert J. Lifton, "Home by Ship: Reaction Patterns of American Prisoners of War Repatriated from North Korea," *American Journal of Psychiatry* 110: 732, 1954; Theodore A. Kotchen, "Existential Mental Health: An Empirical Approach," *Journal of Individual Psychology* 16: 174, 1960.

923. *UCM*, pp. 106-107.

924. *PE*, p. 21.

925. *UCM*, p. 107.

926. *PE*, p. 83.

927. *UCM*, p. 107.

928. *DS*, p. 116. The bracketed explanatory phrase is mine.

929. *WM*, p. 144. The bracketed [are] is mine.

930. *MSUM*, p. 16. Italics are the publisher's. The bracketed [T]s are mine.

931. *MSUM*, p. 80.

932. *VFR*, p. 57. The bracketed uppercase [W] is mine.

933. William Irwin Thompson (PhD, Cornell University, 1966) is an interdisciplinary scholar, having studied anthropology, philosophy, literature, and cultural history.

934. William Irwin Thompson, "Anthropology and the Study of Values," *Main Currents in Modern Thought* 19: 37, 1962, quoted in *WM*, pp. 85-86.

935. *MSM*, p. 150.

936. *MSUM*, p. 10. The quotation is about Viktor Frankl by Swanee Hunt, the United States ambassador to Austria, in the "Foreword" to *MSUM*.

937. *WM*, p. 66.

938. *PE*, p. 85, footnote 13.

939. *MSUM*, p. 62. The bracketed words [world view] are mine. Italics are the publisher's.

940. *MSUM*, p. 142. The bracketed word [are] is mine.

941. *WM*, p. 73.

942. *PE*, p. 88.

943. *MSM*, p. 139.

944. *MSUM*, p. 142. Italics are mine.

945. Frankl's doctrine of transcendence is a response to all forms of reductionism which teach that a human being is "nothing but" matter or "only" a material being. On the contrary, transcendence suggests that a human being is much more than a biological, electro-chemical creature. A human being is much more than a highly advanced animal. To be human is not only to be material but also a spiritual being. Conscience is a property of

the human spirit and, thus, transcends (goes above and beyond) the material dimension of the human body.

946. *MSUM,* p. 60.

947. Time is transitory; it quickly passes. There really isn't a present, for as soon as one says, "The present," it is gone. It becomes a part of one's past. For Frankl, the past need not be a waste of one's life. Rather, the passing of time is an opportunity to "store up," as it were, "rich" meanings (or meaning) in one's own life. Those meanings are safely stored away in one's past. In a sense, they become a part of a person, forever. They may enrich or make one's life better.

948. *UCM,* p. 115.

949. *UCM,* p. 117.

950. *UCM,* p. 118.

951. Although Frankl was influenced by the philosophy of existentialism, he did not accept the radical subjectivism of some its philosophers, expressed by such statements as "A person creates his own truth" again, "Life is objectively meaningless; therefore, each person must created his or her own meaning in life." Although not every truth is objective, Frankl taught that there are many truths which are objective. Frankl rejected the objective meaninglessness of life.

952. *PE,* p. 44.

953. *PE,* p. 49. Objective knowledge means independent or outside of the subject, that is, the person who perceives or apprehends it. A person (subject) knows the truth (objective knowledge). Hence, there is a correspondence between subject (the one who knows something) and object (the thing that is known).

954. *PE,* p. 64.

955. Sigmund Freud, "Book Review," *Wiener medizinische Wochenschrift,* 1889, The German may be translated *Viennese Medical Weekly Review,* quoted in *WM,* p. 114.

956. There is a subjective dimension to knowing reality, because a person cannot totally detach himself or herself from the knowing process. He or she sees the world through his or her own eyes or understands the world with his or her own mind.

957. *WM*, pp. 59, 60. Italics are the publisher's.

958. Supermeaning is ultimate meaning, the highest meaning in life, which is usually discovered by faith in a supreme being or god.

959. *WM*, p. 145.

960. Matthew Scully, "Viktor Frankl at Ninety: An Interview," *First Things*, http://www.firstthings.com/ftissues/ft9504/scully.html. It can also be found in Viktor Frankl at Ninety: An Interview. *First Things*, 52 (April, 1995): 39-43. Frankl's notion of "supermeaning" is expressed in theology as the "incomprehensibility of God." The Latin term for it is *finitum non capax infiniti*, which is translated "the finite cannot contain or grasp the infinite." One can apprehend but not comprehend God; or, one can know something about God but not everything. God can be known truly but not exhaustively.

   Faith in God is not irrational, against reason, but beyond reason, transcending it. Faith in God, then, is more than reason but not less than reason. Faith involves more than just thinking about God but choosing to believe in God. It involves not merely thinking but willing, choosing. Cf. St. Thomas Aquinas, *Summa Theologica*, I, Q. 12, Art. 7; II-II, Q. 10, Art. 8.

961. *MSUM*, p. 143.

962. *MSM*, p. 122. Just because one cannot find an answer to the question "Why do human beings suffer?" now, in this world, does not mean that suffering is meaningless nor does it mean that there is no answer to the question. For if there is a world beyond the present world, if there is a fourth dimensional world beyond the three-

dimensional world that human beings now experience, then there may be an ultimate answer to the question.

The answer to the question "Why do human beings suffer?" requires faith that the suffering one presently experiences will be meaningful, ultimately. It also presupposes that there is a supreme being, a higher power, an infinite, all-knowing, being; in short, a god who has the ultimate answer as to why human beings suffer when they themselves do not understand why. Suffering, then, may have a meaning not only in this world but also in the world to come, not only from a finite, human perspective but also from *sub specie aeternitas* (the Latin phrase, meaning "under the view of eternity"), "from the perspective of eternity."

963. Self-forgetfulness is that state in which a person is not conscious or aware of his or her self. Logotherapy teaches that one is truly he or her self when he or she is not conscious (aware), reflecting, or thinking about his or her self. To think about one's self every movement or to have excessive reflection on one's self is not good—that is, mentally healthy.

964. *MSUM,* p. 37.

965. *MSUM,* p. 31. Italics are the publisher's.

966. *MSUM,* p. 37.

967. *WM,* p. 92. The bracketed [many people] serves as the subject of the sentence.

968. Many people today believe that meaning in life can be found only in paid employment, a salary for one's job. Frankl corrects the notion that the only way human beings can find meaning in life is by the work they do.

969. *DS,* p. 121.

970. *DS,* p. 124.

971. *DS,* p. 123. The bracketed [T] letters and the bracketed [They] are mine.

972. *DS,* p. 123.

973. Frankl says, "For a long time psychoanalysis . . . has seen its assignment as the 'unmasking' of unconscious dynamics underlying human behavior" (*MSUM*, p. 97). Unmasking is "digging deeper and deeper" into a person's unconscious motivations for behavior. In unmasking, the counselor searches for hidden motives to a person's behavior. Those motives may even be base or unworthy of a person. Unmasking may only help another person if he or she believes that what is unmasked is the truth. The problem with unmasking is that it may say more about the counselor than the one being counseled. It may reveal, and thereby unmask, the counselor's own unconscious motivation to actually hurt or wound the counselee.

974. *MSUM*, p. 97. The bracketed words are mine. Italics are the publisher's.

975. *MSM*, p. 106.

976. *VFR*, p. 64. Frankl calls the first group "creative values"; the second, "experiential values"; and the third, "attitudinal values." Cf. *MSM*, pp. 115-119.

977. *MSM*, p. 76.

978. *MSUM*, p. 122.

979. *UCM*, p. 107. Frankl is speaking in general terms, which means that there are still specific cases of sexual frustration and feelings of inferiority.

980. *MSUM*, p. 104.

981. Robert Jay Lifton, *History and Human Survival* (New York, N.Y.: Random House, 1969), quoted in *UCM*, p. 110. Dr. Lifton, MD, is a psychiatrist, professor and author of several books.

982. Frankl's first quotation is from Fredrick Wertham, *American Journal of Psychotherapy*, 26 (1972), p. 216. Frankl's second quotation is from Jerome D. Frank, "Some Psychological Determinants of Violence and Its Control," *Australia New Zealand Psychiatry*, 6 (1972), pp. 158-164. Both quotations are from *MSUM*, p. 103.

Although Frankl's sources date back to 1972, nothing has really changed at the beginning of the twenty-first century. In fact, violence on television is worse today than it was thirty years ago.

983.   Edith Weisskopf-Joelson, "Logotherapy and Existential Analysis," *Acta Psychothrapeutica*, 6:193 (1958), quoted in *PE*, p. 84. Edith was a former professor of psychology at Purdue University.

984.   *PE*, p. 84.

985.   Franz Werfel, quoted in *DS*, p. 195. Frankl gives no source for Werfel's quotation.

986.   Franz Werfel, quoted in *WM*, p. 95. Frankl gives no source for Werfel's quotation. In the context of the quotation, Frankl contends that there are thirst points to the reality, the existence of water. Likewise, a person's search for meaning points to the reality of meaning that there really is meaning in life. However, just as some may miss their search for water, so, too, some may miss their search for meaning. The former may die of thirst; the latter may suffer from the "existential vacuum," which may lead to despair, giving up on the hope of finding a meaning in life. However, just because one does not find it does not mean that it is not there. Meaning is just as real as water. The difference is that water is a material reality, while meaning is a spiritual reality.

987.   *MSUM*, pp. 132-133.

988.   *PE*, p. 102. Italics are the publisher's. There is built within the human person a natural inclination or desire to live, to choose life, to keep oneself alive. In other words, a human person gravitates toward being, not non-being. There would be no sense in Frankl appealing to the prisoners' "will to live" if a human being did not, in fact, have a natural inclination to live. There is, then, a natural law of self-preservation. Human beings normally want to live, not kill themselves. Human beings normally love themselves, which involves caring for and protecting

themselves. It is contrary to self—love to eliminate the self that one loves.

989. Ludwig Wittgenstein, quoted in *MSUM,* p. 153. Frankl gives no source for Wittgenstein's quotation.

990. *DS,* p. 118.

991. *DS,* p. 119.

992. *DS,* p. 126.

993. *DS,* p. 127.

994. *DS,* p. 127. The bracketed words [For the] are mine.

995. *Weltanschauung* (German, *welt,* meaning "world" and *anschauung, meaning* "view") literally means "world view." It is a given, a starting point or premise by which one interprets reality (comprehensively), such as right and wrong, what a human being is, the meaning of life, God, etc.

996. *WM,* p. 15. In other words, every person has a world view, a philosophy or view about human beings and life, whether he or she is aware of it or not. The person who insists: "I have no world view" has actually stated a contradiction, because to have no view of the world is at least to have one view of the world, namely, "I have no view of the world."

997. *PE,* p. 2. A *theoria* is a transliteration of the Greek word *theoria,* which, in turn is derived from two Greek words, *thea,* meaning "a view" and *horan,* meaning "to see." A *theoria,* then, is a person's approach or the way a person looks at, sees or understands the various data or phenomena in the world. It is not necessarily a fact. [L] is mine. I changed it from a lowercase "l" to an uppercase "L."

998. *WM,* pp. 28-29.

999. *MSM,* p. 143. The bracketed [and] is mine.

1000. *MSUM,* p. 134.

1001. The German word *zeitgeist* is derived from two German words: *zeit,* meaning "time" and *geist,* meaning "spirit." It literally means "time spirit." It is the "spirit of the times"—that is, what or how people are generally thinking in a particular culture and at a particular time in history. Hence, a writer, philosopher, psychologist, etc., may have some difficulty escaping from the influence (either conscious or unconscious influence) of the thought forms of his or her society.

1002. *WM*, p. 27. The genius to whom Frankl is referring is Sigmund Freud. See Freud.

1003. Paul Tillich, *The Courage to Be* (New Haven, CT.: Yale University Press, 1952), p. 47.

1004. "Viktor E. Frankl Collection," Graduate Theological Union, Berkeley California, *http://library.gtu.edu/archives/frankl.html*. Retrieved on 15 May, 2003. I owe a special thanks to Lucinda Glenn, the Graduate Theological Union archivist, for allowing me to modify the Bibliography of Works by Viktor Frankl in the GTU Archives and select the various English editions of Frankl's writings. See also Viktor E. Frankl, *Man's Search for Meaning*, 3rd ed. (New York, N.Y.: Simon and Schuster, 1984), pp. 155-189.

9 781413 453362